Transnational Regions in Historical Perspective

National competitiveness has become a misnomer, as competitiveness is increasingly understood as a regional phenomenon and regions are not confined to the boundaries of the nation state. This book focuses on the Port of Rotterdam and its hinterland – i.e. the Lower Rhine and the Ruhr area. A transnational perspective is imperative to understand the historical trajectories of the port, the hinterland and the region itself. This book brings geography and the transnational study of regions back into the historical discipline, linking places to larger geographical scales and to systems of production and consumption and the global chains in which they are organised. This book will be of interest to scholars and practitioners in urban studies, urban planning, public policy, geography and political science.

Marten Boon is researcher at the University of Oslo and an affiliated researcher at the Norwegian University of Science and Technology in Trondheim.

Hein A.M. Klemann is Professor of Social and Economic History at Erasmus School of History, Culture and Communication, Erasmus University Rotterdam.

Ben Wubs is Professor of International Business History at Erasmus School of History, Culture and Communication, Erasmus University Rotterdam and Appointed Project Professor at the Graduate School of Economics, Kyoto University.

Routledge Advances in Regional Economics, Science and Policy

Rural Housing and Economic Development
Edited by Don E. Albrecht, Scott Loveridge, Stephan Goetz and Rachel Welborn

Creative Ageing Cities
Place Design with Older People in Asian Cities
Edited Keng Hua Chong and Mihye Cho

Competitiveness and Knowledge
An International Comparison of Traditional Firms
Knut Ingar Westeren, Hanas Cader, Maria de Fátima Sales, Jan Ole Similä and Jefferson Staduto

Gastronomy and Local Development
The Quality of Products, Places and Experiences
Edited by Nicola Bellini, Cécile Clergeau and Olivier Etcheverria

The Geography of Scientific Collaboration
Agnieszka Olechnicka, Adam Ploszaj and Dorota Celińska-Janowicz

The Canada–U.S. Border in the 21st Century
Trade, Immigration and Security in the Age of Trump
John B. Sutcliffe and William P. Anderson

Economic Clusters and Globalization
Diversity and Resilience
Edited by Francisco Puig and Berrbizne Urzelai

Transnational Regions in Historical Perspective
Edited by Marten Boon, Hein A.M. Klemann and Ben Wubs

For more information about this series, please visit www.routledge.com/series/RAIRESP

Transnational Regions in Historical Perspective

Edited by Marten Boon, Hein A.M. Klemann and Ben Wubs

Routledge
Taylor & Francis Group

LONDON AND NEW YORK

First published 2020
by Routledge
2 Park Square, Milton Park, Abingdon, Oxon OX14 4RN

and by Routledge
605 Third Avenue, New York, NY 10017

First issued in paperback 2021

Routledge is an imprint of the Taylor & Francis Group, an informa business

British Library Cataloguing-in-Publication Data
A catalogue record for this book is available from the British Library

Library of Congress Cataloging-in-Publication Data
Names: Boon, Marten, editor. | Klemann, Hein A. M., 1957– editor. |
    Wubs, Ben, editor.
Title: Transnational regions in historical perspective / edited by Marten
    Boon, Hein A.M. Klemann and Ben Wubs.
Description: Abingdon, Oxon ; New York, NY : Routledge, 2019. | Series:
    Routledge advances in regional economics, science and policy ; 32 |
    Includes bibliographical references and index.
Subjects: LCSH: Ruhr (Germany : Region)—Economic conditions—20th
    century. | Rotterdam (Netherlands)—Economic conditions—20th
    century. | Ruhr (Germany : Region)—Foreign economic relations—
    20th century. | Rotterdam (Netherlands)—Foreign economic
    relations—20th century. | Interregionalism—Germany—Ruhr
    (Region)—History—20th century. | Interregionalism—Netherlands—
    Rotterdam—History—20th century.
Classification: LCC HC288.R8 T73 2019 | DDC 330.943/55087—dc23
LC record available at https://lccn.loc.gov/2019013377

ISBN 13: 978-0-367-78590-1 (pbk)
ISBN 13: 978-1-138-67085-3 (hbk)

Typeset in Bembo
by Apex CoVantage, LLC

Contents

Figures

Tables

Contributors

Marten Boon is researcher at the University of Oslo and an affiliated researcher at the Norwegian University of Science and Technology in Trondheim. He received his PhD from Erasmus University Rotterdam in 2014. His thesis won the dissertation prize of the European Business History Association in 2016. Boon has published in *Business History* and *Business History Review* and is the author of *Multinational Business and Transnational Regions: A transnational business history of energy transition in the Rhine region, 1945–1973*, Abingdon, UK (2018).

Hein A.M. Klemann studied history and economics. After his PhD at the Free University, he worked at the Utrecht University and the Dutch Institute for War Documentation, and widely published on Dutch-German economic relations and its political consequences and the economic development in the German occupied countries during the Second World War. Since 2005 he is full Professor of Economic History and International Relations at Erasmus University Rotterdam.

Klara Paardenkooper-Süli has acquired a PhD in Economic and Business History at the Erasmus University Rotterdam. Currently she is teaching research skills at the Rotterdam Business School, Rotterdam University of Applied Sciences, and she is a Chain Manager Blockchain at the RDM Knowledge Center Sustainable Port City in Rotterdam.

Joep Schenk is a post-doctoral researcher and lecturer in the History of International Relations at Utrecht University. He researches how the emergence of cooperative international river regimes depend on societies' fluctuating and intersubjective understanding of – the relation between – security and prosperity over time.

Ben Wubs is Professor of International Business History at the Erasmus University in Rotterdam and an appointed Project Professor at the Graduate School of Economics Kyoto University. He is engaged in various research projects related to multinationals, business systems, transnational economic regions, Dutch–German economic relations and the global fashion industry.

Acknowledgments

Transnational Regions in Historical Perspective is the result of research undertaken between 2009 and 2015 in the project *Outport and Hinterland. Rotterdam Business and Ruhr Industry, 1870–2010.* The editors wish to express their gratitude to the Netherlands Organisation for Scientific Research (NWO) for funding the project (grant number 360–53–120). We also wish to thank our contributors, who, despite new obligations, took the time to cooperate on the making of this book. The maps in this book would not have materialised without the generous financial aid of the Unger-Van Brero Fund. In addition, we would also like to thank Annelieke Vries for the design and production of the maps. We warmly thank Sally-Ann Ross for language editing and the editorial team at Routledge for their patience.

1 Transnational regions from a historical perspective

Rotterdam's port and Ruhr industry, 1870–2010

Marten Boon, Hein A.M. Klemann and Ben Wubs

Introduction

This book is based on a research project funded by the Netherlands Organization for Scientific Research (NWO) entitled *Outport and Hinterland. Rotterdam Business and the Ruhr Industry, 1870–2000* (NWO Humanities; Project number 360–53–120). The project aimed to explore the development of the economic links between, on the one hand, the Dutch Port of Rotterdam, Rotterdam business and the Rhine's mouth ports, and, on the other, the German Ruhr district and Ruhr industry during the long 20th century. The central research questions concerned: how and why economic interdependencies between Rotterdam and its hinterland evolved over this 130-year period; the ways in which the main actors shaped the cross-border region; and the role that networks or clusters played in this process. Although the term hinterland is a more complex concept, for the time being it is defined as the chief inland area from where traffic arises and passes through a port. The project focused on two main actors in the Lower Rhine economy: firms and governments. The geographical location and natural conditions made the development of Europe's most important cross-border economic region possible, but entrepreneurs and companies used these opportunities and created the economic reality: small, medium-sized and large international firms and (inter)national cartels shaped the Lower Rhine economy. Governments also played a determinative role as regulators of economic activities, owners of public companies and providers of public goods.

In the second half of the 19th century, Germany's heavy industry became increasingly dependent on foreign raw materials, in particular iron ore and wood. As the freight costs of water transport declined compared to railway freight, this industry concentrated in the Lower Rhine area. The Ruhr mines and industry also required an outlet for their finished products and coal, and, simultaneously, the growing population of workers needed cheap food from abroad. As a result, Rotterdam evolved into the most important port for its German hinterland, while the Rhine River became the foremost commercial inland waterway in Europe.

Economic conditions in Germany, particularly in the Lower Rhineland, largely determined Dutch economic developments between the late 19th and late 20th century. When the Prussian Prime Minister Otto von Bismarck created the *Kaiserreich* around 1870, and with that a German nation state, the Netherlands participated in the economic element of this integration process, but remained well away from the political aspects. This did not, however, mean that the much smaller Netherlands was unilaterally dependent on its larger neighbour. German interests in the Netherlands were significant, and the country's dependence on Dutch services was noteworthy. A close link existed between German and Dutch economic growth rates for more than a century, but this narrow link cannot be proven statistically anymore from the 1990s onwards. Indeed, major structural changes in the Ruhr district in this period altered the relationship between the German and Dutch economies.[1]

This NWO research project was particularly significant, because it dealt with the origins, growth and structural changes of the world's largest port, Rotterdam, and Western Europe's largest industrial complex, the Ruhr district, as well as their interrelations in terms of regional economic development. The three sub-themes of the project were:

1   The German *Montan* industry – this is a German word for the combination of coal, iron and steel manufacturers – and its relationships with Rotterdam in the period 1870–1940.[2]
2   The transformation from coal to oil in the German economy and the effects on the Rhine mouth ports after World War II.[3]
3   The effects of globalisation and containerisation on the Lower Rhine economy during the last part of the 20th century.[4]

In 2014 and 2015, all three subprojects were concluded with the production of PhD theses. As well as summarising these theses, this volume is a synthesis of the entire project.

Economic regions and transnational history

Traditionally, when analysing the international relations of the Dutch economy with the outside world in the 19th and first half of the 20th century, the focus is initially on the Dutch colonial empire. Nonetheless, economic contacts with surrounding countries were more important for the development of Dutch industry, agriculture and services. The Dutch economy had been very open since the 1860s, with an export and import ratio of over 50 per cent of GDP, which is a level that is even rare today.[5] In fact, during the first wave of globalisation, the Dutch economy achieved an openness that only developed elsewhere in the 1990s, and even then only in a limited number of small, highly developed countries.[6] These high import and export ratios are an indication that the Dutch economy was so closely interwoven with the economies of its neighbours that it is barely useful to call it a national economy. Such a level of international trade is only possible when the major tradable-producing branches are only adding a little value to imported raw materials or semi-finished products before exporting them again. Apart from the non-tradable sectors, the national economy is then only an accidental geographical coming together of individual links in internationally organised business columns.

It was not only the Dutch economy that could barely be described in national terms in the late 19th century. The German historian Nikolaus Wolf found that the economic contacts between the diverse regions within Germany were no more intense until 1914 than such relations with neighbouring foreign regions:

> before 1914, German trade districts were, if anything, only slightly better integrated with each other than with trade districts across the German border. When we just estimate the effect of two districts being part of Germany as opposed to one being outside Germany, that border effect is not different from zero before 1914: it is insignificant at any reasonable level.[7]

In other words, during the pre-1914 period of liberal economic relations and monetary stability, there was hardly any reason to describe the enormous economic activity within Germany as a national German economy. Due to limited east-west connections within Germany – all the major rivers flow in a north-northwestern direction – the economic activity within the country fell apart in regional economies and such economic regions did not always end at the border.

The idea that the political entity, the nation state, should also be an economic entity reached a climax in the 1930s. National economic isolation in this decade, which was the product of the Depression and the protectionism of the period, created huge problems for highly developed small countries such as the Netherlands. In the same period, instruments were needed to regulate the economy on a national level. Measuring and analysing the national economy became crucial, as economics developed from a purely academic discipline and became increasingly instrumental in national economic and social policy. The emphasis of economic analysis shifted from explaining economic developments to recommending economic policies to improve the national situation, in particular to limit national unemployment. In other words, economics became a servant of politicians.

Nina Glick-Schiller and Andreas Wimmer point out that, in empirical social sciences, societies are analysed within the limits of their national borders, as if this is the natural unit of analysis. As a reason for this, they point to the data that are used and collected at a national level.[8] In the service of economic policy, the establishment of national accounts in the interwar period created an entirely new form of equipment with which to analyse economic development, using national measures such as national income, gross national or domestic product and national savings. In the economic models of the time, international trade was seen as something of an anomaly that undermined national economic developments. Until the 1980s, generations of students of economics first learned to understand the macro-economic models of a closed economy. Equations on international trade came second, quite often in an elective course, as this complicated the model. The national, if not nationalist, bias of economics ignores the fact that, for a trader, selling his products within a country is not so different from selling them across the border, especially if both countries use the same river for transport, the same port as a hub to the outside world or when exporting means just selling to the next village. International trade is a problem for the nation state when it wants to manipulate its economic development with Keynesian instruments; in such cases, import leakages will undermine political targets. Trade is a problem from that perspective; it is not for traders who have contacts with people speaking quite similar dialects within the same river region, even when a national border divides it. Instead, trade is about relations between people and companies, and is therefore not limited to the nation state, or at least not as long as such states do not destroy it by artificial means.

The Rhine river basin is a region where culture, language and geography provide minimal obstacles to economic contacts. Nonetheless, the predominance of national economic modelling and policy prompted the National Statistical Office to collect economic data for the development of national economic policy. Reflecting and analysing economic and trade realities was not its prime concern. So, due to the lack of data, it became almost impossible to analyse the economy on a different level from the nation state. It is not only in statistics, but also in state archives, that one will find data on national economic policy. Newspapers write about the national economy and politicians speak about it and how its problems should be solved. Such politicians claim positive developments as their achievements, even when they are almost completely a result of international economic developments. The politician knows that these are important, and will claim that they are the course of negative developments. However, really analysing the economy on a supra- or international level was, for a long time, rarely done. In the 60 or so years after the Guns of August ended the first period of globalisation, this was less problematic. Protectionism and national isolation created economies that were more or less congruent with nation states, although transnational relations were never completely destroyed. The national instruments used to analyse levels of growth, long-term economic cycles and inflation in this period are, however, less useful at times when economic openness and regional rather than national economies are the rule. When industrialisation began, economic regions typically had both national and transnational contacts. Using standard economic tools and data to analyse these regional economies on a national level creates, on paper, something that, in fact, never existed.

When the Dutch economic historians Jan Luiten van Zanden and Arthur van Riel wrote their book on the Dutch economy in the long 19th century, they concluded that it was only in the 1860s that a Dutch national economy developed from all kinds of fragmented local economies. In fact, as the German economy liberalised at the same time, the local economies in these years integrated not on a national, but on a transnational level. According to reconstructed Dutch national accounts, the Netherlands experienced the start of modern economic growth when Bismarck created the German *Kaiserreich* in the coarsest of

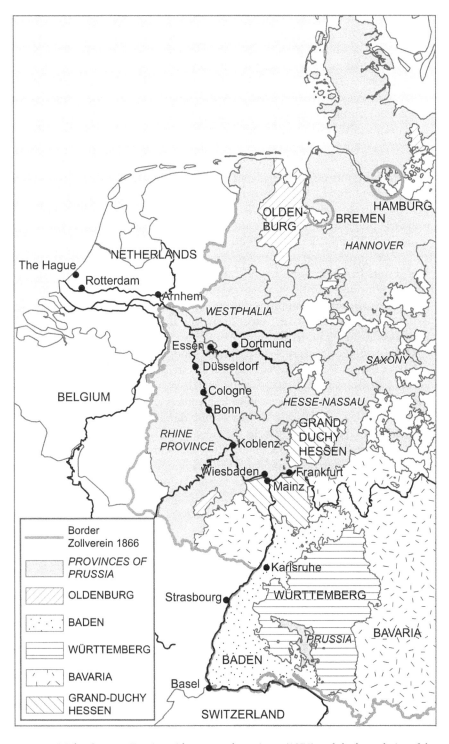

Figure 1.1 The German Empire with states and provinces (1871) and the boundaries of the
Zollverein (1866)

Source: Map produced by Cartographic Studio/Annelieke Vries-Baaijens (2018).

ways (1862–1871).[9] To explain this, Van Zanden and Van Riel emphasise the abolition of all kinds of institutional barriers such as tolls at the city gates, which had caused regional fragmentation. This and the development of railways gave the market its chance and a national economy developed.[10] German industry boomed in the same period. The trade of the German *Zollverein* – the customs union comprising the majority of German states that would integrate into the *Kaiserreich* in 1871 – was encouraged by Bismarck.

Bismarck implemented a relatively high level of free trade. He was no free trader, but hoped to once and for all surpass Austria, Prussia's only rival as leader, in the process of Germany's political integration. Austria was unable to participate in free trade for economic reasons and so had to remain outside the customs union, which was one of the instruments in the process of political integration.[11] At the same time, the second cabinet of the liberal leader J.R. Thorbecke in the Netherlands largely terminated duties, taxes and related production regulations,[12] with the economy rapidly opening up as a result. In 1862, the Netherlands turned to free trade and remained a free trade country until the Depression of the 1930s made it necessary to implement national economic measures. Consequently, in 1864, imports and exports reached a level of, respectively, 59 and 56 per cent of GDP and remained at such a high level until 1914.[13]

Germany's 19th century industrialisation and Dutch economic liberalisation created a transnational economic region. The relatively open economies in the two countries made it possible for the Dutch Port of Rotterdam to become a major hub linking the German industrial centres around the Ruhr and Lower Rhine with the outside world. The Rhine developed into the link between German industry and the port. In the last few decades, economic geographers have developed ways to think about economic activity and competitiveness as a regional, rather than a national, phenomenon. As geographers did not use competitiveness as an explanation for regional economic development, it fell to economists like Michael E. Porter and Paul Krugman to take the lead in the discourse.[14] Porter believes in regional-based drivers of prosperity in concentrated clusters of similar industries and companies.[15] In a project on the economic performance of the US, Porter found huge regional differences in competitiveness, which was reflected in wage levels, wage growth, employment and patenting and a strong clustering of related industries.[16] According to Porter, a cluster "allows each member to benefit as if it had greater scale or as if it had joined with others formally – without demanding that it sacrifices its flexibility." Porter obviously thinks of Hollywood and Silicon Valley as examples of such regions, but emphasises that clusters are everywhere.[17] Externalities resulting from the use of similar technologies, skills or raw materials – functional relations – explain the concentration of related industries. In the Rhine region, his concept could explain the concentration of: mining, blast furnaces, steel factories or machine industry along the Ruhr; machinery, chemistry and car production around Mannheim; Dutch commercialised agriculture and food processing; and barging, transport and other trade services around the Port of Rotterdam. However,

clusters cannot explain the Rhine region as such. Not all links between industries in the region are the result of functional relations. Moreover, clusters come
and go and so cannot explain the continuity of over a century that is visible in
this region.

Core regions, which are central in Krugman's work, are more diverse and
larger than Porter's clusters. The New Economic Geography, of which Krugman is the most prominent representative, started by observing that economic
activity concentrates in agglomerations that can only be explainable by regional
competitiveness.[18] Therefore, Krugman incorporated a geographical dimension in an economic model, using increasing returns to scale and externalities
as explanations.[19] Contrary to Porter's specific externalities, for Krugman any
economic concentration results in positive externalities and increasing returns.
His core regions are urbanised, developed and have wealthy customers, trained
labour and a good infrastructure. New activities are set up in such regions.[20]
"Because of the costs of distance in economic transactions, the preferred locations for producers are those where demand is large or supply particularly
convenient – which in general are locations chosen by other producers."[21]
Therefore, it makes sense "to talk about competitiveness for regions in a way
one wouldn't talk about it for larger units."[22] According to Krugman, the idea
that there is such a thing as national competitiveness is incompatible with
Ricardian ideas on trade that focus on the competitiveness of companies, not
of countries.

As a result of the research by Porter and, especially, Krugman, regional development received growing attention and Krugman even turned analysing economies on a national level into a matter of dispute. The idea that it is better
to analyse economic regions is not new; as far back as the 1980s, the British
economic historian Sidney Pollard wrote about one of the most prominent
topics in economic history, industrialisation, as a process that did not happen in
Britain or Germany, but in Lancashire or the Ruhr area.[23] Recent economic
history research shows that it is not just in the Netherlands, but also in Germany, that a national economy only came into being after 1914, and then only
by political manipulation – wartime measures, tariffs and monetary protection.
The late 19th-century nation state, with monetary stability and a low level of
protection, is hardly an appropriate unit for economic analysis. The same is
probably also true for late 20th-century states.[24]

The concept of regional competitiveness implies that Krugman's division
in core periphery regions is only accidentally congruent with the political
division in nation states, or – when it is – that this is created by protectionism
undermining trade contacts that would otherwise improve the economies of
the diverse parts of such regions. In a continental-wide country like the US,
the political unit will fall apart in a number of regions. In politically divided
Europe, however, a country could well be part of a core periphery pattern that
is larger than the state. In fact, when Krugman found that exports were more
than 50 per cent of Belgian and Dutch GDP in the 1990s, he claimed that
these countries should be "best thought of as part of an integrated economic

region that comprises northern France and, most important, the Ruhr and other nearby areas of Germany." He continued: "different pieces of a productive process tend to be spread across this region in much the same way that manufacturing plants in the modern U.S. automobile industry tend to be scattered across a fairly wide area of the Midwest."[25]

In a cluster of similar industries, externalities stimulate activity, while increasing returns not only motivate other industries to settle in the same region, but therefore also secure the continuity of regions with a high level of economic activity. In an article on the Manufacturing Belt, Krugman concludes that this area, just like the Rhine region, survived as a core region even though the reason for its development disappeared long ago. "Increasing returns and cumulative processes are pervasive and give an often decisive role to historical accident," or as some geographers wrote, "history matters."[26] In the Rhine region, there was a strong tendency towards clustering resource-bound industries, while increasing returns stimulated non-location-bound industries to also settle there during the pre-1914 period. After 1945, the period of coal came to an end, but increasing returns ensured that activities remained at a high level. The rise of the Asian economies in the globalisation wave of the late 20th and early 21st century ultimately caused a renewed period of transnationalisation, as manufacturing was offshored. Former industrial areas such as the German Ruhr or the US regions of the Manufacturing Belt did not manage to survive as major centres of industry, but instead developed in post-industrial crisis areas.

The Rhine basin as a transnational economic region

In Krugman's parlance, the Rhine basin as a core region is the result of a historical accident, perpetuated and sustained by self-reinforcing agglomeration effects. The nature and causes of the accident, however, remain obscure. Moreover, at times, the durability of core regions is threatened by dramatic political dramas, such as world wars, major economic crises, or economic transformations such as the transition from coal to oil. In other words, applying new economic geography reveals precious little as to how and why the Rhine River gave rise to a transnational economic core region. Explaining historical accidents requires an analysis of the actors involved in shaping the hard- and software of cross-border economic relations, i.e. the state as the provider of public goods and regulator of economic activity on the one hand, and risk-taking, innovating entrepreneurs on the other. The national bias of economic statistics and data, however, severely complicates such an analysis. This problem should be addressed by transnational research methods.

Transnational history developed out of a wide variety of research undertaken in cultural, political, post-colonial and global history. Although each proposed a slightly different term – related, connected, transfer, crossing, international, world or global history – they share the realisation that "[w]e can shape our territorial units of research according to the issues we want to study, instead of forcing these issues onto existing territories."[27] Existing notions of the national economy, fixating a national unit out of a regional economy, forego the objective and research question of this book. This implies the need to trace the relations within the wider region to reconstruct and establish the contours, nature and development of the Rhine economic region. Nature shaped the region; these relations were not only determined by entrepreneurs, traders, captains of industry and managers of multinational companies, but also by local and national governments. Over time, relations congealed into business networks, some formal and hierarchical, others loose and flexible. These relations and networks gave rise to circulations of goods, capital, people and knowledge. Although nationalist politics and policies regularly interfered in transnational connections, such relations and circulations are only partially captured by national sources and statistics. The methodology of this study, therefore, looks towards primary sources rather than national (statistical) data to establish and reconstruct the relations between the various ports and industrial and urban clusters within the Rhine basin.

A long-running debate in regional studies is the distinction between space as territory and space as relation.[28] Brought on by the current wave of globalisation, space is increasingly being thought of as constituted by relations. This means that regions are not territorially fixed through inherent characteristics such as climate or discursively delineated by politics or identity, but are open, dynamic and the result of multiple overlapping networks.[29] This has shifted attention away from a preoccupation of boundaries to the study of relations, connectivity and networks. Such an approach sits comfortably with economics – trade, transport, foreign direct investment, values and supply chains. Indeed, within the field of geography, just as in economics, the debate comes down to the question of what to make of the nation state. Some have argued that, given the openness and global connectivity of regions, politics should move away from their territorial, national foundations, while others maintain that territorial politics and identity even greatly affect global and trans-territorial economic relations.[30] A crucial question to ask is: what is related? If everything is more or less related, there is no spatial concept of a region. Applied to the Lower Rhine basin, the unbounded relational perspective would yield a meaningless spatial construct, because it would negate our argument that conceptualising the Lower Rhine basin as a transnational economic region is relevant. Instead, the research presented here balances the twin ideas of the unbounded region constituted by relations and the bounded region in which trans-territorial relations are constrained by politics and the costs of transacting across distance.

The transnational economic relations that shaped the Lower Rhine region were of a varying nature at different points in time, ranging from market-based relations, to networks, to hierarchically integrated multinational enterprises. In some periods, such as in the mid-19th century, transnational relations were mainly market-based. Local industries relied on local and foreign merchants for imports and exports. Increasing scale and price and economic fluctuations in the Ruhr industries fostered the emergence of horizontal and vertical integration. Coal mining companies cartelised production and sales in the late 19th and early 20th century, extending across borders to organise exports to the Netherlands and (via Rotterdam) beyond. The tightly networked structure of the cartelised Ruhr coal industry was instrumental in the dominant role that the Rhine and Rotterdam gained in the organisation of Ruhr coal exports before 1914. Rising tariff barriers and monetary and currency restrictions increasingly stimulated the formation of cross-border hierarchical business relations. After World War I, multinational companies progressively came to dominate economic activities and relations in the Lower Rhine region.[31] Major coal, steel, chemicals, oil, food and fibre companies owned factories on both sides of the border. They also often owned or controlled Rhine fleets, pipelines and transhipment and storage facilities, tightly integrating the Lower Rhine region into their vertically integrated value chains.

Multinationals continued to dominate the transnational economic relations in the Lower Rhine region throughout the 20th century.[32] Containerisation, however, gave rise to the networked and market-based relations that typified globalising supply chains. Although container shipping and terminals became highly concentrated industries themselves, the flow of containerised goods was increasingly dictated by small changes in the cost of transhipment, creating port competition and contested hinterlands to a greater degree than in highly integrated industries like oil and petrochemicals. Analysing the different modes under which cross-border trade and transport was organised in the Lower Rhine region helps us to understand and explain the historical ebb and flow of transnational economic relations in the area. Moreover, it sheds light on the economic geography of infrastructures and production facilities, which are the building blocks of the regional economy. Importantly, tracing these different modes of exchange also brings into focus the political dimension regarding, for instance, issues of foreign ownership, cross-border infrastructure or the impact of national policies and regulations on international trade, business networks and multinational companies.

Such debates are highly relevant for the conception of a transnational region for three reasons. First, a relational approach to regions proposes an actor-oriented geography, emphasising networks as spatial relations. This allows for an open, flexible and dynamic concept of region that is well attuned to studying business networks and transport infrastructures as the basis for economic geography. Second, it is apparent that trans-territorial (or transnational) relations and networks are constrained by bounded political borders, geography and distance. Third, it appears important not to juxtapose a spatial concept based on networks with one based on territory. Although our historical data suggest that the transnational Lower Rhine basin is a highly relevant regional concept for explaining the economic growth of places within it, focusing on the territorial demarcation of the transnational Lower Rhine region is missing the point. The territorial politics on both sides of the Dutch-German border, and the lack of any political, social and cultural initiative or discourse arguing for a Lower Rhine territorial region, makes that clear. Our proposal, therefore, is that the Lower Rhine basin is a region in the relational, but not strictly in the territorial, sense, as it will be hard to define its borders. When it is possible to do so in a certain period, these borders are shifting. Moreover, we argue that the absence of a territorial region has imposed spatial constraints on the relational region, making it vulnerable and dynamic over time.[33] There is growing literature in urban and regional studies, as well as in port and transport geography and economics, that emphasises open, flexible and historically contingent conceptions of places and regions.[34] Although such conceptions of flexible scale have typically emerged in response to globalisation and the perceived diminishing relevance of the nation state, they also have historical significance, in particular with regard to as fickle a concept as the transnational region.

This book is not only preoccupied with measuring and reconstructing relations and circulations in the Rhine region, because this alone cannot explain historical ruptures or continuities. An explanation of sustained (or disrupted) cross-border economic interactions must include an understanding of why and how interrelations developed and evolved. As our book concerns a port city and its historical relations with its hinterland, we have turned to the concept of hinterland to frame and study the relationships between places in the Lower Rhine region. The port-hinterland constellation implies a functional relationship where the port provides transhipment, transport and other trade-related services to productive and consumptive clusters in the hinterland.

In recent years, port-hinterland formations have increasingly been perceived from a global supply chain perspective, due to globalisation, the fragmentation of value chains and the rise of container transport and logistics.[35] A supply chain is a network of organisations that jointly coordinate and organise the activities in the value chain between producer and customer.[36] Supply chain networks in principle encompass all the actors and organisations that engage in one way or the other in the production, transportation and marketing of products or the regulation of any of these activities. Combining the spatial concept of the hinterland with the supply chain's actor-network perspective establishes an empirical and historical connection between the assembly of supply chains and the development of port-hinterland relations.[37] The growing interest in supply chains (or commodity chains) is directly linked to the complex logistics of containerised transport and fragmented value chains, but the basic concepts apply to all types of goods. Bulk chains are typically less complex, and economies of scale often largely explain localisation and logistics. Yet the basic questions remain the same: how are producers connected to consumers, and how does this affect port-hinterland relations?

Notteboom and Rodrigue suggested a particularly encompassing model of the port-hinterland formation: they propose a layered model of the hinterland that consists of two components. The first of these models port development. Investments in port infrastructure and transport capacity derive from a demand pull from the needs of supply chain management and logistics on the one hand, and a supply push from port managers seeking to valorise the port's location and facilities on the other. These port dynamics fit into a port-hinterland model that embeds the port-hinterland formation in global supply chains. The hinterland model, which is the second component, consists of a macro-economic layer, which essentially represents global geographies of production and consumption and the complex of macro-economic and policy factors that affect direct investments, production locations and, ultimately, trade. Trade gives rise to demand for transport, which requires infrastructure and transport capacity represented by the physical layer. The intensity of the regional interrelations is determined on the logistical level. Here, the transport costs of the available infrastructure and transport capacity feed into the logistical decisions of supply chain managers who are coordinating those involved in production, transportation and marketing, resulting in the actual flow of goods. The intensity and variability of these flows depend on the level of flexibility and adaptability of the infrastructure and transport capacities. Among other aspects, the nature of the industry (resource-bound or not), asset specificity, sunk costs, economies of scale and regulation are factors that determine to what extent flows are footloose or fixed. This, in turn, has implications for the intensity, longevity and stability of transnational regional relations. Drivers of historical change can occur on either level of the model, i.e. they can derive from macro-economic, infrastructural or logistical change.

Combined, the port dynamics and hinterland models identify three drivers of infrastructural and transport investment: the macro-economic geography of production and trade, the logistical requirements of supply chains and the locational valorisation of ports. Although infrastructure, transport capacity and the flow of goods represent the measurable, material attributes of the port-hinterland formation, the significance of this model is the emphasis on actors and their interactions, consisting of port managers, local and national governments, local and multinational firms and other organisations and bodies at various levels. Particularly central to the study is the network of organisations that is involved in the supply chain and logistical decision-making. Although this and similar models have been developed in order to study the relationship between port management and the complexity of globalised supply chains with regard to container logistics, there are no impediments to using the model to study any commodity at any point in time. At any one time, there is a macro-economic context where capital flows give rise to international divisions of labour and geographies of production and trade within a specific set of political and international relations and constraints. There are public and private actors involved in orchestrating international trade, and there are public and private investments in infrastructure and transport capacity. Finally, there are ports that attempt to capture trade flows by facilitating efficient transport, transhipment, storage and processing. At any one time, these elements give rise to port-hinterland formations, however limited or expansive.

The chapters in this book are organised chronologically, reflecting periods of major transitions. Chapter 2 traces the origins of the political and institutional foundations for the emergence of the Rhine economy in the 19th century. Chapter 3 considers the emergence of heavy industry in the German Ruhr area and its increasing reliance on foreign resources and markets. Combined, Chapters 2 and 3 explain how the principles of free trade and navigation, German unification, entrepreneurship and technological innovation and the fortuity of natural geography shaped the foundations of the Lower Rhine economic region in the 19th century. Chapter 4 considers how nationalist economic policies resulting from the Depression and World War II complicated Dutch-German business and economic relations between the 1930s and 1950s. It shows that multinational companies and governments created the economic reality and shaped the Lower Rhine economy, but this was frequently against the odds and was often accompanied with conflicts and discontent. The after-effects of protectionism and war after 1945 and the subsequent economic boom of the 1960s is the theme of Chapter 5. The transition to oil decimated the German coal industry – the founding industry of the Lower Rhine region – but the successful transition of related industries and the return to normal economic relations between the Netherlands and the Federal Republic of Germany in the mid-1950s fostered a new period of growth in the Lower Rhine region. Finally, Chapter 6 traces how globalisation, de-industrialisation of the Ruhr area and the diffusion of footloose container logistics from the 1970s onwards unravelled the transnational connections in the Lower Rhine region. After the 1990s, rising port competition for container flows to and from the European interior made the Rhine delta's German hinterland increasingly a contested, rather than a captive, hinterland.

Notes

1 Hein A.M. Klemann, *Waarom bestaat Nederland eigenlijk nog? Nederland-Duitsland: Economische Integratie en politieke consequenties 1860–2006* (Rotterdam: Erasmus University, 2006).
2 Joep Schenk, *Havenbaronnen en Ruhrbonzen. Oorsprong van een wederzijdse afhankelijkheidsrelatie tussen Rotterdam en het Ruhrgebied 1870–1914* (Rotterdam: Erasmus University, 2015). Supervisors: Prof. Dr. H.A.M. Klemann, Prof. Dr. B. Wubs.
3 Marten Boon, *Oil Pipelines, Politics and International Business: The Rotterdam Oil Port, Royal Dutch Shell and the German Hinterland, 1945–1975 (Rotterdam: Erasmus University, 2014). Supervisors:* Prof. Dr. H.A.M. Klemann, Prof. Dr. B. Wubs.
4 Klara M. Paardenkooper [Süli], *The Port of Rotterdam and the Maritime Container: The Rise and Fall of Rotterdam's Hinterland (1966–2010) (Rotterdam: Erasmus University, 2014). Supervisors:* Prof. Dr. H.A.M. Klemann, Prof. Dr. B. Wubs.
5 Centraal Bureau voor de Statistiek, *Tweehonderd jaar statistiek in tijdreeksen* (Voorburg: CBS, 1999); Authors' own calculations.
6 Paul Krugman, "Growing World Trade: Causes and Consequences," *Brookings Papers on Economic Activity* 1 (1995): 327–377, there 330–334.
7 Nikolaus Wolf, "Was Germany Ever United? Evidence from Intra- and International Trade, 1885–1933," *Journal of Economic History* 69, no. 3 (2009): 846–881, there 867–870.
8 Nina Glick-Schiller and Andreas Wimmer, "Methodological Nationalism and Beyond: Nation-State Building, Migration and the Social Sciences," *Global Networks* 2, no. 4 (2002): 301–334; also: Daniel Chernilo, "Social Theory's Methodological Nationalism: Myth and Reality," *European Journal of Social Theory* 9, no. 1 (2006): 5–22.
9 See: Jan Luiten van Zanden and Arthur van Riel, *Nederland 1870–1914. Staat, instituties en economische ontwikkeling* (Amsterdam: Balans, 2000), 218; Jan Pieter Smits, Edwin Horlings, and Jan Luiten van Zanden, *Dutch GNP and Its Components, 1800–1913*

(Monograph Series 5) (Groningen: Rijksuniversiteit Groningen 2000); CBS, *Tweehonderd jaar statistiek*.

10 van Zanden and van Riel, *Nederland 1870–1914*, 218.

11 Helmuth Böhme, *Deutschlands Weg zur Großmacht. Studien zum Verhältnis von Wirtschaft und Staat während der Reichsgründungszeit 1848–1881*, 3rd ed. (Cologne: Kiepenheuer & Witsch, 1974), 95.

12 Jan Pieter Smits, "Economische ontwikkeling, 1800–1995," in *Nationaal goed. Feiten en cijfers over onze samenleving (ca.) 1800–1999*, ed. R. van der Bie and P. Dehing (Voorburg and Heerlen: CBS 1999), 15–36 there 18–19.

13 CBS, *Tweehonderd jaar statistiek*; authors' own calculations.

14 Ron Martin, "Economic Geography and the New Discourse of Regional Competitiveness," in *Economic Geography: Past, Present and Future*, ed. Sharmistha Bagchi-Sen and Helen Lawton Smith (London and New York: Routledge, 2006), 159–172, 163.

15 Mercedes Delgado, Michael E. Porter, and Scott Stern, "Clusters, Convergence and Economic Performance," *US Census Bureau Center for Economic Studies, Paper No. CES-WP-10-34*, 21 October 2010.

16 Michael E. Porter, "Regions and the New Economics of Competition," in *Global City Regions*, ed. A.J. Scott (Oxford: Oxford University Press, 2001), 139–152; Michael E. Porter, "The Economic Performance of Regions," *Regional Studies* 37, nos 6–7 (2003): 571.

17 Michael E. Porter, "Clusters and the New Economics of Competition," *Harvard Business Review* 76, no. 6 (November–December 1998): 80.

18 M. Fujita, P. Krugman, and A.J. Venables, *The Spatial Economy: Cities, Regions, and International Trade* (Cambridge, MA and London: The MIT Press, 1999), 1–12.

19 Paul Krugman, "Increasing Returns and Economic Geography," *The Journal of Political Economy* 99, no. 3 (1991): 483–499, passim.

20 Paul Krugman, "Urban Concentration: The Role of Increasing Returns and Transportation Costs," *International Regional Science Review* 19, no. 1–2 (April 1996): 5–30; Andrew M. Isserman, "'It's Obvious, It's Wrong, and Anyway They Said It Years Ago'? Paul Krugman on Large Cities," *International Regional Science Review* 19, no. 1–2 (April 1996): 37–48.

21 Paul Krugman, *Geography and Trade* (Leuven: Leuven University Press, 1991), 98.

22 Paul Krugman, *Growth on the Periphery: Second Wind for Industrial Regions?* (Strathclyde: Allander Institute, 2003), 23–24.

23 Sidney Pollard, *Peaceful Conquest: The Industrialisation of Europe, 1760–1970* (Oxford: Oxford University Press, 1981), 45–46.

24 Wolf, "Was Germany Ever United?"; Klemann, *Waarom bestaat Nederland eigenlijk nog?*; H.A.M. Klemann and F. Wielenga, "Die Niederlande und Deutschland, oder verschwindet die nationale Ökonomie?," in *Deutschland und die Niederlande Wirtschaftsbeziehungen im 19. und 20. Jahrhundert*, ed. H.A.M. Klemann and F. Wielenga (Münster: Waxmann Verlag, 2009), 7–17.

25 Krugman, "Growing World Trade," 335.

26 R. Martin and P. Sunley, "Paul Krugman's Geographical Economics and Its Implications for Regional Development Theory: A Critical Assessment," *Economic Geography* 72, no. 3 (1996): 263.

27 P.Y. Saunier, *Transnational History* (Basingstoke: Palgrave Macmillan, 2013), 115.

28 Martin Jones, "Phase Space: Geography, Relational Thinking, and Beyond," *Progress in Human Geography* 33, no. 4 (2009): 487–506, there 489–491.

29 Ibid., 493.

30 Ash Amin, "Regions Unbound: Towards a New Politics of Place," *Geografiska Annaler: Series B, Human Geography* 86, no. 1 (2004): 33–44; Henry Wai-chung Yeung, "Rethinking Relational Economic Geography," *Transactions of the Institute of British Geographers* 30, Ano. 1 (2005): 37–51.

31 Ben Wubs, *International Business and National War Interests: Unilever between Reich and Empire, 1939–1945* (London: Routledge, 2008), 11–13, 37–40.

32 Ben Wubs, "A Dutch Multinational's Miracle in Post-War Germany," *Jahrbuch für Wirtschaftsgeschichte/ Yearbook for Economic History* 53, no. 1 (2012): 15–41.

33 Krisztina Varró and Arnoud Lagendijk, "Conceptualizing the Region: In What Sense Relational?," *Regional Studies* 47, no. 1 (2013): 18–28; Jones, "Phase Space"; Bob Jessop, Neil Brenner, and Martin S. Jones, "Theorizing Sociospatial Relations," *Environment and Planning D: Society and Space* 26, no. 3 (2013): 389–401.
34 Peter A. Hall and Markus Hesse, "Reconciling Cities and Flows in Geography and Regional Studies," in *Cities, Regions and Flows*, ed. Peter A. Hall and Markus Hesse (Hoboken: Taylor and Francis, 2013), 3–20.
35 James Wang, *Ports, Cities and Global Supply Chains, Transport and Mobility Series* (Aldershot: Ashgate, 2007).
36 Martin Christopher, *Logistics and Supply Chain Management: Strategies for Reducing Cost and Improving Service*, 2nd ed. (London: Financial Times and Prentice Hall, 1998).
37 Theo Notteboom and Jean-Paul Rodrigue, "Re-Assessing Port-Hinterland Relationships in the Context of Global Commodity Chains," in *Ports, Cities, and Global Supply Chains*, ed. J. Wang, et al. (London: Routledge, 2007), 51–69.

Bibliography

Amin, Ash (2004), "Regions unbound: Towards a new politics of place." *Geografiska Annaler: Series B, Human Geography* 86, no. 1: 33–44. doi: 10.1111/j.0435-3684.2004.00152.x.
Böhme, Helmuth (1974), *Deutschlands Weg zur Großmacht. Studien zum Verhältnis von Wirtschaft und Staat während der Reichsgründungszeit 1848–1881*. 3rd ed. (Cologne: Kiepenheuer and Witsch).
Boon, Marten (2014), *Oil Pipelines, Politics and International Business: The Rotterdam Oil Port, Royal Dutch Shell and the German Hinterland, 1945–1975* (Rotterdam: Erasmus University).
Centraal Bureau voor de Statistiek (1999), *Tweehonderd jaar statistiek in tijdreeksen* (Voorburg: CBS).
Chernilo, Daniel (2006), "Social theory's methodological nationalism: Myth and reality." *European Journal of Social Theory* 9, no. 1: 5–22.
Christopher, Martin (1998), *Logistics and Supply Chain Management: Strategies for Reducing Cost and Improving Service*. 2nd ed. (London: Financial Times and Prentice Hall).
Delgado, Mercedes, Michael E. Porter, and Scott Stern (2010), "Clusters, convergence and economic performance." 21 October. *US Census Bureau Centre for Economic Studies*, Paper No. CES-WP: 10–34.
Fujita, Masahisa, Paul Krugman, and Anthony J. Venables (1999), *The Spatial Economy: Cities, Regions, and International Trade* (Cambridge, MA and London: The MIT Press).
Hall, Peter A., and Markus Hesse (2013), "Reconciling cities and flows in geography and regional studies." In *Cities, Regions and Flows*, edited by Peter A. Hall and Markus Hesse: 3–20 (Hoboken: Taylor and Francis).
Hölscher, Lucian, and Sidney Pollard (1980), *Region und Industrialisierung: Studien zur Rolle der Region in der Wirtschaftsgeschichte der letzten zwei Jahrhunderte*. Vol. 42. Kritische Studien zur Geschichtswissenschaft (Göttingen: Vandenhoeck & Ruprecht).
Isserman, Andrew M. (1996), "'It's obvious, it's wrong, and anyway they said it years ago' Paul Krugman on Large Cities." *International Regional Science Review* 19, no. 1–2: 37–48.
Jessop, Bob, Neil Brenner, and Martin S. Jones (2008), "Theorizing sociospatial relations." *Environment and Planning D: Society and Space* 26, no. 3: 389–401. doi: 10.1068/d9107.
Jones, Martin (2009), "Phase space: Geography, relational thinking, and beyond." *Progress in Human Geography* 33 no. 4: 487–506. doi: 10.1177/0309132508101599.
Jones, Martin, and Anssi Paasi (2013), "Guest editorial: Regional world(s): Advancing the geography of regions." *Regional Studies* 47, no. 1: 1–5. doi: 10.1080/00343404.2013.746437.
Klemann, Hein A.M. (2006), *Waarom bestaat Nederland eigenlijk nog? Nederland-Duitsland: Economische Integratie en politieke consequenties 1860–2006* (Rotterdam: Erasmus University).

Klemann, Hein A.M., and Friso Wielenga (2009), "Die Niederlande und Deutschland, oder verschwindet die nationale Ökonomie?" In *Deutschland und die Niederlande Wirtschafts-beziehungen im 19. und 20. Jahrhundert*, edited by Hein A.M. Klemann and Friso Wielenga: 7–17 (Münster: Waxmann Verlag).

Krugman, Paul (1991a), *Geography and Trade* (Leuven: Leuven University Press).

Krugman, Paul (1991b), "Increasing returns and economic geography." *The Journal of Political Economy* 99, no. 3: 483–499.

Krugman, Paul (1995a), *Development, Geography, and Economic Theory*. Vol. 6. The Ohlin Lectures (Cambridge, MA: MIT Press).

Krugman, Paul (1995b), "Growing world trade: Causes and consequences." *Brookings Papers on Economic Activity* 1: 327–377.

Krugman, Paul, (1996a), "Making sense of the competitiveness debate." *Oxford Review of Economic Policy* 12, no. 3: 17–25.

Krugman, Paul (1996b), "Urban concentration: The role of increasing returns and transportation costs." *International Regional Science Review* 19, no. 1–2: 5–30.

Krugman, Paul (2003), *Growth on the Periphery: Second Wind for Industrial Regions?* (Strathclyde: Fraser Allander Institute).

Martin, Ron (2006), "Economic geography and the new discourse of regional competitiveness." In *Economic Geography: Past, Present and Future*, edited by Sharmistha Bagchi-Sen and Helen Lawton Smith: 159–172 (London and New York: Routledge).

Martin, Ron, and Peter Sunley (1996), "Paul Krugman's geographical economics and its implications for regional development theory: A critical assessment." *Economic Geography* 72, no. 3: 259–292.

Notteboom, Theo, and Jean-Paul Rodrigue (2007), "Re-assessing port-hinterland relationships in the context of global commodity chains." In *Ports, Cities, and Global Supply Chains*, edited by J. Wang and et al.: 51–69 (London and New York: Routledge).

Paardenkooper [Süli], Klara M. (2014), *The Port of Rotterdam and the Maritime Container: The Rise and Fall of Rotterdam's Hinterland (1966–2010)* (Rotterdam: Erasmus University).

Pollard, Sidney (1981), *Peaceful Conquest: The Industrialisation of Europe, 1760–1970* (Oxford: Oxford University Press).

Porter, Michael E. (1990), *The Competitive Advantage of Nations* (Basingstoke: Macmillan).

Porter, Michael E. (1998), "Clusters and the new economics of competition." *Harvard Business Review* 76, no. 6: 77–90.

Porter, Michael E. (2001), "Regions and the new economics of competition." In *Global City Regions*, edited by A.J. Scott: 139–152 (Oxford: Oxford University Press).

Porter, Michael E. (2003), "The economic performance of regions." *Regional Studies* 37, nos 6–7: 549–578.

Pred, Alan (1962), *The External Relations of Cities during "Industrial Revolution"* (Chicago, IL: Chicago University Press).

Saunier, Pierre-Yves (2013), *Transnational History* (Basingstoke: Palgrave Macmillan).

Schenk, Joep (2015), *Havenbaronnen en Ruhrbonzen. Oorsprong van een wederzijdse afhankelijkheidsrelatie tussen Rotterdam en het Ruhrgebied 1870–1914* (Rotterdam: Erasmus University).

Schiller, Nina Glick, and Andreas Wimmer (2002), "Methodological nationalism and beyond: Nation-state building, migration and the social sciences." *Global Networks* 2, no. 4: 301–334.

Smits, Jan Pieter (1999), "Economische ontwikkeling, 1800–1995." In *Nationaal goed. Feiten en cijfers over onze samenleving (ca.) 1800–1999*, edited by R. van der Bie and P. Dehing: 15–36 (Voorburg and Heerlen: CBS).

Smits, Jan Pieter, Edwin Horlings, and Jan Luiten van Zanden (2000), *Dutch GNP and its components, 1800–1913*. Monograph Series 5 (Groningen: Rijksuniversiteit Groningen).

Varró, Krisztina, and Arnoud Lagendijk (2013), "Conceptualizing the region: In what sense relational?" *Regional Studies* 47, no. 1: 18–28. doi: 10.1080/00343404.2011.602334.

Wang, James (2007), *Ports, Cities and Global Supply Chains: Transport and Mobility Series* (Aldershot: Ashgate).

Wolf, Nikolaus (2009), "Was Germany ever united? Evidence from intra- and international trade, 1885–1933." *Journal of Economic History* 69, no. 3: 846–881.

Wubs, Ben (2008), *International Business and National War Interests: Unilever between Reich and Empire, 1939–1945.* London: Routledge.

Wubs, Ben (2012), "A Dutch multinational's miracle in post-war Germany." *Jahrbuch für Wirtschaftsgeschichte/Yearbook for Economic History* 53, no. 1: 15–41.

Yeung, Henry Wai-chung (2005), "Rethinking relational economic geography." *Transactions of the Institute of British Geographers* 30, no. 1: 37–51. doi: 10.1111/j.1475-5661.2005.00150.x.

Zanden, Jan Luiten van, and Arthur van Riel (2000), *Nederland 1870–1914. Staat, instituties en economische ontwikkeling* (Amsterdam: Balans).

2 The Rhine in the long 19th century

Creating the Lower Rhine region[1]

Hein A.M. Klemann and Joep Schenk

Introduction

In 1814–1815, after over 20 years of war, Europe's leaders gathered in Vienna in an attempt to bring peace and security to the war-ridden continent. The congregated princes and diplomats not only discussed territorial issues, but also looked for alternative ways to settle disputes.[2] This resulted in multilateral conferences in which the five most important states made decisions on general European matters, thus limiting the sovereignty of their smaller brothers.[3] However, due to growing rivalry, this "Concert of Europe" system eroded in the following decades. In the economic sphere, though, some outcomes were more lasting. Most prominent was the principle of free navigation on international rivers, as well as the foundation of the Central Commission for Navigation of the Rhine (CCNR).[4]

Even in 1814, the peace treaty that was signed in Paris emphasised the importance of cross-border rivers as commerce arteries. The principle of free river navigation was articulated to stimulate trade between nations.[5] For the Rhine, which was Europe's most important, navigable river, the Vienna Congress put these principles into practice. Nonetheless, the decades after 1815 were characterised by passionate disputes between Prussia and the United Kingdom of the Netherlands (including Belgium and with Luxembourg in a personal union) about the precise application of these principles. Consequently, only weak ties linked the Dutch estuary ports with its hinterland. In the Dutch-Prussian diplomatic struggles, Rhine navigation and economic interests became mixed up with the political tension that existed between the smallest European power – Prussia – and the largest of the smaller states – the United Netherlands.

This chapter analyses how, despite friction between those in favour of free navigation and those opposing it, and notwithstanding recurring tensions between Prussia and the Netherlands, a more liberal river regime was introduced in the course of the 19th century. This regime, in turn, led to a highly competitive international transport market and encouraged the individual riparian states to invest in major hydraulic building activities to improve navigation. These developments made the Rhine estuary Port of Rotterdam highly competitive.

As the Rhine linked the North Sea with what, during the 19th century, became Europe's most important industrial centre – the Rhine-Ruhr area – these developments were vital for the economy of a transnational region that included large parts of the Netherlands and the German Lower and Middle Rhine areas.[6] This region explains Rotterdam's high-ranking position among the ports of Europe, as well as the extremely high level of trade that characterised the Dutch economy from the 1860s onwards.[7] That the Rotterdam port was in a sovereign state other than the industrial centre it served demonstrates that economic regions and political entities did not necessarily – and probably only accidently – cover the same geographical territory. Nonetheless, relations within the region were complicated by the fact that the political and economic geography did not fall together. It is therefore necessary to explain how parts of different states could develop into one economic region during a period of growing nationalism.

Free navigation, modernisation and river canalisation were highly sensitive and politicised topics in the 19th century. In the Netherlands, political agents had reasons to limit free navigation, while in Prussia, especially in Cologne, which was the most important trading centre in Prussia's newly obtained Western provinces, the business community strongly favoured liberalisation. Berlin backed the Cologne business community for economic reasons, but also because the Dutch kingdom was the only rival that was not too big for an argument. The Netherlands also backed its business communities in their endeavours to again become the middlemen in European trade. Accordingly, the country attempted to exploit the monopoly on the connection between the Prussian Rhine provinces and the sea. Simultaneously, King William I hoped to achieve a higher political ranking and obtain a seat in the Concert of Europe by undermining the position of his brother-in-law, King Frederic William III of Prussia. During the entire 19th and early 20th centuries, German-Dutch economic competition, as well as rivalries between economic actors within these countries, became intertwined with political interests. This chapter analyses the position of diverse agents, their rivalries and coalitions on both sides of the border, as well as their cross-border coalitions. This should ultimately answer the question of why, in a period in which railroads destroyed inland navigation almost everywhere else, the Rhine became a completely liberalised and canalised transport route linking dominant German industrial centres with the overseas world through a Dutch port.

Napoleon's legacy and the Vienna Congress

The Vienna Congress did not pluck the idea of a free Rhine out of thin air; even the 1814 Paris Peace Treaty stipulated the principle that "navigation on the Rhine should be free from the point where the river becomes navigable until the sea and vice versa and may not be prohibited to anyone."[8] This idea had its ideological origins in 18th-century liberal principles spread by the Revolution and the Napoleonic armies. In 1804, as a result of Germany's mediatisation to France, the Napoleonic Empire reached an agreement with the crumbling Holy Roman Empire (the first *Kaiserreich*) to reorganise, liberalise and simplify Rhine navigation between the Swiss and Dutch border. From that point on, a French-dominated, Franco-German board, instead of numerous individual states, raised river tolls, which had been markedly reduced. In addition, the staple rights of Mainz and Cologne were abolished, and it was no longer compulsory to offer all cargo for sale when passing through these cities. As shipping on the Cologne-Mainz track remained a monopoly of the Cologne Skippers' Guild, and from Mainz to Mannheim of the Mainz Guild, transhipping nonetheless remained compulsory. As Dutch skippers retained their monopoly over the track to Cologne and the river was barely navigable south of Mannheim, administrative decisions, and not market forces, regulated barging and freight rates on the entire Rhine.

After the defeat of Napoleon Bonaparte, the Dutch track again became subject to the authority of the Dutch sovereign, the later King William I, while the Franco-German track was governed by diverse German princes and the restored French kingdom. In December 1813, before the Paris Peace Treaty marked the end of hostilities and prohibited increased tolls, the Dutch prince reintroduced them on his track.[9] Taxation and regulations were also reintroduced in several German principalities. As a consequence, the Allied powers feared that the Rhine would be reduced to the heavily taxed, over-regulated, inefficient transport route that it was before 1804.[10] Although Napoleon's Continental System had obscured its effects, the fact that Rhine liberalisation encouraged trade was clearly understood. Accordingly, at the Congress of Vienna, the 1804 German-French agreement was taken as a starting point for the future Rhine regime.[11]

In 1815, the Vienna Congress founded the Central Commission for Navigation of the Rhine (CCNR). France, the Netherlands, Prussia and four other German states became members of this Commission, which commenced its activities in 1816. According to the Vienna agreement, Rhine navigation could not be prohibited for anyone and should be free from the point where the river became navigable to the sea. This did not mean free from tolls or taxes, but from discrimination against foreign (riparian) flags or cargo. Furthermore, the CCNR was to ensure that tolls were reduced and used to finance the maintenance of water-courses, channels and towpaths.[12] It was also expected to unify regulations. Initially, it was unsuccessful, as it had to manage resistance from several member states whose monarchs appealed to their sovereignty. Indeed, they protected local interests by continuing to levy tolls and taxes.[13]

Dutch protectionism and Prussian trade

As each CCNR member state interpreted the Vienna Congress and the mandate of the Commission in accordance with its own interests, it took 16 years to agree on a workable set of regulations. In the Netherlands, the king backed the business communities in the port cities, which wanted to exploit their monopoly on connections between the sea and the German Rhineland and Westphalia, which were provinces Berlin obtained in Vienna. The Netherlands was in a position to do this, as it controlled all continental North Sea ports, including

Antwerp. In Vienna, the British had backed the Dutch getting these territories. William Pitt the Younger (1759–1806), the British prime minster during most of the wars against France, described Antwerp as a pistol pointed at the heart of England.[14] Accordingly, as long ago as 1805, he wrote to his ally on the other side of the continent, Tsar Alexander I, stating that the Netherlands should be restored and extended to include Antwerp after Napoleon's defeat. An unchallenged position on the seas, not least the North Sea, was essential for London. Pitt thus hoped to keep all North Sea ports out of the hands of any threatening power. Consequently, to ensure that the new Dutch realm was defendable, it should be enhanced with a bordering territory.[15]

After Napoleon's 1813 defeat, Prince William Frederick of Orange, the future king and eldest son of stadholder William V, hoped to restore the Netherlands and make it larger than the Dutch Republic had ever been. The British Foreign Minister, Lord Castlereagh, a political sympathiser of the deceased Pitt, agreed. Prince William hoped to expand his future principality to cover the former Austrian Netherlands, including the Prince-Bishopric of Liège, as well as all German territory west of the Rhine, including Cologne. This was too much for Castlereagh; he wanted to keep the North Sea ports out of the hands of any major continental power, meaning that the Netherlands should not be allowed to become one. Castlereagh thought that all territory north of the line Antwerp, Malines, Liège and Maastricht to the Rhine, somewhere near Cologne, was sufficient for the Dutch. He also deemed it to be unacceptable for Antwerp to remain French or fall into the hands of any potentially dangerous German power, *in casu* Prussia.[16]

As the guardian of all the North Sea ports, the Dutch could rely on British protection and were in a relatively strong position. As a consequence, the business communities in the Dutch ports hoped to regain the prominence they had enjoyed during the 17th century. It was generally believed then that the prosperity of the Republic was based on staple-markets, and it was therefore deemed essential to restore these. In the "Golden Century" in Dutch port cities, or so it was generally believed, traders bought all the products brought in by sea-traders. This so-called "second hand" stocked the incoming cargo, processing or at least re-dividing it to sell in smaller portions to export traders. As contacts were difficult and other markets obscure, the staple market formed a vital hub in long-distance trade, as it always held stock of all types of product, thus guaranteeing that foreign traders would never come in vain to Dutch ports.

As staple-markets formed the basis of the Republic's prosperity, the Dutch needed to revitalise them if it was to recover. In fact, even in the 18th century, agents of foreign companies obtained direct overseas contacts. Dutch intermediaries thus became superfluous and this proved to be irreversible. After 1815, foreign agents settled in Antwerp or Rotterdam again and organised trade and transport for their own benefit. Brokering was no longer needed,[17] but in Dutch eyes was vital for preventing naked transit, i.e. trade organised by foreigners transporting goods through Dutch ports without using the services of Dutch brokers.[18] Naked transit was therefore burdened with transit taxes and Dutch businessmen were reprieved.[19]

Dutch transit taxes were perceived as a gross injustice in the new Prussian provinces. Cologne businessmen – and substantial elements of the German public – considered the Dutch to be penny-pinching *Krämer* (grocers), who took every opportunity to swindle their neighbours. During the entire 19th century, German nationalists remembered this episode as a time when their Dutch Germanic brothers betrayed them, as they had forgotten their heroic Germanic nature and became a slave to Mammon.[20] The diplomatic dispute between the Netherlands and Prussia focused on the formula that guaranteed freedom of Rhine navigation "*du point ou il deviant navigable jusqu'à la mer.*" The Dutch insisted that this formula stipulated free navigation on the Rhine *to*, and not *into*, the sea and that the sea began where the tide became noticeable, i.e. some distance up the river. Influenced by the great annoyance expressed in German nationalist circles, modern authors often think that the *jusqu'à la mer* clause should be interpreted as *into* the sea,[21] with King William's aberrant analysis only proving his stubborn attitude. In the 1820s, however, the interpretation was different. As transit taxes were a major problem for Cologne's businessmen, who complained to the Prussian government, Berlin asked Wilhelm von Humboldt, a former representative in the Vienna River Commission, for his interpretation. After consulting his British colleague on the Commission, Humboldt agreed with the Dutch king, meaning that the Viennese clauses were taken to be an extension of the 1804 Charter and only affected the river.[22]

Even though the Dutch king rightfully claimed that he was fighting an honest cause, contemporaries believed that his interpretation of the *jusqu'à la mer* phrase was not really in the spirit of the Vienna Treaty. Furthermore, William I hampered the agreement by claiming that only the Lek, the smaller of the two major Rhine branches, was part of the Rhine system. In the Netherlands, just across the Prussian-Dutch border, the river forms a delta system and it is hard to determine which waterway is a continuation of which river. However, by denying that the Waal, the main Rhine branch, was part of it, the king was denouncing what everyone had always taken for granted. Indeed, even in the 18th century, it had been decided that hydraulic engineering works should guarantee that the Waal would get two thirds of all Rhine water. It was evidently nonsense to state that it was not part of the Rhine and highlighted that the king was simply being stubborn, argumentative and dogmatic. His reading of the *jusqu'à la mer* phrase was, however, accepted. As a result, the Rotterdam Chamber of Commerce was able to demand the restoration of the staple market by raising transit taxes in the estuary region, as this was not considered to be part of the river but of the sea. The Cologne Chamber of Commerce reacted by demanding that, as long as the Dutch refused to liberalise the Rhine estuary, Berlin should not abolish the monopoly of the Cologne skippers on the track to Mainz.[23]

Modern 19th-century liberal ideas on free trade and competition in open markets clashed with the conventional view that the government should protect traditional interests. In Prussia, and especially in the Rhineland, which was greatly influenced by revolutionary ideas, the opinion prevailed that modern times required liberal trade. The Dutch were considered to be old-fashioned people who used archaic tools to defend out-dated privileges against free trade, thus cutting off Prussia's opportunities.[24]

The idea of the Cologne Chamber of Commerce to use the remains of the staple market as a tool against the Netherlands was not new. Even in May 1815 (when the Vienna Congress was still going on), the Prussian Minister of Finance, Hans Count von Bülow, wrote to his cousin, State Chancellor Karl August Prince von Hardenberg, to state that the implementation of the concessions on Rhine navigation, including the promise to abolish all the regulations and guild monopolies that Prussia had established only two months earlier, should be delayed until the Dutch agreed to a more liberal trade policy. If this refusal to implement these concessions did not convince the Dutch, Prussia's military power could be used as a crowbar, so Bülow wrote at the time when French troops were regrouping after the return of their self-made emperor from Elba.[25] The Dutch and Prussian armies never did meet in battle, but Bülow convinced his government to preserve the monopoly for Cologne skippers on the track to Mainz until the Dutch accepted the spirit of the Vienna agreement. As Hesse-Darmstadt hoped to develop Mainz into a major trading centre, this grand-duchy used the opportunity to operate in Prussia's shadow and also suspended the Vienna decisions concerning Rhine navigation.

Privately, the Dutch king was looking forward to the moment that Prussia could not resist taking up arms once again and accomplishing its wider territorial ambitions. This was because a war between Prussia and some of the other European powers would give the king the opportunity to kick Prussian troops out of the Luxembourg citadel that they occupied for the German Confederation, merge his principalities, or even conquer the Prussian Rhineland. Such moves would make the king a major power, give him a seat on the Concert of Europe and end the limitations of his sovereignty. A memorandum by his foreign minister anticipated such a move even as late as 1829.[26] A year later, however, the Belgian revolt would end all such illusions. Moreover, Berlin was avoiding all confrontations, let alone military ones: it "stood on the side-lines [. . .], steering in the lee of the great powers, avoiding commitments and shying away from conflict."[27] Nonetheless, the Dutch king continued to dream until the late 1830s.[28]

The struggle on the Rhine was not just a clash of economic interests, but also reflected political tension between the two kingdoms. However, due to the 1828 economic integration of some German states into a Prussian-led customs union that became the German *Zollverein* in 1834, the balance of power shifted in favour of Prussia. In 1831, this finally resulted in the Act of Mainz, in which the Dutch met nearly all Prussian demands regarding Rhine navigation. Until that time, transhipments in Cologne and Mainz remained compulsory, skippers' guilds retained their monopolies and the Dutch continued to exploit their transit monopoly. Indeed, free transport markets were some way off.

Skippers' monopolies

Until the 1831 Act of Mainz, Rhine shipping remained roughly as it had been during the *ancient regime*. Consequently, two types of skippers were active: those who were members of one of the guilds or were registered on Dutch skippers' lists; and small boaters. The latter were only allowed to bring cargo or passengers from a village or small town to a nearby market or exploit a ferry. They were not permitted to participate in transport between major centres like Cologne, Mainz or the Dutch ports; intercity transport was reserved for skippers with special licences. International travel between the Dutch ports and Cologne, which was the central distribution point for goods coming from the Netherlands, remained a Dutch monopoly.[29] In Amsterdam, Rotterdam or Dordrecht, municipal committees decided on which skippers were allowed to participate in Rhine barging, as well as on departure times and tariffs. Only local skippers were on the committees' lists. German barges that arrived at a Dutch port thus had to return empty. As a result, they did not come.[30] In the Netherlands, this was seen as a well-ordered system. In Prussia, though, it was regarded as one of the tools that the rigid Dutch used to undercut Prussia's opportunities.[31] Accordingly, but probably primarily because the German hinterland was still mainly agrarian, with only a few provincial towns, transport was limited. It was only when there was enough cargo available, and so not very regularly, that a barge left from Rotterdam to Emmerich. Furthermore, there was a weekly service from Rotterdam to Duisburg which, according to custom, transhipped in Arnhem. Apart from these services, a Rotterdam barge went to Düsseldorf once a fortnight and to Cologne every 10 days. Altogether, there were no more than three to five barges a week from Rotterdam that crossed the border in an upstream direction. Nevertheless, no fewer than fourteen Rotterdam barges were available for shipping to and from Cologne.[32] This seems too high a number, but, depending on the wind and, above all, towing horses, the circa 200-kilometre journey took 10–20 days. Barging was slow, limited and expensive. This encouraged modern entrepreneurs to implement their own system.

In 1816, Matthias Stinnes, the founder of one of Germany's most prominent industrial empires, was the largest ship-owner in Ruhrort with his one Ruhr and five Rhine barges. However, as there was no licence-office in Mülheim-am-Rhein, his home port, Stinnes claimed to be a small boater and did not, therefore, need a licence.[33] Using this argument, he and some Cologne (Germany) and Arnhem (the Netherlands) businessmen started a shipping service between these cities in 1816.[34] In 1819, with 2,000 tons of cargo, this service only had 2 per cent of the transport of traditional skippers. Nevertheless, the licensed Dutch skippers reacted most aggressively, claiming that Stinnes' enterprise undermined their position.[35] The Dutch authorities thus banned the initiative.[36] Indeed, until the Mainz Treaty, the Netherlands systematically exploited its sovereign position over its ports and rivers.

The 1831 Mainz Treaty established a transnational Rhine regime, introduced a uniform toll system and declared that Rhine navigation was free for residents of all riparian states. Skipper guilds and the remains of staple rights were abolished, and the Waal was recognised as part of the Rhine, making it subject to the Rhine regime. Finally, the Netherlands limited its transit taxes to a fixed rate. Simultaneously, the CCNR was given wider responsibilities. In particular, in the future, it was to urge riparian states to improve towpaths and shipping channels; report annually on the development of navigation; and develop ideas on how to improve barging. Finally, it would also serve as the highest court in relation to Rhine affairs. As a result, the CCNR was, to some extent, empowered with authority that was normally the preserve of sovereigns, thus making it a supranational organisation.[37]

Under foreign pressure, the Dutch would slowly turn towards more pronounced liberalism. In 1839, they accepted Belgian independence and the Antwerp-Cologne railway shattered their monopoly from the mid-1840s onwards. In order not to lose all of its hinterland traffic to railways, the Netherlands unilaterally abolished transit taxes and tolls on the Dutch parts of the river in 1851.[38] This was not enough, however, and did little to increase the competitiveness of Rhine navigation compared to the railways. Indeed, it was Prussia that, in the second half of the 19th century, paved the way for the increased competitiveness of Rhine navigation by putting pressure on all Rhine states to undertake huge hydraulic engineering projects to adapt the river to the needs of a modern 19th-century system.[39]

Transport

Prior to the 1831 Act of Mainz, navigation was small-scale, slow and limited. After 1831, however, Rhine barging started to grow substantially, although the main boom only occurred in the late 19th century. Then, with vast normalisation (canalisation) projects, a huge increase in scale became possible and freight rates fell so much that barging could compete with railways again.[40] Until then, however, it had seemed that Rhine shipping would slowly meet its end.

Transport today has little in common with early 19th-century barging. In 1822, 100 skippers with 140 barges were active on the entire Lower Rhine. Now, about 600 Rhine barges a day, each many times larger than those of 1822, pass over the German-Dutch border, transporting circa 850,000 tons of goods (310 million a year). An estimated 6,900 ships sail on the entire Rhine today. In addition, only a small proportion of transport crosses the Dutch-German border by ship these days, with road transport, railways, planes and pipelines responsible for most of this.

In the early 19th century, freight rates quickly exceeded their value, with many goods produced locally. However, from the mid-19th century onwards, and with the advent of railways and steamships and the related increases in scale, transport became systematically cheaper. Until then, traditional barging remained the main form of inland transport. Pretty pictures of nice sailing ships conceal a harsh reality, though, as they were inefficient, low-yield, highly taxed and, between November and March, when ice blocked the river, out of use.

Figure 2.1 shows that, until the mid-1820s, transport at the border amounted to fewer than 100,000 tons a year. Indeed, it was only in the very first few years after the Napoleonic wars, when the continent was restocked, that the volume of transport exceeded 100,000 tons, mainly in the upstream direction. In other words, on one of the most frequented sections of Europe's most important waterway, the sum of all international transport was only 285 tons a day; it was only after the 1830s that systematic growth became visible.[41] This was the result of the first steps of industrialisation and the introduction of steam navigation, but most of all because of increased coal shipping on the Rhine, as the Netherlands replaced Belgian coal with Westphalian coal after the 1830 Belgian revolt. Consequently, between 1830 and 1850, the annual growth of Rhine shipping (measured at the Dutch-Prussian border) was 7 per cent.[42] Nevertheless, in 1850, cross-border Rhine transport was only half a million tons, which is the amount that crosses the border on the Rhine every day currently.[43] Until the construction of railways, the Rhine was indisputably the prime European highway and barging was the only form of large-scale transport. However, as only a limited number of products could bear the transport costs, overall transport was limited.

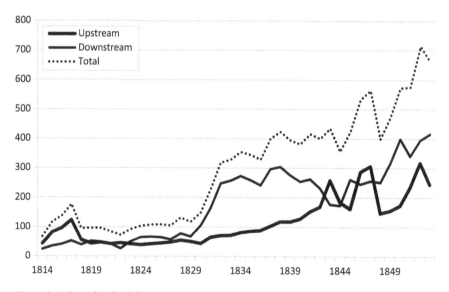

Figure 2.1 Cross-border Rhine navigation near Emmerich, 1814–1853 in 1000 metric tons

Sources: Edwin Horlings, The economic development of the Dutch service sector 1800–1850. Trade and transport in a premodern economy (Amsterdam: Neha, 1995); Authors' own calculations.

During the 1815–1831 period of conflict between Prussia and the Netherlands, and notwithstanding the monopolies in Rhine navigation, freight rates that were corrected for general price developments fell. In the upstream direction, this amounted to 7.3 per cent annually on the Dutch track; downstream, it was 10.4 per cent. This is probably explainable by adaptations made after the first steamers appeared. Wind, the current and muscle power had been used for traction on the Rhine since Roman times. Consequently, before steamers were introduced, the trip to Cologne took 10 to 20 days, with 10–20 kilometres covered per day. As the current was generally stronger than the wind, towing horses were used for upstream traffic. As a result, the tolls used to maintain towpaths were significantly higher for barges travelling upstream than downstream. Horse traction was common, even in the Lower Rhine, where the current was weak and the wind strong. Around 1850, when steamships became more important, 3,000 towing horses were still in use, in addition to 100 steamships.[44] Towing was by no means a part of folklore, but this changed quickly during the second half of the century.

Because manoeuvring spans of more than ca. 10 horses was impossible, up to the mid-19th century, the maximum size of Rhine vessels was limited by the strength of such a span of horses. Obviously, towing horses had to be changed regularly. Shipping was therefore hampered when no horses were available. Moreover, there was an issue because owners did not want their horses crossing the Dutch-Prussian border. As a consequence, more often than not, skippers had to wait up to a week before German horses were available.[45] This explains the rather long duration of a Rotterdam-Cologne trip. A steam-tugged barge, however, made the journey in less than half the time – three to five days – resulting in significant cost reductions. Notwithstanding regulations, steamships created some competition from the 1820s onwards, especially when tugging barges, although it was probably the fear of competition from this new technology that caused Rotterdam skippers to reorganise the horse stations, limiting the duration of horse-towed trips to five-six days.[46] As a result, costs decreased. In addition, steam shipping destroyed the relationship between the scale of transport and the strength of a span of horses. However, for an even larger scale, it was necessary to adapt the channel, which would take half a century.

The 1831 Mainz Treaty, deregulation and the implementation of steaming did not result in the collapse of freight rates. On the contrary, while rates sharply fell up to 1830, they stabilised from 1831 onwards (Figure 2.2). The year of the treaty represented the trough in relation to freight rates. Rhine transport operated in a demand market and the increased demand kept prices high. Between 1829 and 1840, downstream transport increased by 279 per cent, which was 12.9 per cent annually. Meanwhile, growth was less for upstream transport, but was still 206 per cent, or 10.7 per cent annually (Figure 2.1). A price fall could not be expected with such growth figures. Moreover, data show that the 1831 treaty increased tax burdens (Figure 2.3). As the money value of levies was frozen and freight rates fell (Figure 2.2), the share of

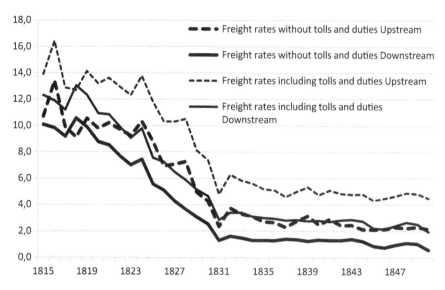

Figure 2.2 Deflated freight rates including and excluding levies and duties, 1816–1850 in guilders per 100 ton/km (Prices 1815=100)

Sources: Edwin Horlings, The economic development of the Dutch service sector 1800–1850. Trade and transport in a premodern economy (Amsterdam: Neha, 1995); Centraal Bureau voor de Statistiek, Tweehonderd jaar statistiek in tijdreeksen (Voorburg: CBS 2001); Authors' own calculations.

Figure 2.3 Shipping duties as a share of the total freight rates, 1815–1850

Sources: Edwin Horlings, *The economic development of the Dutch service sector 1800–1850. Trade and transport in a premodern economy* (Amsterdam: Neha, 1995); Centraal Bureau voor de Statistiek, *Tweehonderd jaar statistiek in tijdreeksen* (Voorburg: CBS 2001); Authors' own calculations.

costs increased. Indeed, from the 1830s onwards, taxes amounted to over half the costs of Rhine shipping.

As long as there was no alternative and everyone who wanted to transport anything between the North Sea and the German Rhineland was dependent on the Rhine, The Hague obstructed steam-tugged barging. However, in 1826, the Netherlands granted concessions to a Rhine steam-shipping company and the Dutch representative in the CCNR stated that the country wanted to increase steam transport in the interests of trade. Only when the Antwerp-Cologne railway became operational in 1843, this showed that the real threat to Dutch transit came from this new technology. The Hague thus wanted to know very little about adjusting the waterway to the requirements of steaming until railways became a threat. That tugging was successful nonetheless resulted from a series of coincidences. Iron barges and steam-tugboats alone did not result in an efficient new technology. When Stinnes considered employing such tugs for coal in 1838, he concluded that it required a larger scale.[47] A form of transport was introduced with steam-tugged iron barges that would make a larger-scale profitable if the infrastructure was adapted. The river needed to become deeper, the channels straightened, and natural obstacles removed. It was only if this occurred that much lower freight rates would become possible. This was essential for making the transport of low-value products like coal or ore feasible on a huge scale.[48] However, as long as there was no alternative to barging, The Hague obstructed modernisation.

Railways

Despite the Netherlands' 1851 unilateral liberalisation of Rhine shipping and the increase in demand for transport that resulted from German industrialisation, from the 1840s the river lost its dominant position on the transport market. German railway construction proceeded quickly from the 1840s onwards, with the first Prussian railway, the 34-kilometre Berlin-Potsdam line, opening in 1838. Twelve years later, 3,602 kilometre of rails were in use and provided Prussia with a backbone to the geographically fragmented state.[49] In Germany as a whole, the first six kilometres opened in 1835 in Bavaria. Then, the country still lacked the technology to produce locomotives.[50] In 1838, the Prussian railways had seven such steam vehicles: six British and one from Belgium. Twelve years later, all 53 new locomotives for the Prussian railways were German-made.[51] By then, 25 per cent of all German transport went by train. Ten years later, this figure was over 50 per cent.[52]

As a result of the discovery of massive coal deposits and iron ore layers just across the Dutch border in the Ruhr area, this Prussian region developed into the heart of industrial Europe from the 1840s onwards. The use of technological innovations like coke blast furnaces marked the start of massive growth in mining and iron and steel production, and this attracted huge investments. In 1854–1857, railways provided the spark that would result in the most spectacular period of growth that Germany had ever experienced.[53] As a consequence, Prussia increased in strength, both politically and economically, from the 1840s onwards. Along with the 1834 foundation of the *Zollverein*, industrialisation made Germany more dominant than ever. Indeed, by the 1870s, it was the largest industrial state on the continent, while in the early 20th century the Prussian-dominated *Kaiserreich* was more important as an industrial nation than Britain, the 19th-century industrial giant. Indeed, only the industrial production of the United States was bigger, but that slumbering colossus seemed far away.[54]

German industrial growth was directly linked to the railways. On the one hand, their construction greatly increased the demand for coal, iron, steel and iron and steel products, while on the other railways provided industries with access to new markets.[55] This was not particularly beneficial for the Dutch ports, because any continental seaport with a railway connection to what was traditionally the Dutch hinterland could now compete. Moreover, as railways were less vulnerable to unfavourable weather conditions than Rhine shipping, they could provide industry with regular, fast and reliable services, including in winter. In a period of increases in scale, predictability was of the utmost importance.[56] Rhine transport was not only losing its competitiveness because railway freight rates were falling, but also because railways were very reliable. For industry, this provided the opportunity to keep less stock and reduce costs.

In the period between 1840 and 1860, German railways grew from below 500 to 14,000 kilometres and rail transport from 3 to 1.675 million tons/km.[57] This is partly explainable by the fall in freight rates from 16.9 to 7.5 *pfennig* per ton/km, equivalent to 4.4 per cent a year.[58] The rail network solved most of the developing industry's transport problems for reasonable prices. Rhine barging was therefore not needed, as the Ruhr area – the vastly industrialising hinterland of the Dutch ports – built one of the densest rail networks in Europe. Indeed, between 1852 and 1865, the share of rail in relation to coal transport within the Ruhr increased from 30 to 78 per cent, while the lion's share of transport in the Rhine catchment area went by train around 1870.[59] It was only by the end of the century that inland navigation would reassert its dominance.[60] Mid-century developments were conclusive for both the rise of railways and the return of the Rhine.

Around the 1850s, Germany's enthusiasm for railways manifested itself in huge oversubscriptions for railway shares.[61] Consequently, soon after 1843, when the Rhineland obtained a rail connection with Antwerp, another railway connected it with Bremen. The Cologne-Antwerp track was an initiative of the Belgian government, but Cologne businessmen encouraged it as they saw it as an opportunity to avoid the Dutch. Already in 1831, just after the Belgian rebellion started, the Cologne merchant and liberal politician David Hansemann proposed establishing a Prussian-Belgian customs union to gain free access through Antwerp to the sea.[62] By then, Cologne businessmen had all kinds of ideas about railways as a way to circumvent the Dutch.[63] However, the authoritarian Berlin regime did not like to collaborate with the liberal Belgians, who they considered to be rebellious. Apart from political reluctance, the problem was that Antwerp was only accessible through Dutch territory, as the West-Scheldt, the sea-arm leading to Antwerp, was Dutch. Although the French and British put an end to a Dutch blockade in 1832 by threatening to seize Dutch ships, proclaim an embargo and send in the French army, the situation around Belgium remained uncertain.[64]

In the liberal Dutch press, Cologne's sympathy for Belgian railways was considered to be a threat, especially because Belgian railway construction plans were not private initiatives, but an instrument in a strategic process of nation-building.[65] In response to the Cologne-backed Belgian proposal, ideas surfaced about connecting the Dutch ports (initially Amsterdam) with Cologne, including by means of a railway. In 1832, Colonel W.A. Bake (1783–1843) asked for a concession to build such a railway. The Dutch government had sent Bake to Manchester in 1830 to buy guns for the war against Belgium. He thus happened to be present at the opening of the Liverpool-Manchester railway, which was the first modern line in the world. Impressed, he wrote numerous articles about the prospects of railways for the Netherlands.[66]

As Bake's idea was seen as a typical Amsterdam notion – the capital struggled with its hinterland connection – Rotterdam businessmen opposed it. Traditionally in Rotterdam, Amsterdam was considered to be the main rival. Accordingly, a Rotterdam businessman, C.M. Roentgen, director of the *Nederlandsche Stoomboot-Maatschappij* (Dutch Steam Boat Company), used the Amsterdam newspaper *Algemeen Handelsblad* to set out an elsewhere-unknown opposition to the new technology. He accentuated the nonsense of investing in railways in the country with Europe's finest waterways. This was not just unpatriotic, but, he warned, would also lead to a financial debacle. In the end, investors would be left with a pile of dirt and some old rust.[67] Notwithstanding this opposition, in 1839, the Haarlem-Amsterdam line opened only a year after the first Prussian line. However, the idea of an Amsterdam-Cologne line was abandoned, as its opponents' lobbying was so strong that the king would not give his permission.[68] The Dutch clayey soil and the need to bridge countless canals and rivers made construction slow. As a consequence, the entire Dutch railway network amounted to just 181 kilometres in 1851.[69]

Roentgen agreed that the Rhine was far from perfect as a hinterland connection. However, this could be resolved by introducing steam-tugboats on more tracks. This was consistent with his personal interests as the owner of a steam boat company, but also with those of Rotterdam and inland shipping. As lobbying created much doubt, a special state commission was appointed to analyse the feasibility of railways. In 1837, it concluded that the Rhine was a reliable link, as low freight rates were more important than speed, and there was no reason to believe that rail tariffs would ever fall below those of barging.[70] It was therefore decided that, before investing large sums, it was better to wait and see what the railways would bring to Belgium.[71]

Among Cologne's businessmen, the Antwerp railway was considered to be a solution to their dependence on the Dutch, and its opening in 1843 was therefore seen as a victory. Moreover, rail transport was not just vaster and more reliable, but was also cheaper. Although the 1845 freight rate per ton/km was 13.6 *pfennig*, and for Rhine barging only 3.4 *pfennig*, the fixed Dutch transit taxes, the longer distance to Rotterdam, the need to use a horse and carriage or rail for the last few miles, and so the necessity to tranship, offset the price differences per ton/km.[72] Indeed, railways were an existential threat to barging.[73]

Until 1856, the Netherlands lacked international rail connections from its major commercial cities. However, railways were needed if the country wanted to compete with foreign seaports,[74] and members of parliament from Rotterdam insisted on this.[75] After parliament approved the Railway Bill in 1860, the construction of a state-paid network could begin. Three years later, the government also initiated improvements in the accessibility of the seaports. To provide both major port cities, Amsterdam and Rotterdam, with a better connection with the sea, two straight canals from these ports to the sea began with the construction of the *Noordzeekanaal* and the *Nieuwe Waterweg*.[76] Smaller ports were also developed, with Vlissingen seeming to be the most promising.[77] The costs of these infrastructural upgrades amounted to almost 17 per cent of the government's budget in the period 1870–1880, but the Dutch could afford this thanks to huge colonial revenues.[78]

Competition

As coal no longer came from Belgium but from Westphalia from 1830 onwards, the demand for Rhine shipping increased. Accordingly, in the early 1840s, the Rotterdam entrepreneur Roentgen and his Cologne rival Camphausen pretty much simultaneously started to use standardised iron barges. For steamship companies, tugging wooden barges of different sizes and shapes was barely profitable. The new barges took one type of cargo at a time: coal, ore, grain or wood; previously, they had been laden with a variety of products, all handled as general cargo. Bulk was transported in bags or barrels. Transport became so large scale from the mid-19th century onwards that it was profitable to fill a barge with only one product. Iron barges and steaming were steps in a process of standardisation that would last until the end of the century. In the Netherlands, they were considered to be a threat to traditional skippers. The Hague therefore examined ways to hinder them by imposing charges, but abandoned the idea because of negotiations with the Prussian-led *Zollverein*; as luxury products from the Dutch Indies were primarily sold on the German market, and the treasury was filled with their yields, The Hague had to keep German interests in mind.

The need to compete also led to the introduction of trains of four to six iron barges tugged by a steamer from 1843 onwards. Each of these barges was loaded with only one product. Such transport was impossible, but also unnecessary, in the early 19th century, as the main commodities transported were luxury goods like coffee, sugar or wine. The most important exception was wood from the Black Forest and the Neckar regions that floated on rafts down the river.[79] After the Napoleonic era, luxury goods were increasingly supplemented with

British semi-finished products like pig iron and yards. Germany made such products itself from the mid-19th century onwards. Consequently, large-scale imports of raw materials were required. In addition, the well-paid working-class population of the Ruhr industrial centres needed foodstuffs, while the growing production of the Westphalian coal mines increasingly had to discharge large quantities of coal. A larger industrial scale, of course, required larger-scale transport. The train solved this problem in most places, but Rhine navigation survived in the Ruhr area.

In the 1850s, when it became clear to The Hague that something must be done to prevent Dutch ports and Rhine barging from losing the competition with foreign ports with railway connections, Dutch efforts to liberalise the Rhine were not met with enthusiasm by the German states. The small states of Nassau and Hesse were financially dependent on their tolls, whereas Prussia, which was willing to reduce these burdens, had an interest in stimulating rail traffic with the German ports for political reasons.[80] The railway to Antwerp had opened eyes in The Hague, and the Dutch proposed that all Rhine states should stop charging tolls in 1847.[81] Under pressure due to competition, the Dutch became liberal, but it was now the Germans that were not in a hurry. Accordingly, in 1851, the Dutch unilaterally stopping charging all tolls and taxes, as they faced the growing threat from Antwerp. The results of this were disappointing, however.[82] Barging seemed to be doomed, but this caused cross-border cooperation between all those interested in this type of transport. In 1853, Dutch and German traders, boatmen and steamship companies together sent petitions to the CCNR asking it to speed up liberalisation.[83] According to Prussia, however, taxation was only part of the problem; the conditions of the navigable waterway were also in dire need of improvement.

In 1847, just after a new railway wiped out barging on the Basel-Strasbourg track, the Prussian Commissioner initiated a technical inspection of the river's navigability, fearing the collapse of barging altogether.[84] If Rhine barging came to an end, Ruhr industry would become dependent on monopolistic rail transport markets. It was therefore in Prussia's interests to prevent that from happening, and large-scale steam barging was the only solution. However, modern steam-towed trains of ships required a straight, deep channel, with width for manoeuvring less relevant than it was for traditional sailing-barges. Adapting the river to these modern needs was a giant project, and after an 1849 inspection, the Rhine commissioners of Prussia, Nassau and Hesse wrote a memo that was particularly negative about the Dutch track.

In Prussia, it was still thought that the Dutch tried to cut off Germany's overseas contacts by hampering river navigation. In reality, as a result of the delta nature of the Dutch part of the Rhine, the water level in each branch was much lower than in Germany, while the slow current and floating ice caused sediment to settle and the height of the river bed to rise. Only heightening the dikes kept the water within the channel, but this caused massive floods whenever ice prevented a quick flow.[85] In Germany, however, it was simply not believed that the Dutch could not solve the water level problem.[86] The Dutch channels, though, were in terrible shape. The depth of the Waal – the main shipping route – was at some points little more than a metre and Rotterdam could only be reached from the sea during high water. The situation was not much better in some German states, but Berlin insisted on a smooth channel from its industrial centres to the sea and demanded Dutch cooperation. In 1850, the year after the inspection, the relevant minister, Rudolf Thorbecke, initiated the construction of summer dikes and groins in order to limit the width and so increase the depth of the rivers. The resulting increased current was expected to remove all superfluous sediment.[87]

After 1849, the CCNR regularly organised inspections to control the condition of the Rhine and set targets for improvement. In 1851, Prussia took the lead again by founding the *Rheinstrombauverwaltung*, an agency to organise hydraulic engineering projects to transform the Prussian Rhine into a straight, deep and easily navigable waterway. It also put pressure on other Rhine states to normalise their tracks.[88] Everyone agreed that something should be done, but it was only in 1856 that a special CCNR meeting gave a committee of engineers the authority to make decisions whenever problems arose. By then, the CCNR seemed to be Prussia's executioner.[89] In 1861, this committee of engineers set uniform targets for the entire river. When the water level was low (1.5 metres in Cologne), the depth of the channel should be at least 1.5 metres on the Strasbourg-Mannheim track, two metres from Mannheim to Koblenz, 2.5 metres from Koblenz to Cologne and three metres from there to the sea. Complicated engineering projects were required, but when these were finished, steam-tugged trains of huge barges could sail from Rotterdam to Mannheim without facing any obstacles.[90] The member states were responsible for the execution of the building activities, but the CCNR's technical committee supervised them.

Robert Keohane emphasises that supranational agencies create "the capability for states to cooperate in mutually beneficial ways," thus "reducing the costs of making and enforcing agreements."[91] Such organisations are tools to make international politics more efficient and economise on transaction costs in international relations. Supranational organisations do not change the division of power, but the decision-making process. As member states depend on them, they are bound by its regulations, thus limiting conflicts.[92] Berlin used the CCNR to obtain what it needed in territories outside its jurisdiction. That the Commission became of vital importance to Berlin was clear when Prussia wanted to build the Cologne Railway Bridge but had to make concessions to Rhine navigation to keep the CCNR going. Nonetheless, Berlin used the Commission to get what it wanted and put pressure on the other members. This would become especially clear in 1866 and 1868. In the former year, Berlin became indisputably dominant within Germany after the Austro-Prussian war and used this to liberalise Rhine navigation once and for all. Not only did it annex small Rhine states like Nassau and Frankfurt, but in the Peace of Prague also dictated to all other German Rhine states (which all fought on the Austrian side) that navigation should be free from tolls, taxes

or flag discrimination and the CCNR should supervise normalisation.[93] The
Netherlands and France were not involved.[94]

The Dutch position was difficult. Napoleon III wanted to be compensated
for not supporting Austria. Rumour had it that the Prussian Prime Minister
Otto von Bismarck and the French Emperor had discussed dividing the Low
Countries, but the former possibly spread these stories to intimidate the small
powers.[95] In 1868, the Prussian CCNR Commissioner attempted to persuade
France and the Netherlands to accept the Rhine paragraphs of the Peace of
Prague Treaty. During the negotiations that followed, a situation arose when
The Hague refused to accept the idea that, in the future, every Rhine state
should be allowed to control all the hydraulic engineering activities related
to Rhine water, as this would involve the Dutch defense system of the New
Holland Waterline. The Hague feared Prussia, as it had just annexed neighbouring Hannover. By then Prussia was considered to be a threat to all small
European nations. The Hague nonetheless withdrew its delegation from the
negotiations concerning a renewed Rhine Treaty adapted to the principles
of the Peace of Prague agreement.[96] As a result, and in a by-the-way manner
discussing whether an independent kingdom of the Netherlands was still an
advantage to anyone in Europe, it was suggested in more or less official Prussian
newspapers that the Dutch had again tried to cut off Germany's access to the
sea. The Hague was duly intimidated.[97] With hindsight, it seems that Berlin
considered the Dutch panic to be a Prussian interest that should be carefully
manipulated. The Hague accepted what became the Mannheim Convention
of 1868,[98] whereby the Rhine became free of all tolls and taxes, regardless of
the flag or cargo, and the riparian states agreed to remove all physical barriers
and normalise their part of the river.

The Dutch approach

In 1849, some German Rhine states produced a memo condemning the conditions of the Dutch Lower Rhine, whereupon minister Thorbecke admitted
that the Netherlands should have paid more attention to river maintenance
and changed the river policy. His admission was also governed by his view that
this issue was in the interests of the Dutch. Summer dikes and groins would
limit the width of the river to improve its depth.[99] The idea behind the new
river policy was to transform the entire river, not just a single dike or a problematic section. However, the hope that a narrow river would flow faster and
deepen due to its current proved to be in vain; the lowland rivers flowed too
slowly. Moreover, at the point where rivers came together – and in a delta
this happens often – very little current remained. Nonetheless, navigability
was still a minor issue for the Dutch, whose main concern was protecting
the land from the floods that occurred frequently in winter when ice blocked
the flow to the sea. Consequently, between 1861 and 1874, the major Dutch
river improvement project involved digging the New Merwede, a Waal estuary
with a huge drainage capacity. German engineers feared that this would result

in even lower water levels during summer. They proved to be right during the period between the Austro-Prussian War and the Prussian-French conflict, when tensions all over Europe were high and the Dutch felt threatened; low water blocked shipping during the summer, especially near Loevesteijn Castle, where the Waal (Rhine) and Meuse flow together. Accordingly, in 1871, the government decided to dredge at least the most problematic parts of the river. Nonetheless, Rhine shipping was frequently blocked in the summer, much to German chagrin. In October 1877, a Ruhr industrialist wrote that he had himself observed how "400 ships were stranded for 3–4 weeks because (. . .) of sandbanks, which are caused by gross negligence of these waterways. With the equivalent of the money these stranded ships lose each day, sufficient precautions could be taken to guarantee a free passage."[100] Ruhr industrialists in general demanded that the Prussian government took action, while German nationalists used the opportunity to emphasise that the Dutch should be annexed anyway. Prussian pressure thus increased.

In the 1860s and 1870s, when the system of colonial exploitation filled the Dutch treasury with enormous sums of money, the budget for river normalisation could be raised and the management of the major rivers was centralised in a national river board in 1875. Nevertheless, inexperience meant that it took years before effective results were achieved.[101] Consistent with the 1851 plans of the Prussian Rhine Building Administration, the target was not, as it had always previously been, to remove a single obstacle or improve a dike, but to straighten and deepen an entire river.[102] This took the greater part of the second half of the 19th century.

Rhine shipping 1850–1880

The German transport market changed completely from the moment the railways were operational. In 1840, less than half a per cent of German transport involved rail. Ten years later this was 25 per cent and in another ten years over 50 per cent, peaking in 1875 at 81 per cent.[103] The reason for this is not hard to uncover: between 1840 and 1850, the ton/km costs on German rail fell by 40 per cent.[104] Simultaneously, the costs of international river shipping fell by only 13 per cent.[105] Figure 2.4 shows that this tendency of German rail freights to fall faster than those of barging continued until the mid-1870s, when Rhine freight rates began to fall faster. The figure also shows that Dutch railways were not competitive; while the costs of German rail transport fell by over 75 per cent between 1840 and 1880, in the Netherlands they increased by 20 per cent.[106] Railways came to dominate transport all over Germany, but construction was slow in the Netherlands, and when the government took this over in the 1860s, it did not lead to falling transport costs.

That the vast development of German rail not only characterised regions where inland navigation was not an option demonstrates that the Ruhr area was a region with good facilities for rail and barge traffic. The share of rail in terms of Ruhr coal transport increased from 30 to 78 per cent between 1852 and

Figure 2.4 Index transport costs, 1850–1880 (1850=100)

Sources: Jan Pieter Smits, Edwin Horlings and Jan Luiten van Zanden, *Dutch GNP and it components, 1800–1913* (Groningen: RUG, 2000) 142–147; Rainer Fremdling, *Eisenbahnen und deutsches Wirtschaftswachstum 1840–1879* (Dortmund: Gesellschaft für Wirtschaftsgeschichte, 1975); Rainer Fremdling, "Freight Rates and State Budget: The Role of the National Prussian Railways 1880–1913," *Journal of European Economic History*, 9, no. 1 (1980) 21–39; Authors' own calculations.

1865. In 1852, 38 per cent of all Ruhr coal still went by horse-drawn carts from the mine to a barge port or a railway station. As large mines could have their own rail connection, but no direct link with the Rhine, the increased competitiveness of railways was not just a matter of freight rates: rail transport could reach its final destination without transhipment, which reduced costs. However, in 1852, 32 per cent of Ruhr coal transport still went by barge. In 1860, this was only 18 per cent. Nonetheless, between 1852 and 1860, the overall transport of coal by barge increased by 30 per cent.[107] Thereafter, this also started to decline. In other words, railways took over in the Ruhr district, but the development of industry was so fast that, although the share of barging in terms of total coal transport fell dramatically, total coal barging initially increased.

In view of the advantages of rail transport, it is no surprise that the Westphalian Coal Export Union – *Westfälische Kohlenausfuhrverein* – considered Rhine transport to be inferior in 1878 and therefore put Dutch ports, including Rotterdam, behind Antwerp.[108] Figure 2.5 shows however that, notwithstanding the enormous growth of rail transport, Rhine barging on the German-Dutch border grew by a dramatic 454 per cent, or 5.9 per cent a year, between 1850 and 1880. German industrialisation created such a huge transport demand that even a barely competitive sector such as Rhine shipping grew, especially in the upstream direction.

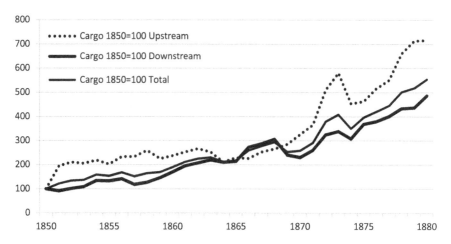

Figure 2.5 Index cargo cross-border Rhine transport near Emmerich, 1850–1880 (1850=100)

Sources: CBS, Statistiek van den handel en de scheepvaart in het koningrijk der Nederlanden (The Hague); Authors' own calculations.

That Rhine shipping felt the competition is clear from the fact that, notwithstanding the still far from ideal channel, the costs of Rhine barging fell by 35 per cent, or 1.4 per cent annually, between 1850 and 1880 (Figure 2.4). Apart from the removal of tolls and taxes, the growing scale of barging was important. In this 30-year period, the average cargo per barge increased by 66 per cent, or 1.7 per cent a year.[109] Normalisation had, however, only just begun; a real, spectacular growth in scale was not yet possible, as the channel simply did not have the capacity.

Normalisation

As Prussian industrialisation was land-locked, it was essential that it had cheap sea port connections. Railways could provide these for the Ruhr, but it was feared that if rail marginalised barging, it would demand monopolistic freight rates. Transforming the Rhine into an efficient, cheap transport route thus became a Prussian interest. The ever-stronger Prussia pressed the other Rhine states to participate. The Hague understood from the 1843 opening of the Antwerp railway that cheap Rhine barging was also a Dutch interest. Accordingly, it wanted to liberalise Rhine shipping from tolls and regulation, but river normalisation would cost enormous sums that the Dutch just did not have after their prolonged military conflict with Belgium and the outcome was uncertain. Nonetheless, in 1850, under Prussian pressure, the first steps were taken.

German unification in 1871 created a new reality, including within the CCNR, which now, apart from the Netherlands, had only German members. However, as the 1868 Act of Mannheim had solved all political problems and discussing these again was not an option, the CCNR turned more and more into a technical commission. It had already been agreed in 1861 how deep and wide each track should be, and now the member states had to accomplish this. The Dutch track was complicated, and normalising it cost more than for any other section. When the targets were more or less reached in 1882, Prussia had spent 20 million guilders and the Netherlands 35 million.[110] As the Dutch also built the *Nieuwe Waterweg* (New Waterway) connecting Rotterdam in a straight line to the sea, it was possible to sail from Mannheim into the North Sea without any serious obstacles from the mid-1880s onwards. This meant that Rhine shipping could now become competitive again.

Increasing the scale of barging, and so using the advantages of steam-tugged trains of barges, only became possible from the late 1880s onwards (Figure 2.6). The average cargo per barge increased by 95 per cent, or 1.8 per cent annually, between 1850 and 1888. Then, from 1888 to 1913, these figures were 188 per cent, or 4.3 per cent annually. Consequently, steam-tugged barge-trains of four to six ships, together 400 metres long and with a loading capacity of up to 6,000 tons, appeared on the river in the early 20th century. In the 1840s, these barge-trains had been only 50–100 metres, with a capacity of 600 tons. Nonetheless, tubular boilers and compound engines reduced fuel consumption.[111] Rhine shipping grew by 65 per cent between 1870 and 1880; it then grew again by 68 per cent between 1880 and 1890, 118 per cent in the next decade and 97 per cent between 1900 and 1913. Thus, Rhine barging became almost six times as large between 1870 and 1913.[112] The new navigability of the river, the implementation of novel techniques in Rhine navigation and transhipment,

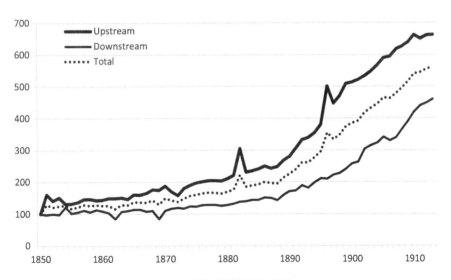

Figure 2.6 Average cargo per barge, 1850–1913 (1850=100)

Sources: CBS, Statistiek van den handel en de scheepvaart in het koningrijk der Nederlanden (The Hague); Authors' own calculations.

and the resulting decline of freight rates by 76 per cent between 1880 and 1913 (4.3 per cent annually) made this possible. As freight rates for rail transport were more or less stable from the 1880s onwards (Figure 2.7), the compatibility of Rhine shipping in comparison with that of rail transport improved spectacularly.

German rail transport increased by 123 per cent in terms of ton/km between 1875 and 1892, and inland navigation by 140 per cent.[113] Inland navigation was duly fighting back, especially as a result of the increased scale of Rhine shipping. Large Ruhr companies built their own fleets of steam-tugged iron barges from the late 1880s onwards (for reasons of labour costs and taxes often under the Dutch flag) to transport enormous quantities of ore, coal, cereals and wood through the straight and deep new channel to their new industrial centres (Figure 2.8). Downstream, the development was less spectacular, as the transport of coal, organised by the Rhenish-Westphalian Coal Syndicate for internal company reasons, was still primarily carried out by train until the early 20th century.[114] The scale of Rhine shipping increased, nevertheless, resulting in an unprecedented fall in freight rates. Consequently, just before World War I, almost a quarter of all German international trade (in tons) crossed the German-Dutch border in Rhine barges.[115] The relationship between the costs of rail transport compared to Rhine transport and the growth of Rhine transport in terms of total transport is statistically significant, as is the relationship

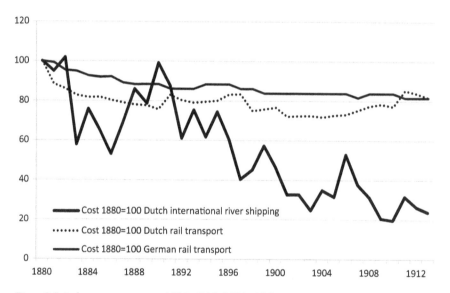

Figure 2.7 Index transport costs, 1880–1913 (1880=100)

Sources: Jan Pieter Smits, Edwin Horlings and Jan Luiten van Zanden, *Dutch GNP and it components, 1800–1913* (Groningen: RUG, 2000) 142–147; Rainer Fremdling, *Eisenbahnen und deutsches Wirtschaftswachstum 1840–1879* (Dortmund: Gesellschaft für Wirtschaftsgeschichte, 1975); Rainer Fremdling, "Freight Rates and State Budget: The Role of the National Prussian Railways 1880–1913," *Journal of European Economic History*, 9, no. 1 (1980) 21–39; Authors' own calculations.

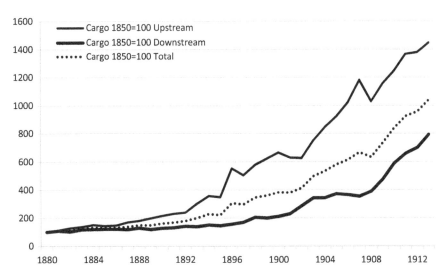

Figure 2.8 Index cargo cross-border Rhine transport near Emmerich, 1880–1913 (1880=100)

Sources: Statistiek van den handel en de scheepvaart in het koningrijk der Nederlanden (The Hague); Authors' own calculations.

between Rhine transport and the growth of the Port of Rotterdam.[116] Indeed, the Dutch port became vital for Germany's most important industrial centre.

German nationalism and the free Rhine

Germany introduced a new toll policy from the 1890s onwards, and ideas about how to redirect trade towards the German seaports emerged. German nationalism became a reason to undermine the transnational character of the Lower Rhine economy. In the late 1870s, Reich Chancellor Otto von Bismarck had leaked the idea of imposing an extra charge on overseas products that entered the country through a non-German port. Possibly, he just wanted to encourage Hamburg, Bremen and Lübeck to finally become members of the *Zollverein*, thereby integrating these port cities economically into the rest of the *Kaiserreich*. In the end, this only occurred in 1888. The idea of these extra charges was possibly also posed to a Dutch diplomat as a way to intimidate the Netherlands.[117] The German government also used special freight rates for rail transport to encourage Germans to use their own national ports, but these rates never were low enough to compensate for the difference in distance and the much lower Rhine freight costs. The construction between 1892 and 1899 of a new canal connecting the Ruhr area with the German Port of Emden was expected to do the job. By this canal, Berlin directly intervened in a nationalistic manner in the supply route of its most important industrial centre. The initial idea to build a canal from the Rhine to the

German coast had already emerged in the 1820s, when Cologne was suffering due to Dutch transit taxes, but the motivation was different now. In the early 1880s, awareness was growing that the railways were bumping against the limits of their capacity, and so only canals could redirect transport from the Rhine to its own sea-ports. Even in the early 19th century, some extreme German nationalists thought that the Netherlands should become part of the future German empire in order to accomplish this.[118] The construction of the Dortmund-Ems Canal must be seen as part of a comprehensive campaign to improve the waterway system to the advantage of the national industry, but also to redirect German trade to German ports.[119] Industrialists were strongly in favour of the expansion of the waterways, partly because of the nationalisation of the Prussian railways in 1879.[120] Although the Ruhr area possessed (with the Rhine) a waterway that would be perfect for bulk transport after normalisation, Germany remained dependent on the Dutch. Berlin preferred a connection with the North Sea that was independent of any foreign power. In 1886, Albert von Maybach, the German Minister of Public Works, rancorously remembered once again the German nationalist story of the conflicts from the early century: "The Netherlands has not always approached us benevolently in this regard."[121] The Dortmund-Ems Canal would favour trade and transport to national ports. However, 20 locks and a ship lift were needed to connect Emden with the Rhine. Consequently, this trip was not only long, but also expensive as a result of high freight rates and duties. Accordingly, as long as the Mannheim Convention was respected, the Dortmund-Ems Canal would never be able to outperform the Rhine.[122]

It was not only the interests of the German ports that were threatened by cheap Rhine transport; Prussian agrarian interests were also affected. In the industrial centres along the Rhine, it was cheaper to obtain overseas cereals than Prussian rye from the territories east of the Elbe River. Agrarian protection substantially raised food prices, but not enough to overcome the differences in costs between cereals from East Germany and America or the Ukraine.[123] The railways also protested against the subsidised advantages of Rotterdam. Rail-ways paid taxes and, after being nationalised, became a prime source of income for the Prussian state, while the Rhine was free from tolls and taxes and its nor-malisation and maintenance was paid for by the Rhine states. In 1906, the steel company *Rote Erde* grumbled about the excessive transport costs for pig iron, ore and coal; these costs were high, as it only could transport these materials by train. The company complained that the Dortmund-Ems Canal, paid for by the state, put rivals with water connections in a better position.[124] Indeed, factories well away from waterways lost their competitiveness.[125] In reality, however, the implicit subsidy for Rhine transport was limited. By regulating the river and not passing on the costs to its users, governments subsidised Rhine transport by an average of 11 per cent.[126] Given the enormous difference in freight rates between railways and river navigation in the early 20th century, this hardly was relevant. Nonetheless, from the late 19th century onwards, German railways, ports and agriculture opposed the fact that Rhine ships did not pay any tolls and thus had their infrastructure for free.[127]

In 1905, the Prussian House of Representatives adopted the Canal Law. The objective of the bill was to construct the *Mittelland Kanal*, which would connect the Rhine with the Elbe in order to provide the agrarian territories with an alternative to the expensive railways. Conservatives from the East Elbe territories opposed the plans for a considerable period, fearing the increased importation of cereals via the canal. Moreover, they thought this could harm the position of Silesian mining in favour of Ruhr mining. In order to address these concerns, the Prussian government made a concession by introducing shipping rights on all German rivers, thus providing Prussia with great control over inland shipping. Raising tolls on waterways was, however, at odds with the 1871 German Constitution, which stipulated that all inland navigation must be free apart from tolls or charges for the maintenance and improvement of these waterways. However, even such tolls went against the Mannheim Convention, which prohibited levying any dues on the Rhine.[128]

The issue was considered to be a serious threat in the Netherlands. Indeed, during a parliamentary debate, the Foreign Minister even called it "a disaster to our country" and confirmed that the government would strongly oppose the Rhine tolls, which could serve as a protectionist tool and would impede imports to Germany via the Netherlands or stimulate the flow through German ports. Resistance to the tolls was not confined to the Dutch;[129] in Germany, it was not a matter of fact that all federal states would accept the change to the constitution. After the Prussian House of Representatives adopted the 1905 law, all the Chambers of Commerce in the Ruhr area protested. Taxing Rhine shipping was not just contrary to the Act of Mannheim, but was primarily against the vital interests of Germany's prime industrial centre.[130] Unsurprisingly, it was the conservative agrarians east of the Elbe, the German sea ports and the railways that were in favour of the new tolls, but the modern industry in the Ruhr area and along the Rhine opposed them. As a result, they lobbied against the plans and coordinated their activities with Dutch stakeholders.[131] The opposition to Rhine tolls was not Dutch or German, but an expression of the cross-border integration of interests against the nationalistic German policy.

Nationalism was a strong reason for the new policy. The regime of *Kaiser* Wilhelm II was much more nationalistic than that of Bismarck. This policy fell on fertile ground all over Germany, but businessmen had other interests. They were not motivated by nationalism or other political targets, but by profits, ensuring the continuity of their companies and the wealth and position of their families.[132] Professional arguments, not nationalistic emotions, motivated them and major industries along the Rhine and the Ruhr therefore opposed the toll policy of the German-Prussian government. For these industries, the Rhine was a way to secure an efficient and cheap supply of overseas raw materials like wood, iron ore and foodstuffs. Tolls that would hinder this supply were against their interests. Accordingly, the cities along the Rhine did not see the advantages of the tolls either, while Saxony and Baden expressed major objections, as they would allow Prussia to control inland navigation. This would harm these states, which were both located on the upper part of a river (the

Rhine and Elbe, respectively) that was Prussian in a lower part. As a concession, Berlin proposed using the revenues to only finance new hydraulic engineering schemes, promising important projects to these states. In 1911, the federal states finally endorsed the amendment and the law was approved by the German parliament. Once the Rhein-Herne Canal – linking the Rhine with the Embden Canal – was completed, tolls would be introduced. Germany now had to prepare for negotiations with the Netherlands on modifying the Convention of Mannheim.[133] Via campaigns in Dutch newspapers and meetings with influential entrepreneurs, German diplomats tried in vain to convince the Netherlands that the revenues would enable the Rhine states to further improve the waterway. The public and politicians were not, however, convinced that funding the preservation of the waterway was the main objective. Indeed, it was generally thought that the tolls were there to provide Prussia with a tool to centralise its transport policy. In fact, revenues anticipated in the Canal Law did not correspond with the actual cost of planned engineering activities.[134] Moreover, the introduction of the high shipping rights and tug dues for eastwards-moving traffic on the Rhine-Herne Canal in 1913, and the confidential proposal to charge additional Rhine tolls on traffic north of Duisburg, indicated that an integrated transport policy and favouring the German ports were the actual targets.[135]

Rhine tolls would also provide Prussia with a strong political tool to use against the Netherlands, as there was no guarantee that Berlin would not increase them. Accordingly, in 1914, the Netherlands resolutely rejected entering into negotiations. As a result, the German Finance Ministry even discussed terminating the 1851 German-Dutch trade agreement, without which import tariffs on many products would be so high that transit through the Netherlands would *de facto* come to an end. Rotterdam was thus at risk of losing its position. Transport could simply be directed to the Rhine from Antwerp, as the Mannheim Convention prohibited the Netherlands from imposing any restrictions on Rhine traffic. If the Netherlands did that nonetheless, the Convention would be revoked, and Germany would still have achieved its goal. However, the outbreak of World War I prevented the matter from escalating further: no Rhine tolls were introduced, and river navigation remained the most important way of connecting Rotterdam to the German hinterland and the Ruhr to the world.

Conclusion

It is a strange fact that in political history the period between 1880 and 1913 is known as a time of nationalism, while in economic history it is considered to be the era of the first wave of globalisation. During this period of globalisation, the Dutch Port of Rotterdam and the Rhine was able to develop into a major hub between the most important German industrial centre and the outside world. As a result, a substantial part of Dutch economic activity became dependent on Germany, while the major German industrial centre was reliant on the Netherlands at the same time. Of course, there were other economic interests in Germany. All economic theorists may agree that free trade is favourable for every economy, but this does not mean that this is the case for every economic activity. The German ports, old-fashioned agriculture east of the Elbe River, railways and some industries without a waterway connection protested against the cheap and efficient import and export route that was opened up by normalisation of the Rhine, as this was not in their interests. As a consequence, just when the process of normalisation achieved its target and the Rhine and Rotterdam provided the Ruhr with the most efficient transport it could wish for, these other interests not only started to protest, but, because of growing German nationalism, also found a listening ear. Indeed, from the late 1880s onwards, when the Rhine was normalised and Rhine transport became cheaper than any other form of transport, thus integrating the Lower Rhine area into one transnational economic region, German nationalism started to back these protests and almost destroyed what had been built in the previous decades. That this early 20th-century equivalent of Brexit was not followed through to its conclusion was related to the other major event where political nationalism prevailed over economic rationality, namely World War I.

Notes

1 Part of this research has received funding from the European Research Council under the European Union's Seventh Framework Programme (FP/2007–2013)/ERC Grant Agreement n.615313.
2 Beatrice de Graaf, "Second-Tier Diplomacy: Hans von Gagern and William I in Their Quest for an Alternative European Order, 1813–1818," *Journal of Modern European History* 12, no. 4 (2014): 546–566 there 546.
3 See: Richard B. Elrod, "The Concert of Europe: A Fresh Look at an International System," *World Politics* 28, no. 2 (1976): 163.
4 Joep Schenk, "The Central Commission for Navigation of the Rhine: A First Step towards European Economic Security?," in *Securing Europe after Napoleon: 1815 and the New Security Order*, ed. Beatrice de Graaf, Ido de Haan, and Brian Vick (Cambridge: Cambridge University Press 2018); F.S.L. Lyons, *Internationalism in Europe 1815–1914* (Leiden: A. W. Sijthoff, 1963), 12; Bob Reinalda, *Routledge History of International Organizations: From 1815 to the Present Day* (New York: Routledge 2009), 3–34. In 2015, the CCNR published: CCNR, *1815–2015: 200 Years History* (Strasbourg: CCNR, 2015).
5 Marc de Decker, *Europees Internationaal Rivierenrecht* (Antwerp: Maklu Uitgevers, 2015), 129–133.
6 P. Krugman, "Growing World Trade: Causes and Consequences," *Brookings Papers on Economic Activity* 1 (1995): 330–334.
7 Hein A.M. Klemann, *Waarom bestaat Nederland eigenlijk nog? Nederland-Duitsland: Economische integratie en politieke consequenties 1860–2000* (Rotterdam: Erasmus Universiteit, 2006), 11–12.
8 "No. 38, Pariser Friedensvertrag, 30 Mai 1814," in *Rheinurkunden, Sammlung zwischenstaatlicher Vereinbarungen, landesrechtlicher Ausführungsverordnungen und sonstiger wichtiger Urkunden über die Rheinschiffahrt seit 1803. Vol. 1. 1803–1860* (The Hague: Martinus Nijhoff, 1918), 36–37; W.J.M. van Eysinga, *Geschichte der Zentralkommission für die Rheinschiffahrt 1816 bis 1969*, 2nd ed. (Strasbourg: CCNR, 1994), 11.
9 Van Eysinga, *Geschichte der Zentralkommission*, 8.
10 Hein A.M. Klemann, "The Central Commission for the Navigation on the Rhine, 1815–1914: Nineteenth Century European Integration," in *The Rhine: A Transnational Economic History*, ed. Ralf Banken and Ben Wubs (Baden-Baden: Nomos, 2017), 13–16.

11 Joep Schenk, "National Interest versus Common Interest: The Netherlands and the Liberalization of Rhine Navigation at the Congress of Vienna, 1814–1815," in *Shaping the International Relations of the Netherlands, 1815–2000: A Small Country on the Global Scene*, ed. R. van Dijk, et al. (London and New York: Routledge 2018), 13–31; Klaus Müller, "Politische und rechtliche Veränderungen der Rheinschifffahrt zwischen der Französischen Revolution und dem Ersten Pariser Frieden 1814," in *Der Rhein als Verkehrsweg. Politik, Recht und Wirtschaft seit dem 18. Jahrhundert*, ed. Clemens von Looz-Corswarem and Georg Möllich (Bottrop: Pomp Verlag, 2007), 50–55; Robert Mark Spaulding, "Changing Patterns of Rhine Commerce in the Era of French Hegemony, 1793–1813," *Vierteljahrschrift für Sozial- und Wirtschaftsgeschichte* 100, no. 4 (2013): 413–431; CCNR, *200 Years*, 23–35; J.L. Wolterbeek, *Proeve eener geschiedenis van de scheepvaartwetgeving op den Rijn* (Amsterdam: Frederik Muller, 1854), 39–58.

12 CCNR, *200 Years*, 44.

13 Van Eysinga, *Geschichte der Zentralkommission*, 25.

14 "Un pistolet braqué au cœur de l'Angleterre." Olivier Chapuis, *À la mer comme au ciel: Beautemps-Beaupré & la naissance de l'hydrographie (1700–1850)* (Paris: Presses de l'Université de Paris-Sorbonne, 1999), 426; According to others it was Napoleon who said this. Willem Bevaart, "Vormende jaren (1815–1870)," in *Met man en macht. De militaire geschiedenis van Nederland 1550–2000*, ed. J.R. Bruijn and C.B. Wels (Amsterdam: Balans, 2003), 287.

15 N.C.F. van Sas, *Onze Natuurlijkste Bondgenoot Nederland, Engeland en Europa, 1813–1831* (Groningen: Wolters-Noordhoff and Bouma's Boekhuis, 1985), 37; "No. LXXIV: Castlereagh to Liverpool, Basle, January 22nd, 1814," in *British Diplomacy, 1813–1815: Selected Documents Dealing with the Reconstruction of Europe*, ed. C.B. Webster (London: G. Bell and Soon Ltd, 1921).

16 "No. 2048: Memorandum Respecting Holland, Submitted to the Powers, 1813," in *Gedenkstukken der Algemeene Geschiedenis van Nederland van 1795 tot 1840, Book 6, Volume 3, GS 17*, ed. H.T. Colenbrander (The Hague: Martinus Nijhoff, 1912), 1951.

17 P.J. Bouman, *Rotterdam en het Duitsche achterland 1831–1851* (Amsterdam: Paris, 1931), 7 and 102–103.

18 See: Ibid.; P.J. Bouman, "Der Untergang auf dem Niederrhein, 1831–1851," *Vierteljahrschrift für Sozial- und Wirtschaftsgeschichte* 26, no. 3 (1933): 244–245.

19 Hein A.M. Klemann and Joep Schenk, "Competition in the Rhine Delta: Waterways, Railways and Ports, 1870–1914," *Economic History Review* 66, no. 3 (2013): 827–828.

20 Friedrich List, *Das national System der politischen Ökonomie* (Stuttgart: Cotta'schen Verlag, 1841), 112; Heinrich Von Treitschke, *Politics*, Vol. 1 (New York: Macmillan, 1916), 33; K. Pabst, "Der übermächtige Nachbar. Belgische, niederländische und luxemburgische Urteile über das Deutsche Reich," in *Das Deutsche Reich im Urteil der großen Mächte und europäischen Nachbarn 1871–1945*, ed. Klaus Hildebrand and Elisabeth Müller (Munich: Oldenbourg, 1995), 27–47 there 32.

21 See: Jean-Marie Woehrling, "Introduction of Free Navigation on the Rhine," in CCNR, *200 Years*, 23–70, 46; Bouman, *Rotterdam, en het Duitsche achterland*, 14; Bouman, "Der Untergang," 246; H.P.H. Nusteling, *De Rijnvaart in het tijdperk van stoom en steenkool 1831–1914: een studie van het goederenvervoer en de verkeerspolitiek in de Rijndelta en het achterland, mede in verband met de opkomst van de spoorwegen en de concurrentie van vreemde zeehavens* (Amsterdam: Holland Universiteits Press, 1974), 1–13.

22 Van Eysinga, *Geschichte der Zentralkommission*, 26.

23 Eberhard Gothein, *Die Schifffahrt der deutschen Ströme. Geschichtliche Entwicklung der Rheinschifffahrt im XIX. Jahrhundert* (Leipzig: Verein für Sozialpolitik, 1903), 87.

24 Bouman, *Rotterdam en het Duitsche achterland*, 22; Joachim F.E. Bläsing, *Das goldene Delta und sein eisernes Hinterland 1815–1851. Von niederländisch-preußischen zu deutsch-niederländische Wirtschaftsbeziehungen* (Leiden: Stenfert Kroese, 1973), 50.

25 "No. 5, von Bülow aan von Hardenberg, Mei 13, 1815," in *Documenten betreffende de Buitenlandsche Politiek van Nederland in de negentiende eeuw. Part III: Onderhandelingen met*

Pruisen en andere Duitsche staten tot aan de oprichting van het Duitsche Tolverbond (1814–1833), ed. N.W. Posthumus (The Hague: Martinus Nijhoff, 1923), 5–6; M. Schwann, "Grundlagen und Organisation des Wirtschaftsleben," in *Die Rheinprovinz 1815–1915. Hundert Jahre preußischer Herrschaft am Rhein, I. Teil*, ed. Joseph Hansen (Bonn: A. Marcus & E. Webers Verlag, 1917), 202.

26 "No. 235, Rapport over de Buitenlandsche Staatkunde der Nederlanden, 23 Januari 1829," *Gedenkstukken*. Book 9, Vol. 2, 442–487.

27 Christopher Clarck, *Iron Kingdom: The Rise and Downfall of Prussia 1600–1947* (London: Penguin Books, 2006), 510.

28 H.T. Colenbrander, *De afscheiding van België* (Amsterdam: Meulenhof, 1936), 120; C. Smit, *De conferentie van Londen: het vredesverdrag tussen Nederland en België van 19 april 1839* (Leiden: E.J. Brill, 1949), 204–205.

29 Jürgen-Heinz Schawacht, *Schifffahrt und Güterverkehr zwischen den Häfen des deutschen Niederrheins (insbesondere Köln) und Rotterdam vom Ende des 18. bis zur Mitte des 19. Jahrhunderts (1794–1850/51)* (Cologne: Rheinisch-Westfälisches Wirtschaftsarchiv, 1973), 82 ff.

30 Woltersbeek, *Proeve*, 39–41; Ulrich S. Soénius, "Wirtschaftliche Selbstverwaltung – Ein Erbe der französischen Zeit," in *Frankreich am Rhein. Die Spuren der "Franzosenzeit" im Westen Deutschlands*, ed. Kerstin Theis and Jürgen Wilhelm (Cologne: Greven Verlag, 2009), 152–153.

31 Bouman, *Rotterdam en het Duitsche achterland*, 22; Bläsing, *Das goldene Delta*, 50.

32 Bouman, *Rotterdam en het Duitsche achterland*, 22–23.

33 Ibid., 87–88.

34 Ibid., 16; Bernhard-Michael Domberg and Klaus Rathje, *Die Stinnes. Vom Rhein in die Welt. Geschichte einer Unternehmerfamilie* (Vienna: Signum, 2009), 10–11; Haniel, *Haniel 1756–2006. Eine Chronik in Daten und Fakten* (Duisburg: Haniel, 2006), 74.

35 Bouman, *Rotterdam en het Duitsche achterland*, 16–18; Bläsing, *Das goldene Delta*, 50–51; Schawacht, *Schifffahrt und Güterverkehr*, 88.

36 Bouman, *Rotterdam en het Duitsche achterland*, passim.

37 Klemann, "The Central Commission"; CCNR, *200 Years*, 45–49; Nusteling, *De Rijnvaart*, 5–12; Van Eysinga, *Geschichte der Zentralkommission*, 26–27.

38 Nusteling, *De Rijnvaart*, 74–84.

39 Klemann, "The Central Commission."

40 Klemann and Schenk, "Competition in the Rhine Delta," passim.

41 Van Zanden and Van Riel believe that Rhine navigation shrank by 60 per cent from 1818–1822. This is not wrong but is related to the downturn after the spectacular revival of trade after the Napoleonic War. Jan Luiten van Zanden and Arthur van Riel, *Nederland 1780–1914. Staat, instituties en economische ontwikkeling* (Amsterdam: Balans, 2000), 186–187.

42 Edwin Horlings, *The Economic Development of the Dutch Service Sector 1800–1850: Trade and Transport in a Pre-Modern Economy* (Amsterdam: NEHA, 1995), 406 ff; author's own calculations.

43 Website Cenrale Commissie voor de Rijnvaart (23 May 2014). www.ccr-zkr.org/ 12030100-nl.html.

44 Heinrich Meidinger, *Die deutschen Ströme und ihren Verkehrs- und Handels-Verhältnissen. Teil 2: Der Rhein und seine schiffbaren Nebenflüsse und Kanäle* (Frankfurt-am-Main: Joh. Chr. Hermanns'sche Buchhandlung, 1861), 73.

45 Schawacht, *Schiffahrt*, 133.

46 Bernhard Weber-Brosamer, "'Die Weltordnung will weder Stillstand noch Rückschritt': zur Einführung der Dampfschiffahrt auf dem Rhein und ihren wirtschaftspolitischen Auswirkungen," in *Der Rhein als Verkehrsweg. Politik, Recht und Wirtschaft seit dem 18. Jahrhundert*, ed. Clemens von Looz-Corswarem and Georg Möllich (Bottrop: Pomp Verlag, 2007), 101 ff; "No. 204 De Kommissaris bij de Centrale Kommissie voor de Rijnvaart Travers aan de Minister van Buitenlandse Zaken Schimmelpennick, 6 april 1848," in *Rijksgeschiedkundige Publicatiën (RGP), Bescheiden betreffende de Buitenlandse Politiek van Nederland, 1948–1919, 1.1. 1848-GS 139* (The Hague, 1972), 205; Ibid., 3 mei 1848, Ibid., 141.

47 Bouman, *Rotterdam en het Duitsche achterland*, 96–97.
48 Edwin Jones Clapp, *The Navigable Rhine: The Development of Its Shipping, the Basis of the Prosperity of Its Commerce and Its Traffic in 1907* (Boston and New York: Houghton Mifflin Company, 1911), 28–30.
49 Rainer Fremdling, *Eisenbahnen und deutsches Wirtschaftswachstum, 1840–1879: ein Beitrag zur Entwicklungstheorie und zur Theorie der Infrastruktur* (Dortmund: Gesellschaft für Wirtschaftsgeschichte, 1975), 48; See: A.J.P. Taylor, *The Course of German History: A Survey of the Development of German History since 1815* (London: Routledge, 1945), 120.
50 Johannes Bähr, Ralf Banken, and Thomas Flemming, *Die MAN: eine deutsche Industriegeschichte* (München: C.H. Beck, 2008), 175.
51 Fremdling, *Eisenbahnen*, 48.
52 Ibid., 86.
53 Werner Abelshauser and Wolfgang Köllmann, *Das Ruhrgebiet im Industriezeitalter. Geschichte und Entwicklung* (Düsseldorf: Schwann, 1990), 263; Gerhard Gebhardt, *Ruhrbergbau: Geschichte, Aufbau und Verflechtung seiner Gesellschaften und Organisationen* (Essen: Glückauf, 1957), 13–19; Wilfried Feldenkirchen, *Die Eisen- und Stahlindustrie des Ruhrgebiets 1879–1914: Wachstum, Finanzierung und Struktur ihrer Großunternehmen* (Wiesbaden: Franz Steiner Verlag, 1982), 22; Gutehoffnungshütte Oberhausen, *Rheinland: zur Erinnerung an das 100 jährige Bestehen 1810–1910* (Oberhausen: August Bagel, 1910), 2; *Die Entwickelung des niederrheinisch-westfälischen Steinkohlen-Bergbaues in der zweiten Hälfte des 19. Jahrhunderts*, Hrsg. vom Verein für die bergbaulichen Interessen im Oberbergamtsbezirk Dortmund, 3. Teil, Band X (Berlin: Springer, 1904), 190–193.
54 Paul Kennedy, *The Rise and Fall of the Great Powers: Economic Change and Military Conflict from 1500 to 2000* (New York: Vintage Books, 1987), 98 ff.
55 Dieter Ziegler, *Eisenbahnen und Staat im Zeitalter der Industrialisierung. Die Eisenbahnpolitik der deutschen Staaten im Vergleich* (Frankfurt-am-Main: Frans Steiner Verlag, 1996), 16–17; Rainer Fremdling, "Railroads and German Economic Growth: A Leading Sector Analysis with a Comparison to the United States and Great Britain," *Journal of Economic History* 37, no. 3 (1977): 601.
56 Ralf Banken, "The Diffusion of Coke Smelting and Puddling in Germany 1796–1860," in *The Industrial Revolution in Iron: The Impact of British Coal Technology in Nineteenth-Century Europe*, ed. Chris Evans and Göran Rydén (Burlington: Routledge, 2017), 63–64; Abelshauser and Köllmann, *Das Ruhrgebiet*, 256–260.
57 Ziegler, *Eisenbahnen und Staat*, 9–19.
58 Fremdling, *Eisenbahnen*, 17, 48, 57.
59 Ibid., 67.
60 See: Klemann and Schenk, "Competition in the Rhine Delta," passim.
61 Lothar Gall and Manfred Pohl, *Die Eisenbahn in Deutschland. Von dem Anfangen bis zum Gegenwart* (München: C.H. Beck, 1999), 18–20.
62 Wilhelm Gerloff, "Grundlinien der belgischen Zoll- und Handelspolitik von der Gründung des Königsreich bis zur Gegenwart," *Weltwirtschaftliches Archiv* 12 (1918): 159–161.
63 "No. 39, Maandbericht over Juli 1821 van de Handelskamer te Keulen, 1821, Augustus 2," *Documenten III*, ed. Posthumus: 49; Bouman, "Der Untergang," 259.
64 M.G. de Boer, *Leven en werken van Gerhard Moritz Roentgen. Grondvester van de Nederlandsche Stoomboot-maatschappij thans Maatschappij voor scheeps- en werktuigbouw "Fijenoord" 1823–1923* (Groningen: Noordhoff, 1923), 92–93.
65 *Arnhemsche Courant*, 28 February 1832, Dag. *Algemeen Handelsblad*, 6 September 1834, Dag; David Hansemann, *Abhandlung über die muthmaßliche Frequenz der von Cöln bis zur belgischen Grenze bei Eupen projectirten Eisenbahn bei unmittelbarer Berührung der Städte Aachen und Burtscheid* (Aachen: Beaufort, 1835); J.C. Boogman, *Nederland en de Duitse bond, 1815–1851. Deel 1, 1815–1848* (Groningen en Djakarta: J.B. Wolters, 1955), 77; Horst Lademacher, *Zwei ungleiche Nachbarn. Wege und Wandlungen der deutsch-niederländischen Beziehungen im 19. und 20. Jahrhundert* (Darmstadt: Wissenschaftliche Buchgesellschaft, 1990), 64–65; Greet de Block, "Designing the Nation: The Belgian Railway Project, 1830–1837," *Technology and Culture* 52, no. 4 (October 2011): 703–732.

66 W. van den Broeke, "Het spoor terug gevolgd. De eerste honderd jaar (1839–1939)," in *Het spoor. 150 jaar spoorwegen in Nederland*, ed. J.A. Faber (Amsterdam: Meulenhoff, 1989), 15.

67 Ibid., 17.

68 Jeroen Koch, *Koning Willem I, 1772–1843* (Amsterdam: Boom, 2013), 382.

69 CBS, *Tweehonderd jaar statistiek in tijdreeksen* (Voorburg: CBS, 2001), 65.

70 Bouman, *Rotterdam en het Duitsche achterland*, 63–65.

71 "IJzeren spoorweg van Amsterdam naar Keulen," *Arnhemsche Courant*, 4 February 1834, Dag.

72 Fremdling, *Eisenbahnen*, 18, 57; Jan Pieter Smits, Edwin Horling, and Jan Luiten van Zanden, *Dutch GNP and It Components, 1800–1913* (Groningen: Rijksuniversiteit Groningen, 2000), 198–200; authors' own calculations; Klemann and Schenk, "Competition in the Rhine Delta," 830.

73 Nusteling, *De Rijnvaart*, 85–103; Weber-Brosamer, "Die Weltordning," 100.

74 Guus Veenendaal, *Spoorwegen in Nederland van 1834 tot nu* (Amsterdam: Boom, 2008), 100–104; Auke van der Woud, *Een nieuwe wereld. Het ontstaan van het moderne Nederland* (Amsterdam: Bert Bakker, 2011), 305–308.

75 *Handelingen van de Tweede Kamer der Staten-Generaal*, 1859–1860, 8 November 1859, 115–118.

76 Paul van de Laar, *Stad van formaat. Geschiedenis van Rotterdam in de negentiende en twintigste eeuw* (Zwolle: Waanders, 2000), 65–70; W.C. Mees, *Man van de daad. Mr Marten Mees en de opkomst van Rotterdam* (Rotterdam: Nijgh & Van Ditmar, 1946), 145; Van der Woud, *Een nieuwe wereld*, 243.

77 Hein A.M. Klemann, "Vlissingen als haven voor het Duitse achterland," in *Zeeland en de wijde wereld*, ed. Tobias van Gent and Pieter van Ippel (Middelburg: De Drukkery, 2012), 27–47; Van der Woud, *Een nieuwe wereld*, 243–244, 314.

78 Van Zanden and Van Riel, *Nederland 1780–1914*, 199, 218–225, 335, table 7.3.

79 Pim Kooij, "Stad in het isolement, 1813–1850," in *Geschiedenis van Dordrecht III, 1813 tot 2000* (Hilversum: Verloren, 2000), 31–33; S. Mohr, *Die Flößerei auf dem Rhein* (Mannheim: Walther, 1897), passim.

80 Nusteling, *De Rijnvaart*, 58, 85–103.

81 *Algemeen Handelsblad*, 30 October 1847.

82 Klemann, "Vlissingen," 27–29; *Dagblad van Zuidholland en 's Gravenhage*, 9 October 1861, Dag, *Opregte Haarlemsche Courant*, 26 April 1852, Dag.

83 *De Grondwet*, 4 October 1853, Dag; *Nieuwe Rotterdamsche Courant*, 30 May 1856, Dag.

84 Van Eysinga, *Geschichte der Zentralkommission*, 78.

85 Auke van der Woud, *Het lege land 1798–1848*, 4th ed. (Amsterdam: Olympus, 1998), 95 ff.

86 Alex van Heezik, *Strijd om de rivieren. 200 jaar rivierenbeleid in Nederland of de opkomst en ondergang van het streven naar de normale rivier* (Haarlem and The Hague: Alex van Heezik, 2008), 73–74.

87 Van der Woud, *Het lege land* 87ff.

88 Ibid., 58; Van Heezik, *Strijd om de rivieren*, 22–35.

89 Van Eysinga, *Geschichte der Zentralkommission*, 81–84.

90 W. Nasse, *Die Schifffahrt der deutsche Ströme. Untersuchung über deren Abgabenwesen, Regulierungskosten und Verkehrsverhältnisse. 3 Der Rhein als Wasserstraße* (Leipzig: Verein für Sozialpolitik, 1905), 32.

91 Ibid.

92 Ibid., 86.

93 Hans A. Schmitt, "Prussia's Last Fling: The Annexation of Hanover, Hesse, Frankfurt, and Nassau, June 15–October 8, 1866," *Central European History* 8, no. 4 (1975): passim.

94 A. Doedens, *Nederland en de Frans-Duitse oorlog. Enige aspecten van de buitenlandse politiek en de binnenlandse verhoudingen van ons land omstreeks het jaar 1870* (Zeist: Doedens, 1973), 18; J.R. Thorbecke, *De Briefwisseling Uitgegeven door G.J. Hooykaas en F.J.P. Santegoets. Vol. 7, 1892–1872* (The Hague: RGP, 2002), 487.

95 *The Times*, 16 November 1866; *Nieuwe Rotterdamsche Courant*, 13 August 1866, Dag; *Nieuwe Rotterdamsche Courant*, 17 August 1866, Dag.

96 *Dagblad van Zuidholland en's Gravenhage*, 30 August 1868.
97 *Handelingen Tweede Kamer*, 1868–1869, 5 Maart 1869, 973–975; *Dagblad van Zuidholland en 's-Gravenhage*, 25 August 868, Dag; Idem., 9 October 1861, Dag; *Algemeen Handelsblad*, 5 September 1868, Dag; *Nieuwe Rotterdamsche Courant*, 30 August 1868, Dag.
98 *Handelingen Tweede Kamer*, 1868–1869, 5 Maart 1869, 973–975; Klemann and Schenk, "Competition in the Rhine Delta," 831.
99 Van Heezik, *Strijd om de rivieren*, 87ff.
100 William Thomas Mulvany, "Deutschlands Wasserstraßen und deren Verwendung in ihrem jetzigen Zustande für den Export vermittelst Verbesserungen im Schiffsbau," *Glückauf* 59 (23 July 1881).
101 R.P.J. Tutein Nolthenius, "De nieuwe Rijn (Rhenus Renatus)," *De Gids* 60 (1896): 494–501; Klemann and Schenk, "Competition in the Rhine Delta," 835–836; Van Heezik, *Strijd om de rivieren*, 75–104. CCR, *200 Years*, 89–90.
102 Nasse, *Die Schiffahrt der deutsche Strome*, 58; Van Heezik, *Strijd om de rivieren*, 22–35.
103 Fremdling, *Eisenbahnen*, 86.
104 Ibid., 57.
105 Smits et seq, *Dutch GNP and It Components*, 143–144.
106 Ibid., 145–146; Fremdling, *Eisenbahnen*, 57.
107 Fremdling, *Eisenbahnen*, 67.
108 J. Rive, "De tegenwoordige steenkool-handel," *De Economist*, 26, 1878, 585–589; "Het Goederen-vervoer langs den Rijnspoorweg," *De Economist*, 9, 1861, 196–199; Ernst Heubach, *Wasserstraßen und Eisenbahnen des Elbe-Odergebietes in dem Zeitraum von 1882–1895* (Berlin: Siemenroth & Troschel, 1898), 35.
109 CBS, *Statistiek van den handel en de scheepvaart in het koningrijk der Nederlanden* (The Hague: CBS 1898 ff); own calculations.
110 "No. 84a. Nota behorende bij de brief van Waterstaat, Handel en Nijverheid van 19 maart 1887, 38, Waterstaat A." Rijksgeschiedkundige Publicatien, *Bescheiden betreffende de Buitenlandse Politiek van Nederland, 2.4. 1886–1890-GS 126* (The Hague: Martinus Nijhoff, 1968), 119–120.
111 Clapp, *The Navigable Rhine*, 44.
112 Andreas Kunz, "The Performance of Inland Water Navigation in Germany, 1835–1935," in *Inland Navigation and Economic Development in Nineteenth-Century Europe*, ed. Andreas Kunz and John Armstrong (Mainz: Philipp von Zabern, 1995), passim.
113 Viktor Kurs, "Schifffahrtsstraßen im Deutschen Reich. Ihre bisherige und zukünftige Entwicklung und ihre gegenwärtige wirtschaftliche und finanzielle Ausnützung," *Jahrbücher für Nationalökonomie und Statistik* 4 (1895): 670–671.
114 See Chapter 3.
115 Klemann and Schenk, "Competition," 840–841.
116 Ibid., 845.
117 CCNR, *200 Years*, 81–82.
118 List, *Das national System*, 113 and 519–520; Ernst Moritz Arndt, *Der Rhein, Deutschlands Strom, nicht aber Deutschlands Grenze. Mit einer zeitgemäßen Einleitung von Edgar Wildberg* (Dresden: Carl Reissner, 1921), 21; Lademacher, *Zwei ungleiche Nachbarn*, passim; Treitschke, *Politics*, I, 33.
119 Feldenkirchen, *Die Eisen- und Stahlindustrie*, 68–69.
120 H. Rentzsch, "Der Kanal von Dortmund nach den Emshäfen," *Stahl und Eisen* 5 (1883): 267–273.
121 "Het Rijn-Emskanaal," *Algemeen Handelsblad*, 17 June 1886, 5.
122 Kamer van Koophandel en Fabrieken Rotterdam, *Jaarverslag van de Kamer van Koophandel en Fabrieken Rotterdam* (Rotterdam: Kamer van Koophandel 1889).
123 Nicolaus Wolf, "Was Germany Ever United? Evidence from Intra- and International Trade, 1885–1933," *Journal of Economic History* 69, no. 3 (2009): 846–881; S. Broadberry and C. Burhop, "Real Wages and Labor Productivity in Britain and Germany, 1871–1938: A Unified Approach to the International Comparison of Living Standards," *Journal of Economic History* 70, no. 2 (2010): 409.

124 Wilhelm Rabius, *Der Aachener Hütten-Aktien-Verein in Rote Erde 1846–1906. Die Entstehung und Entwicklung eines rheinischen Hüttenwerks* (Jena: Gustav Fischer, 1906), 69–75.
125 Wallace E. McIntyre, "Canalization of the Moselle," *Scientific Monthly* 84, no. 5 (May 1957): 255–263; Kenneth Warren, "The Changing Steel Industry of the European Common Market," *Economic Geography* 43, no. 4 (1967): 323.
126 Klemann and Schenk, "Competition," 837.
127 M. Mees, "De vrije vaart op den Rijn," *De Economist* 146 (1898): 38–41; *Algemeen Handelsblad*, 5 November 1909, Avond.
128 Nusteling, *De Rijnvaart*, 367–370; André Beening, *Onder de vleugels van de adelaar. De Duitse buitenlandse politiek ten aanzien van Nederland in de periode 1890–1914* (PhD diss., Amsterdam, 1994), 297–301; Klemann and Schenk, "Competition," 831.
129 Nusteling, *De Rijnvaart*, 374–379; Beening, *Onder de vleugels*, 301–303.
130 H. Schwabe, *Die Entwicklung der deutschen Binnenschifffahrt bis zum Ende des 19. Jahrhunderts* (Berlin: Siemenroth & Troschel, 1899), 3–4.
131 A. Wirminghaus, *Zur Frage der Wiedereinführung von Rheinschifffahrtsabgaben* (Leipzig: Duncker & Humblot, 1905); "Progrès du port de Rotterdam," *Annales de Géographie* 9 (1900): 277.
132 Carl Strikwerda, "The Troubled Origins of European Economic Integration: International Iron and Steel and Labor Migration in the Era of World War I," *American Historical Review* 98, no. 4 (1993): 1106–1129.
133 Nusteling, *De Rijnvaart*, 374–379; Beening, *Onder de vleugels*, 301–303.
134 Nusteling, *De Rijnvaart*, 377.
135 Beening, *Onder de vleugels*, 331–332.

Bibliography

Abelshauser, Werner, and Wolfgang Köllmann (1990), *Das Ruhrgebiet im Industriezeitalter. Geschichte und Entwicklung* (Düsseldorf: Schwann).
Arndt, Ernst Moritz (1921), *Der Rhein, Deutschlands Strom, nicht aber Deutschlands Grenze. Mit einer zeitgemäßen Einleitung von Edgar Wildberg* (Dresden: Carl Reissner).
Bähr, Johannes, Ralf Banken, and Thomas Flemming (2008), *Die MAN: eine deutsche Industriegeschichte* (München: C.H. Beck).
Banken, Ralf (2017), "The diffusion of coke smelting and puddling in Germany 1796–1860." In *The Industrial Revolution in Iron: The Impact of British Coal Technology in Nineteenth-Century Europe*, edited by Chris Evans and Göran Rydén (Burlington: Routledge).
Beening, André (1994), *Onder de vleugels van de adelaar. De Duitse buitenlandse politiek ten aanzien van Nederland in de periode 1890–1914* (PhD diss., Amsterdam).
Bevaart, Willem (2003), "Vormende jaren (1815–1870)." In *Met man en macht. De militaire geschiedenis van Nederland 1550–2000*, edited by J.R. Bruijn and C.B. Wels: 287–312 (Amsterdam: Balans).
Bläsing, Joachim F.E. (1973), *Das goldene Delta und sein eisernes Hinterland 1815–1851. Von niederländisch-preußischen zu deutsch-niederländische Wirtschaftsbeziehungen* (Leiden: Stenfert Kroese).
Block, Greet de (2011), "Designing the nation: The Belgian Railway Project, 1830–1837." *Technology and Culture* 52, no. 4: 703–732.
Boogman, Johan C. (1955), *Nederland en de Duitse bond, 1815–1851. Deel 1, 1815–1848* (Groningen en Djakarta: J.B. Wolters).
Bouman, Pieter Jan (1931), *Rotterdam en het Duitsche achterland 1831–1851* (Amsterdam: Paris).
Bouman, Pieter Jan (1934), "Der Untergang auf dem Niederrhein, 1831–1851." *Vierteljahrschrift für Sozial- und Wirtschaftsgeschichte* 26, no. 3: 244–266.
British Diplomacy (1921), *1813–1815: Selected Documents Dealing with the Reconstruction of Europe*, edited by C.B. Webster (London: G. Bell and Soon Ltd.).

Broadberry, S., and C. Burhop (2010), "Real wages and labor productivity in Britain and Germany, 1871–1938: A unified approach to the international comparison of living standards." *Journal of Economic History* 70, no. 2: 400–427.

Centraal Bureau voor de Statistiek (1898 ff.), *Statistiek van den handel en de scheepvaart in het koningrijk der Nederlanden* (The Hague: CBS).

Centraal Bureau voor de Statistiek (2001), *Tweehonderd jaar statistiek in tijdreeksen* (Voorburg: CBS).

Central Commission for the Navigation of the Rhine (2015), *1815–2015. 200 Years History* (Strasbourg: CCNR).

Chapuis, Olivier (1999), *À la mer comme au ciel: Beautemps-Beaupré & la naissance de l'hydrographie (1700–1850)* (Paris: Presses de l'Université de Paris-Sorbonne).

Clapp, Edwin Jones (1911), *The Navigable Rhine: The Development of Its Shipping, the Basis of the Prosperity of Its Commerce and Its Traffic in 1907* (Boston and New York: Houghton Mifflin Company).

Clarck, Christopher (2006), *Iron Kingdom: The Rise and Downfall of Prussia 1600–1947* (London: Penguin Books).

Colenbrander, Herman Theodoor (1936), *De afscheiding van België* (Amsterdam: Meulenhof).

De Boer, M.G. (1923), *Leven en werken van Gerhard Moritz Roentgen. Grondvester van de Nederlandsche Stoomboot-maatschappij thans Maatschappij voor scheeps- en werktuigbouw "Fijenoord" 1823–1923* (Groningen: Noordhoff).

De Decker, Marc (2015), *Europees Internationaal Rivierenrecht* (Antwerp: Maklu Uitgevers).

De Graaf, Beatrice, (2014), "Second-tier diplomacy: Hans von Gagern and William I in their quest for an alternative European order, 1813–1818." *Journal of Modern European History* 12, no. 4: 546–566.

Documenten, betreffende de Buitenlandsche Politiek van Nederland in de negentiende eeuw. Part III: Onderhandelingen met Pruisen en andere Duitsche staten tot aan de oprichting van het Duitsche Tolverbond (1814–1833), edited by N.W. Posthumus (The Hague: Martinus Nijhoff).

Doedens, Anne (1973), *Nederland en de Frans-Duitse oorlog. Enige aspecten van de buitenlandse politiek en de binnenlandse verhoudingen van ons land omstreeks het jaar 1870* (Zeist: Doedens).

Domberg, Bernhard-Michael, and Klaus Rathje (2009), *Die Stinnes. Vom Rhein in die Welt. Geschichte einer Unternehmerfamilie* (Vienna: Signum).

Elrod, Richard B. (1976), "The concert of Europe: A fresh look at an international system." *World Politics*, 28, no. 2: 159–174.

Entwickelung (1904), *Die, des niederrheinisch-westfälischen Steinkohlen-Bergbaues in der zweiten Hälfte des 19. Jahrhunderts*, Hrsg. vom Verein für die bergbaulichen Interessen im Oberbergamtsbezirk Dortmund, 3. Teil, Band X (Berlin: Springer).

Feldenkirchen, Wilfried (1982), *Die Eisen- und Stahlindustrie des Ruhrgebiets 1879–1914: Wachstum, Finanzierung und Struktur ihrer Großunternehmen* (Wiesbaden, Franz Steiner Verlag).

Fremdling, Rainer (1975), *Eisenbahnen und deutsches Wirtschaftswachstum, 1840–1879: ein Beitrag zur Entwicklungstheorie und zur Theorie der Infrastruktur* (Dortmund: Gesellschaft für Wirtschaftsgeschichte).

Fremdling, Rainer (1977), "Railroads and German economic growth: A leading sector analysis with a comparison to the United States and Great Britain." *Journal of Economic History*, 37, no. 3: 583–604.

Fremdling, Rainer (1980), "Freight rates and state budget: The role of the national Prussian railways 1880–1913." *Journal of European Economic History* 9, no. 1: 21–39.

Gall, Lothar, and Manfred Pohl (1999), *Die Eisenbahn in Deutschland. Von dem Anfangen bis zum Gegenwart* (München: C.H. Beck).

Gebhardt, Gerhard (1957), *Ruhrbergbau: Geschichte, Aufbau und Verflechtung seiner Gesellschaften und Organisationen* (Essen: Glückauf).

Gedenkstukken (1912), *der Algemeene Geschiedenis van Nederland van 1795 tot 1840*, edited by H.T. Colenbrander (The Hague: Martinus Nijhoff).

Gerloff, Wilhelm (1918), "Grundlinien der belgischen Zoll- und Handelspolitik von der Gründung des Königsreich bis zur Gegenwart." *Weltwirtschaftliches Archiv* 12: 159–172.

"Goederen-vervoer, (1861), Het, langs den Rijnspoorweg." *De Economist*, 101, no. 1: 196–199.

Gothein, Eberhard (1903), *Die Schifffahrt der deutschen Ströme. Geschichtliche Entwicklung der Rheinschifffahrt im XIX. Jahrhundert* (Leipzig: Verein für Sozialpolitik).

Gutehoffnungshütte Oberhausen (1910), *Rheinland: zur Erinnerung an das 100 jährige Bestehen 1810–1910* (Oberhausen: August Bagel, 1910).

Haniel (2006), *Haniel 1756–2006. Eine Chronik in Daten und Fakten* (Duisburg: Haniel).

Handelingen (1859–1860), *van de Tweede Kamer der Staten-Generaal*.

Hansemann, David (1835), *Abhandlung über die muthmaßliche Frequenz der von Cöln bis zur belgischen Grenze bei Eupen projectirten Eisenbahn bei unmittelbarer Berührung der Städte Aachen und Burtscheid* (Aachen: Beaufort).

Heubach, Ernst (1898), *Wasserstraßen und Eisenbahnen des Elbe-Odergebietes in dem Zeitraum von 1882–1895* (Berlin: Siemenroth & Troschel).

Horlings, Edwin (1995), *The Economic Development of the Dutch Service Sector 1800–1850: Trade and Transport in a Pre-Modern Economy* (Amsterdam: NEHA).

Kamer van Koophandel en Fabrieken Rotterdam (1889), *Jaarverslag van de Kamer van Koophandel en Fabrieken Rotterdam* (Rotterdam: Kamer van Koophandel).

Kennedy, Paul (1987), *The Rise and Fall of the Great Powers: Economic Change and Military Conflict from 1500 to 2000* (New York: Vintage Books).

Klemann, Hein A.M. (2006), *Waarom bestaat Nederland eigenlijk nog? Nederland-Duitsland: Economische integratie en politieke consequenties 1860–2000* (Rotterdam: Erasmus Universiteit).

Klemann, Hein A.M. (2012), "Vlissingen als haven voor het Duitse achterland." In *Zeeland en de wijde wereld*, edited by Tobias van Gent and Pieter van Ippel: 27–47 (Middelburg: De Drukkery).

Klemann, Hein A.M. (2017), "The central commission for the navigation on the Rhine, 1815–1914: Nineteenth century European integration." In *The Rhine: A Transnational Economic History*, edited by Ralf Banken and Ben Wubs, 13–32 (Baden-Baden: Nomos).

Klemann, Hein A.M., and Joep Schenk (2013), "Competition in the Rhine delta: Waterways, railways and ports, 1870–1914." *Economic History Review* 66, no. 3: 826–847.

Koch, Jeroen (2013), *Koning Willem I, 1772–1843* (Amsterdam: Boom).

Kooij, Pim (2000), "Stad in het isolement, 1813–1850." In: *Geschiedenis van Dordrecht III, 1813 tot 2000* (Hilversum: Verloren).

Krugman, Paul (1995), "Growing world trade: Causes and consequences." *Brookings Papers on Economic Activity*, 1: 327–377.

Kunz, Andreas (1995), "The performance of inland water navigation in Germany, 1835–1935." In *Inland Navigation and Economic Development in Nineteenth-Century Europe*, edited by Andreas Kunz and John Armstrong: 47–78 (Mainz: Philipp von Zabern).

Kurs, Viktor (1895), "Schifffahrtsstraßen im Deutschen Reich. Ihre bisherige und zukünftige Entwicklung und ihre gegenwärtige wirtschaftliche und finanzielle Ausnützung." *Jahrbücher für Nationalökonomie und Statistik Dritte Folge*, 10: 641–705.

Lademacher, Horst (1990), *Zwei ungleiche Nachbarn. Wege und Wandlungen der deutsch-niederländischen Beziehungen im 19. und 20. Jahrhundert* (Darmstadt: Wissenschaftliche Buchgesellschaft).

List, Friedrich (1841), *Das national System der politischen Ökonomie* (Stuttgart: Cotta'schen Verlag).

Lyons, Francis Steward Leland (1963), *Internationalism in Europe 1815–1914* (Leiden: A. W. Sijthoff).

McIntyre, Wallace E. (1957), "Canalization of the Moselle." *Scientific Monthly* 84, no. 5: 255–263.

Mees, M. (1898), "De vrije vaart op den Rijn." *De Economist* 146: 38–41.

Mees, Willem C. (1946), *Man van de daad. Mr Marten Mees en de opkomst van Rotterdam* (Rotterdam: Nijgh & Van Ditmar).

Meidinger, Heinrich (1861), *Die deutschen Ströme und ihren Verkehrs- und Handels-Verhältnissen. Teil 2: Der Rhein und seine schiffbaren Nebenflüsse und Kanäle* (Frankfurt-am-Main: Joh. Chr. Hermanns'sche Buchhandlung).

Mohr, S. (1897), *Die Flößerei auf dem Rhein* (Mannheim: Walther).

Müller, Klaus (2007), "Politische und rechtliche Veränderungen der Rheinschifffahrt zwischen der Französischen Revolution und dem Ersten Pariser Frieden 1814." In *Der Rhein als Verkehrsweg. Politik, Recht und Wirtschaft seit dem 18. Jahrhundert*, edited by Clemens von Looz-Corswarem and Georg Möllich: 50–55 (Bottrop: Pomp Verlag).

Mulvany, William Thomas (1881), "Deutschlands Wasserstraßen und deren Verwendung in ihrem jetzigen Zustande für den Export vermittelst Verbesserungen im Schiffsbau." *Glückauf*, 59 (23 July).

Nasse, W. (1905), *Die Schifffahrt der deutsche Ströme. Untersuchung über deren Abgabenwesen, Regulierungskosten und Verkehrsverhältnisse. 3 Der Rhein als Wasserstraße* (Leipzig: Verein für Sozialpolitik).

Nusteling, Hubertus P.H. (1974), *De Rijnvaart in het tijdperk van stoom en steenkool 1831–1914: een studie van het goederenvervoer en de verkeerspolitiek in de Rijndelta en het achterland, mede in verband met de opkomst van de spoorwegen en de concurrentie van vreemde zeehavens* (Amsterdam: Holland Universiteitspers).

Pabst, Klaus (1995), "Der übermächtige Nachbar. Belgische, niederländische und luxemburgische Urteile über das Deutsche Reich." In *Das Deutsche Reich im Urteil der großen Mächte und europäischen Nachbarn 1871–1945*, ed. Klaus Hildebrand and Elisabeth Müller: 27–47 (Munich: Oldenbourg).

"Progrès du port de Rotterdam (1900)." *Annales de Géographie*, 9, no. 45: 277.

Rabius, Wilhelm (1906), *Der Aachener Hütten-Aktien-Verein in Rote Erde 1846–1906. Die Entstehung und Entwicklung eines rheinischen Hüttenwerks* (Jena: Gustav Fischer).

Reinalda, Bob (2009), *Routledge History of International Organizations: From 1815 to the Present Day* (New York: Routledge).

Rentzsch, H. (1883), "Der Kanal von Dortmund nach den Emshäfen." *Stahl und Eisen* 5: 267–273.

Rheinurkunden (1918), *Sammlung zwischenstaatlicher Vereinbarungen, landesrechtlicher Ausführungsverordnungen und sonstiger wichtiger Urkunden über die Rheinschiffahrt seit 1803*. Vol. 1. 1803–1860 (The Hague: Martinus Nijhoff).

Rijksgeschiedkundige Publicatiën (RGP) (1972), *Bescheiden betreffende de Buitenlandse Politiek van Nederland, 1948–1919*, 1.1. 1848–GS 139 (The Hague: ING).

Rive, J. (1878), "De tegenwoordige steenkool-handel." *De Economist*, 26: 585–589.

Schawacht, Jürgen-Heinz (1973), *Schifffahrt und Güterverkehr zwischen den Häfen des deutschen Niederrheins (insbesondere Köln) und Rotterdam vom Ende des 18. bis zur Mitte des 19. Jahrhunderts (1794–1850/51)* (Cologne: Rheinisch-Westfälisches Wirtschaftsarchiv).

Schenk, Joep (2018), "National interest versus common interest: The Netherlands and the liberalization of Rhine navigation at the Congress of Vienna, 1814–1815." In *Shaping the International Relations of the Netherlands, 1815–2000: A Small Country on the Global Scene*, edited by R. van Dijk et al.: 13–31 (London and New York: Routledge).

Schenk, Joep (2019), "The Central Commission for Navigation of the Rhine: A first step towards European economic security?" In *Securing Europe after Napoleon. 1815 and the New Security Order*, edited by Beatrice de Graaf, Ido de Haan and Brian Vick (Cambridge: Cambridge University Press, Forthcoming).

Schmitt, Hans A. (1975), "Prussia's Last Fling: The annexation of Hanover, Hesse, Frankfurt, and Nassau, June 15–October 8, 1866." *Central European History* 8: 316–347.

Schwabe, H. (1899), *Die Entwicklung der deutschen Binnenschifffahrt bis zum Ende des 19. Jahrhunderts* (Berlin: Siemenroth & Troschel).

Schwann, M. (1917), "Grundlagen und Organisation des Wirtschaftsleben." In *Die Rheinprovinz 1815–1915. Hundert Jahre preußischer Herrschaft am Rhein, I. Teil*, edited by Joseph Hansen: 196–249 (Bonn: A. Marcus and E. Webers Verlag).

Smit, Cornelis (1949), *De conferentie van Londen: het vredesverdrag tussen Nederland en België van 19 april 1839* (Leiden: E.J. Brill).

Smits, Jan Pieter, Edwin Horling, and Jan Luiten van Zanden (2000), *Dutch GNP and it components, 1800–1913* (Groningen: Rijksuniversiteit Groningen).

Soénius, Ulrich S. (2009), "Wirtschaftliche Selbstverwaltung – Ein Erbe der französischen Zeit." In *Frankreich am Rhein. Die Spuren der „Franzosenzeit" im Westen Deutschlands*, edited by Kerstin Theis and Jürgen Wilhelm: 145–159 (Cologne: Greven Verlag).

Spaulding, Robert Mark (2013), "Changing patterns of Rhine commerce in the era of French Hegemony, 1793–1813." *Vierteljahrschrift für Sozial- und Wirtschaftsgeschichte* 100, no. 4: 413–431.

Strikwerda, Carl (1993), "The troubled origins of European economic integration: International iron and steel and labor migration in the era of World War I." *American Historical Review* 98, no. 4: 1106–1129.

Taylor, Alan J.P. (1945), *The Course of German History: A Survey of the Development of German History since 1815* (London: Routledge).

Thorbecke, Johan Rudolph (2002), *De Briefwisseling Uitgegeven door G.J. Hooykaas en F.J.P. Santegoets*. Vol. 7, 1892–1872 (The Hague: RGP).

Treitschke, Heinrich von (1916), *Politics*. Vol. 1 (New York: Macmillan).

Tutein Nolthenius, Rudolph P.J. (1896), "De nieuwe Rijn (Rhenus Renatus)." *De Gids*, 60: 494–501.

Van de Laar, Paul (2000), *Stad van formaat. Geschiedenis van Rotterdam in de negentiende en twintigste eeuw* (Zwolle: Waanders).

Van den Broeke, Willem (1989), "Het spoor terug gevolgd. De eerste honderd jaar (1839–1939)." In *Het spoor. 150 jaar spoorwegen in Nederland*, edited by J.A. Faber: 11–49 (Amsterdam: Meulenhoff).

Van der Woud, Auke (1998), *Het lege land 1798–1848*. 4th ed. (Amsterdam: Olympus).

Van der Woud, Auke (2011), *Een nieuwe wereld. Het ontstaan van het moderne Nederland* (Amsterdam: Bert Bakker).

Van Eysinga, Willem J.M. (1994), *Geschichte der Zentralkommission für die Rheinschiffahrt 1816 bis 1969* (Strasbourg: CCNR sec.ed.).

Van Heezik, Alex (2008), *Strijd om de rivieren. 200 jaar rivierenbeleid in Nederland of de opkomst en ondergang van het streven naar de normale rivier* (Haarlem and The Hague: Alex van Heezik).

Van Sas, Niek C.F. (1985), *Onze Natuurlijkste Bondgenoot Nederland, Engeland en Europa, 1813–1831* (Groningen: Wolters-Noordhoff/Bouma's Boekhuis).

Van Zanden, Jan Luiten, and Arthur van Riel (2000), *Nederland 1780–1914. Staat, instituties en economische ontwikkeling* (Amsterdam: Balans).

Veenendaal, Guus (2008), *Spoorwegen in Nederland van 1834 tot nu* (Amsterdam: Boom).

Warren, Kenneth (1967), "The changing steel industry of the European common market." *Economic Geography*, 43, no. 4: 314–332.

Weber-Brosamer, Bernhard (2007), "'Die Weltordnung will weder Stillstand noch Rück-schritt': zur Einführung der Dampfschiffahrt auf dem Rhein und ihren wirtschaftspoli-tischen Auswirkungen." In *Der Rhein als Verkehrsweg. Politik, Recht und Wirtschaft seit dem 18. Jahrhundert*, edited by Clemens von Looz-Corswarem and Georg Möllich: 93–116 (Bottrop: Pomp Verlag).

Wirminghaus, A. (1905), *Zur Frage der Wiedereinführung von Rheinschifffahrtsabgaben* (Leipzig: Duncker & Humblot).

Wolf, Nicolaus (2009), "Was Germany ever united? Evidence from intra- and inter-national trade, 1885–1933." *Journal of Economic History*, 69, no. 3: 846–881.

Wolterbeek, Johannes L. (1854), *Proeve eener geschiedenis van de scheepvaartwetgeving op den Rijn* (Amsterdam: Frederik Muller).

Ziegler, Dieter (1996), *Eisenbahnen und Staat im Zeitalter der Industrialisierung. Die Eisenbahn-politik der deutschen Staaten im Vergleich* (Frankfurt-am-Main: Frans Steiner Verlag).

Journals

Algemeen Handelsblad (1834–1909).
Arnhemsche Courant (1832–1834)
Dagblad van Zuidholland en 's Gravenhage (1861)
De Grondwet (1853)
Nieuwe Rotterdamsche Courant (1856–1868)
Opregte Haarlemsche Courant (1852)
The Times (Great Britain, 1866).

Websites

Webside Centrale Commissie voor de Rijnvaart, www.ccr-zkr.org/12030100-nl.html

3 Coal, iron ore and the rise of the Rotterdam-Ruhr relationship, 1850–1914

Joep Schenk

Introduction

The geographic reality of the River Rhine seems to be the most obvious explanation for the rapid development of industry in the German Ruhr district at the turn of the 20th century. The Rhine provided a cheap and efficient highway for the transport of raw materials and goods to and from the industrial agglomerations that emerged in the Ruhr area, namely the district situated between the Lippe and Ruhr rivers to the north and south and bordering the Rhine in the west and the city of Hamm in the east (Figure 3.1).

The Rhine empowered this hinterland district to reach the global market, join the disposition of the international division of labour and start competing with producers of coal, iron and steel worldwide. In the slipstream of this process of industrialisation in the hinterland, it seems almost as if the Port of Rotterdam was predestined to cash in on its auspicious position on the estuary of the Rhine. It was roughly in the period between 1860 and 1914 that the Dutch port and the German hinterland engaged in a relationship of ever-stronger interdependency.[1]

In fact, as this chapter shows, the interdependent relationship reached its zenith between 1900 and 1914, when 60 to 75 per cent of pig iron production in the Ruhr depended on iron ore that was imported through Rotterdam. Simultaneously, a sixth of total Ruhr coal exports were marketed in or via Rotterdam. Conversely, between 1900 and 1914, about 40 per cent of the volume of the total throughput in Rotterdam consisted of iron ore and coal coming from and going to the Ruhr.

It is true that no history of the Ruhr, or any self-respecting study on the Port of Rotterdam, fails to mention the economic importance of the relationship between the port and its hinterland.[2] Nevertheless, most of these studies apply strict national or sub-national perspectives that do not allow for further scrutiny of the transnational relations. Moreover, the relationship seems so evident that historians have generally maintained that it is unnecessary to analyse it in detail. After all, the presence of the River Rhine, it is assumed, adequately explains the formation of the relationship between the two economic centres.

However, such an approach is problematic.

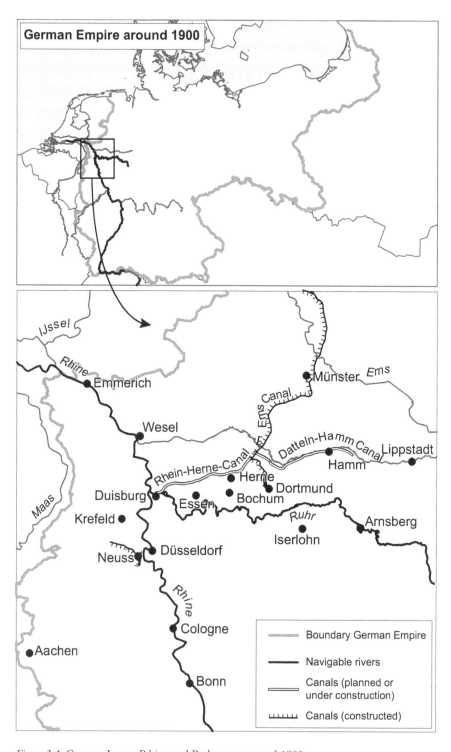

Figure 3.1 German Lower Rhine and Ruhr area, around 1900

Source: Map produced by Cartographic Studio/Annelieke Vries-Baaijens (2018).

First, it ignores the influence of actors in the economic relations between the Netherlands and Germany in general, and between Rotterdam and the Ruhr district in particular. This chapter shows that entrepreneurs shaped, for good or ill, the scope, intensity, velocity and impact of the interrelationship between Rotterdam and the two areas from 1850–1914.[3]

Second, a focus on the Rhine as the sole explanatory factor of the rise of the Rotterdam-Ruhr relationship is troublesome in the historiographical context. The supposedly self-evident importance of this relationship seems to be incompatible with the prime significance that historians have ascribed to the railways in the rise of the Ruhr industry in the 19th century. If Ruhr industrialists focused on railways, however, a shift to river navigation in the Rotterdam-Ruhr connection needs to be explained. Moreover, until at least the 1890s, if the Rhine was such a self-evident connector, why would contemporaries – such as the Dutch government and the Port of Rotterdam especially – largely focus their economic and transport policies on improving the rail infrastructure?

Third, taking the Rotterdam-Ruhr relationship to be self-evident presumes that Rotterdam was always predestined to become the outport for the Ruhr industry. This teleological perspective does not allow for a better understanding of the ups and downs of this relationship. Indeed, it obscures the fact that the transformation into industrial mass production in the Ruhr in the 1860s was a relatively isolated process in the sense that it did not depend on foreign, let alone overseas, raw materials. At that point in time, Rotterdam was not in the picture at all, whereas ten years later, Antwerp and, another ten years later, the German North Sea ports were viable alternatives for reaching the global market. It was only after the turn of the century that Rotterdam became the uncontested port for the Ruhr industry, i.e. 30 years after the start of industrialisation in the Ruhr, 20 years after the completion of the Nieuwe Waterweg – the canal linking Rotterdam more directly with the sea that allowed the largest sea steamers to enter the Port of Rotterdam – ten years after the port had expanded with large and deep basins and, finally, about ten years after the Rhine had regained its competitiveness on the transport market.

This chapter does not take the Rotterdam-Ruhr relationship for granted. It explains its origins in detail by historicising the level of interdependence over time. What is more, the chapter scrutinises the role of entrepreneurs in establishing this relationship. It particularly studies the intermediating actors within the coal mining and iron and steel industries, i.e. coal and iron ore merchants. The chapter is organised in chronological order. To understand the origins of Rotterdam-Ruhr relations, it first returns to the origins of the industrialisation in the Ruhr area around 1850 and tries to understand what need there was to encroach upon more distant markets and which tools contemporaries had at their disposal to realise these connections. The second part explains how industrialisation in the 1870s unleashed a real quest for distant markets and why the organisation of new supply routes did not favour the Rhine. Part three, starting around 1880, shows how it is possible that Ruhr industry increasingly depended on distant and overseas markets, while its dependence on Rotterdam did not unequivocally increase. Part four, finally, covers the 1900–1914 period, explaining what structural amendments were necessary within the organisation of the raw material supply chain in the Ruhr for establishing its strong connections to the Port of Rotterdam.

A silent revolution of perception: small profits and quick returns (1860–1870)

On 5 May 1865, the Irishman William Thomas Mulvany (1806–1885) was subject to cross-examination by a Royal Commission on the issue of the nation's railways; rumours about illicit price fixing in the sector had reached London. The Commission, chaired by the Duke of Devonshire, investigated whether it was socially and economically desirable to adopt a drastic measure and subjugate the private British and Irish railways to the state.[4] Mulvany was invited as a hands-on expert. He had been a senior government clerk and had been responsible for the improvement and expansion of the transport network in Ireland. Remarkably, the Commission showed no interest in his competence as a civil servant. Instead, it interrogated him lengthily on his experience as an entrepreneur in the mining sector in the Ruhr district; there, in the late 1850s, Mulvany had managed single-handedly to connect Prussian railway companies with the mining sector, so changing the coal market forever.[5]

The coal industry in the Ruhr region took off from 1850–1856. This development followed on from the liberalisation of the mining industry in Prussia, which allowed entrepreneurs to establish a mining company and freely extract, sell and distribute the obtained commodities.[6] The mining rush also coincided with technical innovations such as the introduction of the coke blast furnace.[7] In addition, the infrastructure improved considerably. The construction of hundreds of kilometres of railways resulted in an unprecedented market expansion. Simultaneously, the skyrocketing demand for railways, locomotives and wagons was an enormous boost for the iron and steel industry.[8] These circumstances, along with the entrepreneurial optimism and ample availability of capital that was the result of a cyclical upswing, attracted dozens of entrepreneurs in both the iron and steel industry and the coal mining sector. The fastest industrial development Germany had ever experienced reached its climax after 1854, a period also known as the first *Gründerzeit* – founders' period.[9]

It was in these years that Mulvany, backed by a consortium of largely Irish investors, acquired a mine near the village of Gelsenkirchen and another one near Herne. Both mines were situated in the newly explored northern parts of the district, further away from the Rhine, but within a stone's throw of the recently constructed Cöln-Mindener railway.[10] However, by the time Mulvany could put his mines into production, the world had suffered a major financial crisis and the demand for coal and cokes imploded. The expansion of the coal industry between 1850 and 1857, entailing an average production growth of more than 9 per cent a year, now quickly turned into an enormous coal surplus.[11] Indeed, with the growing dependence on the continuity of the iron and steel industry, the mining sector became part of a cyclical movement upon which it could exercise barely any influence.[12]

During his cross-examination in 1865, Mulvany looked back at his extraordinary attempt to circumvent the toxic struggle between mine owners and coal traders in the favour of consumers:

> My partners and I being strangers in the country, and having commenced the working of the collieries in the midst of 200 or 300 existing collieries, the necessity arose to find markets for our produce, and we resolved at an early period to seek the most distant markets, where we would come least in competition with the existing collieries.[13]

These more distant markets had long been physically accessible by road or waterway and, more recently, by rail. However, the relatively high costs of transporting low-value bulk cargo such as coal made the long-distance displacement of such commodities economically unfeasible. Mulvany, however, addressed this distribution problem in a radically different way to his competitors by focusing exclusively on the most modern means of transport: the railways.

Transporting low-value bulk over the expensive railways seemed to be utterly foolish. However, this is not to say that coal mines did not make any use of rail. After all, the railway was born in the caverns of the mineshaft. Moreover, the new collieries in the Ruhr were increasingly located northwards, further away from any waterways. Railway transport, including of coal, therefore increased. However, this only involved short distance transportation from the shaft to the blast furnace, local industrial consumers or the waterway. As a rule, in the 1850s, railways carried coal no further than 75 kilometres outside the Ruhr;[14] in cases of more distant markets, transport costs would exceed the value of Ruhr coal, preventing it from competing with cheap English coal or alternative fuels such as peat. Nevertheless, this was precisely what Mulvany had been aiming for: sales in more distant markets via the railways.[15]

To make long-distance rail transport for coal distribution profitable, freight rates had to be reduced significantly. However, in the late 1850s, freight reduction was an organisational problem and a highly charged political issue in the German Confederation. The large number of states, governments and railway companies that were involved in the determination of freight rates hampered any renegotiation of tariffs. Moreover, the issue of freight rate reduction was entirely politicised by the actions of the Prussian Minister of Commerce, August von der Heydt (1801–1874), in 1852. In an attempt to boost the region's coal mining industry and push back against the dominance of British coal in Berlin, von der Heydt had forced the Upper Silesian railway company to adjust its freight rates for coal to the so-called *Einpfennigtarif*. If a company refused to comply, the minister threatened to put it under control.[16] In von der Heydt's eyes, a drop in the dependence on foreign coal was a political interest that transcended the profitability of a railway company. From then on, railways saw freight rate reduction as a symbol of political coercion in favour of the domestic mining sector. Consequently, Mulvany's attempts to generate enthusiasm for freight rate reduction among the railway companies in the German Confederation repeatedly floundered. Nevertheless, Mulvany insisted that the transport of coal over long distances could be profitable for railways.[17] In England, railway companies carried mineral fuels over large distances, making a 50 per cent gross profit.[18] "The fact is," a contemporary British news article said:

> the more the subject is investigated, the more apparent it is that under good management, and in consideration of large quantities and long distances, coals can be profitably carried for the charge of about one-half penny per ton per mile.[19]

The German railway companies hesitated. Unlike British firms that were accustomed to determining their freight rates based on actual operating costs plus a reasonable profit, railways on the European continent determined their freight rates relative to the market value of alternative means of transportation. On this point, Mulvany failed to convince the German railway companies, and, without their cooperation, it was impossible to extend the distribution of his coal to, for example, the North German markets. If Mulvany could not soon find new channels of distribution, his company could perish, as so many others, in the fierce competition in the Ruhr area.

Faced with these circumstances, Mulvany shifted his attention to the Netherlands. Although the country's industrial activity was limited and it still raised duties on fuel, he expected to find new markets in the seaports and profit from the Dutch trade networks.[20] Moreover, since 1856, the Netherlands had been connected to the Ruhr district by means of a direct railway. The Dutch Rhenish Railway Company (*Nederlandsche Rhijnspoorweg-Maatschappij*) operated the lines between Amsterdam, Rotterdam, Utrecht and the German hinterland. Coincidentally, the new director of Dutch Rhenish was a Brit, James Staats Forbes (1823–1904), who was familiar with the special rates for coal transportation in his homeland. Forbes was also a personal friend of Mulvany.[21] It therefore did not take long before the two would meet.

Forbes had been appointed to reorganise Dutch Rhenish. In the mid-1850s, the company was ailing, not least because its freight transport was not doing well. Mediocre management and political friction between the Netherlands and Prussia delayed the establishment of the connection with the latter to 1856.[22] Nevertheless, despite this connection, the company's finances did not improve and its shares were valued as "worth less than nothing." This was because the volume of freight traffic was insufficient and hundreds of unemployed wagons were rusting away in the marshalling yards of Amsterdam and Utrecht.[23] In these circumstances, Forbes met Mulvany and listened to his plan, which basically consisted of two components: high frequency and large scale. New flat rates should apply to the direct transport of coal from the Ruhr to the Dutch ports and to major consumers such as gas factories. The elimination of stopovers ensured the regularity and speed of coal trains and minimised the cost per ton-kilometre. Standardisation in the handling of transhipments and scale increases further reduced the relative costs.[24] "(. . .) Being for the greater part English," Mulvany declared in 1865, "the majority of them [the shareholders JS] were more open to conviction on such a matter."[25]

Indeed, Forbes, who was in need of goods to keep his locomotives and wagons on track, and Mulvany, who was looking for a way out for his coal, soon recognised that they could help each other. They calculated that, as long as it was in large volumes, coal could be cost-effectively transported from Gelsenkirchen to the Netherlands by rail at a rate of 2.2 *pfennigs* per ton-kilometre. In return for these low freight rates, Mulvany would keep the level of his margins low and thus secured a large and continuous coal supply from his mines. As *Dutch Rhenish* reported internally in 1859, the two companies would: "make an equal sacrifice in the usual price of coal and in the coal transport price respectively."[26] When Mulvany finally succeeded in convincing the Cöln-Mindener railway to run the same pilot scheme from the mine to the German-Dutch border at the end of that year, a two-year experiment took off. Indeed, after months of irregular sales, the Ruhr coal trade in Amsterdam finally came on stream.[27]

Despite high expectations, including among Dutch newspapers, the main goal of reaching global markets through Dutch ports was not achieved.[28] Indeed, Ruhr coal could not compete with English coal on the world market and, by 1860, Mulvany shifted his attention to the Dutch inland market. However, distributing large volumes of coal in the Dutch market was also problematic. Apart from capacity shortages, which *Dutch Rhenish* could gradually resolve, it was mostly a problem of reaching the consumers.[29] Coal merchants were hostile towards the introduction of yet another coal product, while they were generally not interested in acting as agents of Ruhr coal for a very limited fee. Moreover, they could not accept the economic viability of coal distribution by rail.[30] Mulvany therefore established a private agency in the Netherlands that actively started recruiting new clients. Simultaneously, *Dutch Rhenish* switched from English to Ruhr coal for its own consumption. In addition, it actively brought Ruhr coal to the attention of large-scale consumers and also developed a unique sales organisation.[31] Station managers were encouraged to take-up coal sales on provision themselves, thereby establishing an ever-expanding intricate network of Ruhr coal sales points.[32]

The cooperation between Mulvany and Forbes benefitted both companies. On the one hand, Ruhr coal sales in the Netherlands increased and, by 1861, more than 40 per cent of Mulvany's total production was being sold on the Dutch market.[33] On the other hand, *Dutch Rhenish* increased its freight traffic from 103,000 tons in 1856 to 846,000 tons in 1870. Gross revenue per kilometre per year also increased in the same period by 180 per cent. Accordingly, while *Dutch Rhenish* was on the verge of bankruptcy at the end of the 1850s, it restored its profits due to the increased freight traffic in the course of the 1860s, becoming a role model for other railway companies in the Netherlands. Ruhr coal was soon being transported and sold along all major rail lines, which increased competition in the Dutch transport market considerably.[34] In the Ruhr, more and more mines became interested in marketing their coal in the Netherlands via the railways.[35]

It was only a matter of time before Mulvany was able to employ his demonstrable success in the Netherlands as a crowbar for opening negotiations with Prussian railway companies.[36] In 1861, he gathered a group of 32 Ruhr coal mines around him. Together, they guaranteed to supply the North German railway companies with 25,000 tons of coal annually for the city of Magdeburg. This assured scale and continuity allowed the companies to finally reduce their freight rates to 2.2 *pfennigs* per ton-kilometre. In two years, the volume of these coal shipments tripled, which also increased the profitability of the North German railway firms.[37]

Mulvany's persistence in changing the distribution structure of coal would completely transform the position of the Ruhr mining industry in the coal market. Whereas coal was transported by rail no further than 75 kilometres outside the Ruhr district in 1858, by 1865 it was moved to locations some 750 kilometres from the Ruhr. In 1871, the special coal rate was included in the German constitution as the normative tariff for railway transport of bulk cargo.[38] This success story cannot, however, be assigned to Mulvany alone; it had required transnational cooperation. "(. . .) there was a disposition to go into the matter," Mulvany clarified to the Royal Commission in London, "but I should have failed had it not been for the assistance afforded to me by the manager of the Dutch-Rhenish Railway, from Amsterdam and Rotterdam to Germany."[39]

The entrepreneurial initiative of exporting Ruhr coal via the Dutch ports to the world market failed. However, the economic notion of increasing transit trade was an idea that also penetrated Dutch politics in the mid-19th century. In the 1850s, the liberalisation of Dutch trading policies entailed an increasing appreciation for transit trade and an expansion of its transit connections to neighbouring countries, mostly via the River Rhine.[40] Rotterdam also strongly supported the emerging idea that transit trade was a good supplement to (and in some cases could even contribute to) trade on its own account.[41] Critics, however, felt that, as long as the Netherlands was in danger of infrastructural isolation, the act of navigation and the liberalisation of the Rhine were "but an adhesive bandage on a fatal wound."[42]

The Rotterdam Chamber of Commerce concluded that the port would not be able to compete with the Port of Antwerp for the European transit trade if it had no way other than the Rhine to reach its German hinterland. It therefore urged the national government to take a leading role in expanding the Dutch railway network and improving its connections with the port and neighbouring countries.[43] In the national parliament, the Rotterdam representative Anthony Hoynk van Papendrecht tirelessly expressed his belief in the need to expand the transit trade by improving international railway connections. He also condemned the indifference shown by Amsterdam's representatives, but was able to explain his ideas.[44] Whereas Rotterdam and Dordrecht covered about three quarters of the total transit trade in the Netherlands, worth 100 million guilders,[45] Amsterdam had stuck to the traditional focus on trade on its own account. Indeed, it barely participated in the country's transit trade and therefore did not share in its benefits.

One of the advantages of transit trade was that it offset lower profits with a lower risk. This meant that less wealthy entrepreneurs could find a way of earning a living in it. In addition, transit trade was a continuous source of income for the working classes; the unloading, transhipping and loading of abundant goods created employability and prosperity for many. The biggest advantage of transit trade was its positive impact on trade on its own account and the development of a merchant class. According to Hoynk van Papendrecht, transit trade triggered the entrepreneurial spirit. This explained the emergence of many major trading houses in Rotterdam. Indeed, with increasing traffic and the numerous relationships that transit trade produced, Rotterdam's entrepreneurs were able to develop trade on their own account. Furthermore, the growing number of unloading ships anchored in the port demanded return cargo and provided Dutch merchants with a cheap means of distribution for domestic produce. Finally, Hoynk van Papendrecht concluded there was no alternative; if the Netherlands was to not lose the transit trade to Belgium completely, it was of the greatest importance to have the shortest and cheapest transport routes from the North Sea to the German industrial hinterland, and this entailed, first and foremost, railways.[46]

In the eyes of government officials, merchants (for the most part, but not exclusively, Rotterdam merchants) and port officials, transit trade was directly connected to the improvement of the railways. The Rhine was considered to be no more than a convenient extra feature of the Dutch transport market. This "railway paradigm," as we propose to call it, also explains the course of Dutch economic policies in the 1860s and 1870s. This policy focused on the improvement of the accessibility of the four Dutch seaports as complementary to the construction of multiple international railway connections.[47] The Dutch Prime Minister, Johan Rudolph Thorbecke (1798–1872), openly declared that he would turn the Netherlands into a funnel with this policy: "so world trade will enter into direct relations with half of Europe, with all countries that lie behind and next to us (. . .)."[48]

Mulvany's entrepreneurship and ability to put friendships to good commercial use brought into operation a whole new set of dynamics in the distribution and sale of coal that corresponded to the new conditions of mass production and market expansion. The Dutch example had shown that low coal transport tariffs could be profitable, not only in Britain, but also on the European continent, even in a region where waterways competed fiercely with the railways. Mulvany materialised, for the first time, the ideas of high frequency and the large-scale transportation of coal or any other low-value commodities such as iron ore, strictly encapsulated in the cost-plus principle. Small profits and quick returns proved to be as good or even better than occasional large profits. In fact, the re-emergence of *Dutch Rhenish* because of increased coal transport was openly celebrated by the most important Dutch trade magazine, *De Economist*:

> These figures prove that regardless [of] the complaints made against the board of this company, it at least has had the talent to increase the transport greatly; and that it therefore promoted not only the interests of shareholders, but no less the interests of the general public and above all those of trade, and that this shows again that both interests usually go hand in hand.[49]

It was this silent revolution of perception that was unfolding among contemporary Dutch government officials, merchants and port and city authorities in Rotterdam. However, as long as the railways were in the spotlight of this new dynamics in the distribution and sale of industrial commodities, Rotterdam would lose its competitive advantage; other seaports with an international rail connection could be as fit for transit trade as Rotterdam. Moreover, Mulvany failed in his original idea to use the Dutch ports as springboards to the world market. The coal consumption in the ports themselves also remained insignificant for producers in the Ruhr. It should be concluded that, at this point in time, there was no interdependence between Rotterdam and the Ruhr. Nevertheless, in the early 1870s, the structures upon which Rotterdam and other seaports would have to compete for pole position in the transit trade market were established. This was a time in which the greatest industrial growth that ever had taken place in the Ruhr was about to begin.

Unleashing industrialisation: the quest for outlets and supply routes begins, 1870–1880

During the industrial wave in the 1850s, the coal mining industry and the iron and steel sector in the Ruhr experienced unprecedented growth *and* decline. During the latter phase, coal mining was forced to rely on more distant markets to sell its products. In the iron and steel sector, however, reliance on distant markets for bulky goods was insignificant. The blast furnaces in the Ruhr had been self-supporting in their ore provision until 1870. Blackband had been an important local source, as were ores from the Siegerland and the Lahn-Dill regions. This would, however, soon change.

With the introduction of the Bessemer-refining process in the Ruhr in the 1860s, all stages of iron and steel production had been mechanised. The industry started refining iron on a massive scale, which allowed pig iron production to increase significantly. The demand for ore rose correspondingly. However, at the same time, it became clear that the scope and quality of the Blackband deposits had been seriously overestimated, while the costs of ore exploitation in both the Siegerland and the Lahn-Dill areas were increasing. Furthermore, and this was far more important, the Bessemer process required pig iron with a low level of phosphorus ores, which was not available from any of these areas. The large-scale industry thus became increasingly dependent on a voluminous and continuous ore or pig iron supply from abroad.[50]

In 1871, after the war against France was won and the German Empire established, the steel industry experienced such glorious years that this period is also known as the second *Gründerzeit*. Entrepreneurs were confident of a lasting peace and were keen to invest. Moreover, piles of orders that could not have been entered into production during the war were now to be finished.[51] With the demand for iron and steel increasing, a growing need for ore took hold. The little accurate and sometimes even misleading data in German statistics make it impossible to identify the origin and exact composition of the ores used in the Ruhr in this period.[52] However, from the data of the *Oberbergamtsbezirk* Dortmund (the administrative name for the German mining region corresponding to what is now called the Ruhr), a quite dramatic increase in the use of foreign ore, from 1 per cent in 1872 to 19 per cent seven years later, can be observed. In subsequent years, the share of foreign ore in Ruhr production rose further to nearly 30 per cent in 1882.[53] In Germany as a whole, in 1870 about 7 per cent of the consumed ores were imported from abroad. Ten years later, that figure had risen to around 9 per cent.[54] This means that, in this period, the ironworks of the Ruhr were much more dependent on foreign ores than industry in the rest of Germany.

It is not known where the first foreign ores for the Ruhr industry came from. It is likely, though, that they consisted of Dutch ore. Locals had long been extracting bog ore, or *oer*, in small quantities in the eastern parts of the Netherlands.[55] The sudden appearance of German agents in the early 1870s revealed the increasing importance of these resources just across the border. The agents of the Ruhr industry started organising ore extraction on a scale that had never been seen before. Locals observed the spectacle with some astonishment, while farmers took double advantage of the extraction:

> Many moors are thereby transformed into arable land, because while earlier the owners used to incur major expense for ploughing their lands, now the German agents do this for them, while in addition, they receive considerable sums of money for the ore (. . .).[56]

The amount of Dutch ores that ended up in the ovens in the Ruhr cannot be reported with certainty, but it cannot have been much. Nevertheless, the Netherlands played an important role in supplying ore to industry in the Ruhr, which imported virtually all its foreign ores through Dutch seaports. Judging from Dutch import statistics in the first half of the 1870s, the Ruhr industry depended on foreign ores mainly from North African, Spanish and Italian sources.[57] Unsurprisingly, these ores contained a high iron and a very low phosphorous content and were especially appropriate for the Bessemer process. It was, however, Spanish ores that would soon become a vital resource for the Ruhr industry.

With the objective of securing "perpetual independence" in its ore supply, Krupp was the first, and for decades the only, steel company from the Ruhr operating a mining company (Orconera) in the ore rich environment of the Basque region around Bilbao.[58] Krupp transported these ores to the new Dutch

Port of Flushing from 1875 onwards; at that time, this was the most accessible seaport with deep basins in the Netherlands. Moreover, it had a new and direct rail connection to the hinterland. Cargos were easily transhipped from the ship to the wagons at the quays and transported further to the factories in the Ruhr.[59] By 1877, Krupp shifted the supply route to Rotterdam, however, and established the transport company the *Kruppsche Spedition und Rhederei Comptoir*, managing part of the ore transports at sea using his own vessels. Admittedly, Flushing was a much more state of the art seaport, but it connected the hinterland using only a single track while its number of wagons was limited. Due to sandbanks, Bilbao ores could only head to sea in shallow ships, and only during spring tide. As a consequence, only twice a month the ores arrived at the port in large quantities, meaning that an adequate transport capacity was indispensable. In Rotterdam, the hinterland connections were far better. The port not only had access to a rail connection, but was also equipped with the Rhine. Moreover, Rotterdam, unlike Flushing, was already a developed transit trade and transport hub. Even the poorly navigable waterway to the sea could not scare off Krupp, or other Spanish ore importers for that matter, as ore vessels coming from Bilbao also had a limited draught.[60]

By 1880, 21 per cent of Krupp's ore supply originated from Orconera; 20 years later this share had risen to 45 per cent.[61] Thanks to Orconera and Krupp's domestic mines, the company had become virtually independent from the ore market at the turn of the century, producing 10 per cent cheaper than competing German blast furnaces. Krupp's Spanish investments turned out to be very lucrative and drove much of the company's developments and strategies until World War I.[62]

Despite its significant success, Krupp's strategy remained exceptional in both the Ruhr and Germany. Krupp was certainly not the only one importing Spanish ores. By the end of the 1870s, ironworks in the Ruhr with Bessemer installations and coke blast furnaces imported about 300,000 tons of Spanish ore via the Netherlands, which was about half of the total amount of imported ores.[63] Krupp was exceptional, as it remained the only company in the Ruhr that secured its ore supply at such an early stage by participating in an international mining company and by establishing a transport firm in the Netherlands (*Kruppsche Spedition und Rhederei Comptoir*). All other companies in the Ruhr depended fully on the market for their foreign ore supply. Naturally, both Krupp and the independent ore merchants designated Rotterdam as the most appropriate ore import port. Indeed, after 1877, most of the ore imports in the Netherlands were transported via this port to the German hinterland.[64]

For the coal mining industry, the glorious years of the early 1870s were heaven, but the economic downturn that began with the stock market crash in Vienna in late 1873 was a disaster. The manufacturing industry went into decline, causing stagnating coal sales. At the time the new mines in the northern part of the Ruhr coal basin started their large-scale production, there was no longer a market for such enormous quantities of high-quality coal, or at least no nearby market.[65] The situation was worsened by the automatic impulse of the new large-scale mines not to limit, but to increase their production even further, with the aim being to reduce the costs per unit produced and stabilise their margins. Unsurprisingly, this strategy resulted in a larger coal supply, creating an even more competitive market. The importance of breaking the vicious circle of increasing supply and decreasing prices in the second half of the 1870s was as urgent (or even more so) as it had been in the 1860s.[66]

The coal mining industry in the Ruhr sought refuge from this race to the bottom in two strategies between 1870 and 1880. Both required close cooperation among the mining companies. The first aimed to create further market expansion, while the goal of the second was to exert market manipulation by means of price fixing and production agreements. This strategy could have had consequences for the way the coal market was organised, if it had not been so inefficacious. Market expansion, on the other hand, could have direct consequences for the relationship between the Ruhr and seaports like Rotterdam, depending on its exact range, starting with national all the way to international and overseas exports.

While he had been successful in expanding the market through the railways to the Netherlands and Magdeburg in the 1860s, Mulvany now continued his efforts to conquer the market for coal in the North German ports. In collaboration with other mining companies and the *Bergbau-Verein* – the branch organisation in the Ruhr – he wanted to come to an agreement with the railway companies. Only special tariffs enabled mining firms in the Ruhr to reach the ports and compete with the dominant English coal on the world market.[67] In 1874, Mulvany and Hugo Haniel, the head of one of the largest mining and steel conglomerates in the Ruhr, travelled to the North German ports and made a non-conclusive deal with two large shipping companies to supply them with 200,000 tons of coal annually. Mulvany and Haniel both used the logic of numbers and the language of the national interest to convince and put pressure on the local railway companies to put in place special coal tariffs. In a memorandum, published only three years after the establishment of the new German Empire, they publicly stated that the development of the industry was in the national interest, as it glued the young nation together in an expanding web of interdependent relations. Railway companies were thus charged with a special public responsibility; by decreasing the tariffs on bulk goods, specifically those of coal, they could provide the nation with the necessary transport connections. After all, the large-scale transport of cheap domestic coal was in the interests of the railway companies and was key to the healthy industrial development of the country as a whole. Furthermore, and this was the logic of numbers, Mulvany and Haniel accused the German railways of inefficiency. In England, the average transport costs amounted to 1.62 marks per kilometre. In the Netherlands, Mulvany could tell from his own experience that the average amounted to 1.65 marks. Given that the German railways did not need to import their locomotives or wagons and paid lower wages overall, how was it possible that the average transport costs here amounted to 2.01 or even 3.08 marks per kilometre?[68] In reality, this was a sign of the monopolistic structure of the German railway market. Mulvany's strategies worked and, in 1875, the Cöln-Mindener railway company finally introduced special tariffs for coal transport to Hamburg. As a result, Ruhr coal was able to compete successfully with English coal in the German port for the first time.[69]

From that moment on, it was only a matter of time before the coal mining companies in the Ruhr would target overseas markets as their next prey. However, this required lower rail tariffs to other seaports, an improvement in the reputation of Ruhr coal, the necessary adjustments to be made to the tranship-ment installations in existing ports, close cooperation with the German ship-ping companies and the establishment of a worldwide network of Ruhr coal depots.[70] In 1877, 23 mines founded a trading company, again under the lead-ership of Mulvany. This enterprise, the *Westfählische Kohlen-Ausfuhr-Verein*, had the exclusive aim of stimulating coal exports through the Western European seaports. One year before then, however, the Dutch professional journal *De Economist* had observed, rather piqued, that instead of approaching the Dutch, the Ruhr tycoons had come to secret tariff, tax and logistical agreements with the Belgian authorities, the railway companies and the German shipping firms, which made exporting Ruhr coal via the Port of Antwerp very advantageous for both the industrialists and the port. The availability of an easy and market-able commodity like coal solved the problem of the usual lack of return freight that many ports were dealing with. "Is it surprising," *De Economist* wrote, "that I directly (. . .) thought of the Dutch ports that suffer even more from a lack of return freight, thereby (. . .) increasing freight rates." If Antwerp were to suc-ceed in becoming the preferred export port for Ruhr coal, the journal warned, the Dutch ports, and especially Amsterdam, should fear for their international trade position.[71]

Meanwhile, the *Ausfuhr-Verein* represented more than five million tons of coal per year and was able to gently play no fewer than 22 Western European ports off against each other. It organised international conferences that were attended by almost 100 Western European delegates from port authorities, governments, coal traders and railway engineers. All of them were interested in putting an increasing part of Ruhr coal exports under their control.[72] By 1878, the *Verein* had reached a definite agreement with the railway companies, agreeing to run regular services and introducing uniform, low and all-inclusive tariffs for coal transport from the Ruhr to all Western European seaports.[73]

Coal tariff reforms, as proposed by W.T. Mulvany, 10 July 1879

Despite these arrangements, the mining companies still had little success on the world market,[74] as no port dared to invest heavily in new transhipment equip-ment to achieve the necessary efficiencies.[75] At the end of the 1870s, the efforts of Mulvany and the *Ausfuhr-Verein* to reach the global market via the railways and the Western European ports failed once again. Nonetheless, the endeavours by the Ruhr mining companies did not go unnoticed. The British newspaper

The Times observed that although Ruhr coal was not competing with English coal on the world market, it was becoming a major player in Germany's neighbouring countries:

> Germany now supplies Holland with about 2,000,000 tons of coal per annum, where England only supplies 400,000 tons; and in the markets of Switzerland, Austria and even France the one country runs the other a hard race.[76]

There was a clear discrepancy between 1870 and 1880 in the strategies of the iron and steel companies in the Ruhr on the one hand, and the mining companies on the other. Whereas the transportation and distribution of ore imports in the Ruhr were being organised through both the waterways and the railways, coal exports from the Ruhr were increasingly and exclusively organised via rail. The mining industry in the Ruhr was counting on continuing along the road already travelled and paved by their Irish brother William T. Mulvany since the economic downturn in the 1850s. By collaborating in consortia, they could guarantee scale and frequency, which enabled them to cut advantageous deals with the railway firms. In turn, the rail companies could guarantee speed, regularity and stable and long-term price agreements. Moreover, the new coal mines in the Ruhr were located further away from the Rhine and therefore made increasing use of the railways from 1870–1880. The ironworks, on the other hand, were located along the Rhine and could receive their ores via both the river and railways. At this point, they did not operate in consortia and predominantly depended on independent merchants for their foreign ore supply. These merchants coordinated the ore imports all the way to the Ruhr and played the railways off against the Rhine skippers. The discrepancy in the transportation and distribution strategies of imports and exports and the rather limited dependence on overseas markets did not allow for growing interdependencies between Rotterdam and the Ruhr. Dutch ports were not preferred over other European ports when it came to coal exports. Indeed, as long as the obsession of industrialists and policy makers with rail transport continued, Rotterdam would not be key for Ruhr tycoons when it came to entering the world market. Accordingly, in the 1870s, Rotterdam's comparative transport advantage over the Rhine remained largely untapped.

The Ruhr industry looking outwards, 1880–1900

The period 1880–1900 was a time in which the Ruhr's iron industry became increasingly dependent on the importation of foreign ores via Rotterdam and the Rhine. In 1880, with the introduction of a refining process that was, in contrast to the Bessemer procedure, also able to refine high phosphorous pig iron (Thomas process), the large reserves of high phosphorus Minette ore in Lorraine could finally be employed.[77] Simultaneously, the structurally increasing coal production and the endemic economic downturns forced the local mining industry to expand its market. By the 1890s, more coal was sold outside the Ruhr than inside it. What is more, an ever-larger share of coal was being transported via the Rhine. However, the interdependence between the Port of Rotterdam and the Ruhr with regard to coal sales still did not increase. Remarkably, Rotterdam failed for the third time in 40 years to attract Ruhr coal exports to its port, thereby nullifying a potential complementary advantage of coordinated coal and iron ore transport up and down the Rhine. This failure is even more remarkable given that the Rhine was perfectly navigable at that time and Rotterdam had finally achieved an impeccable form of entry from and to the sea (see Chapter 2). In addition, the port had also started mechanising bulk transhipments. It remains to be seen how it is possible that Ruhr industry increasingly depended on distant and overseas markets, while its dependence on Rotterdam did not obviously rise.

The growing dependence of the Ruhr industry on more distant and overseas markets for its iron ore supply is a much-overlooked fact of the 19th century history of the industrialisation of the Ruhr. Often, the introduction of the Thomas process is regarded as the moment when Germany became independent from foreign ores. After all, ironworks were enabled to increase their production by employing the rich mineral resources in Lorraine and Luxembourg, which were part of the German customs union. Scholars understand the introduction of the Thomas process in the Ruhr in terms of an industrial raw material strategy, with the objective being to become independent from foreign ore markets.[78] Sources from the time do mention this autarchic argument. The annual report of the iron and steel concern *Dortmunder Union*, for example, wrote in 1882:

> Above all (. . .) we need to concern [ourselves with] the increasing importance that the Thomas-Gilchrist process has won for Germany and especially for the *Union*, as it allows us also to become independent from foreign ore imports.[79]

However, such statements should be considered with caution, especially if companies from the Ruhr made them. The Thomas process did not have the same denotation for the Ruhr as it had for the rest of Germany. Moreover, the extent to which the national iron and steel sector really counted on Lorraine and Luxemburg as "*Erzkammer deutschlands*" (i.e. Germany's ore deposit) before the turn of the century is questionable.[80] Until that time, the increasing Minette production did not contribute to the growing pig iron production in the Ruhr. Contemporaries calculated that little more than 10 per cent of the total Minette production was marketed on the German market – excluding Lorraine. Minette imports to the Ruhr were simply too expensive. Indeed, because of the relatively low iron value of Minette ore and the high transport costs, pig iron production in the Ruhr by means of Spanish ore was always cheaper, and could be up to 24 per cent less expensive than Minette ore until the turn of the century.[81] It is not a convincing argument to state that Ruhr tycoons did not see, let alone anticipate, these conditions. As a result, the introduction of the Thomas process around 1880 must have had other aims than a raw material strategy.

The true breakthrough of the Thomas process in the Ruhr followed in 1881, when it became clear that Thomas steel could be processed into more kinds of semi-finished product than Bessemer steel. The market for rails, the main product of Bessemer steel, had been in decline for some years and the Ruhr tycoons grabbed the opportunity to diversify their product lines with both hands.[82] The reason why *Dortmunder Union* wrote so euphorically about a presumed upcoming independence from foreign ores can be found elsewhere; it wanted to appeal to the politics of self-sufficiency and other nationalist economic policies under Chancellor Otto von Bismarck in those years.[83] The *Union* adapted this rhetoric as it sought to settle the ongoing negotiations with the Prussian state railways in favour of the Ruhr lobby by introducing special rates for Lorraine ore. It would be regarded as useful if, due to an autarkic policy and corresponding lower rail freight rates, the Minette ore reserves could be added to the ore resources that were already available to the ironworks. Minette ores were never meant to completely replace them. The *Union*'s statements were nothing but rhetoric, and in fact the import of foreign ores would only really become significant in the years following the introduction of the Thomas process. Thomas pig iron production in Lorraine and Luxemburg skyrocketed and started to seriously compete with the blast furnaces in the Ruhr. Securing a vast supply of cheap phosphorus ore, if necessary from abroad, thus became a matter of survival.[84]

Krupp was the only entrepreneur in the Ruhr to operate iron ore mines overseas before the turn of the century. Other companies, such as *Gutehoffnungshütte*, relied completely on the market. For the blast furnaces in the Ruhr, the foreign ore market was dominated by only a few trading houses. In the 1880s, the Düsseldorf trading company Wm. H. Müller & Co. managed to achieve control over almost the entire market in Spanish ore in the Ruhr. Ten years later, the company was also one of the largest suppliers of Swedish ore. Up and until the turn of the century, Müller & Co. would be the most important independent ore supplier in the Ruhr. As a young man, Wilhelm Heinrich Müller (1838–1889) already possessed the spirit of enterprise. Aged 16, after he completed business school, he left to go to the United States for several years. On his return to Germany, he was left with nothing financially, but in terms of experience he was a rich man. In the Ruhr, he caught the eye of one of Germany's most famous industrialists, Friedrich Grillo, who appointed Müller as director of one of his iron and steel factories. Müller was a rising star and successfully pulled the company out of the doldrums. Nonetheless, after a difficult reorganisation, he decided to leave his position and start his own business. In 1876, and capitalising on his experience within the sector, Müller established an international trading company in mining and metallurgical products, Wm. H. Müller & Co.[85] Iron ore trade was not part of its initial business activities, and it was only a year later that Spanish ores came into the picture. After Krupp, Müller was one of the first German entrepreneurs to reach the Spanish ore market. This first mover's advantage allowed him to control about half of Germany's Spanish ore imports within a year.[86]

The rather unforeseen spectacular increase in ore transactions via Rotterdam forced Müller to establish a branch office in the port that would be charged with shipping activities both at sea and in the hinterland.[87] He was even contemplating moving the company's seat altogether: "We have (. . .) to consider that (. . .) also our business in mining and metallurgical products will gravitate more and more to Rotterdam," he wrote in 1878.[88] Müller established the freight and forwarding company Wm. H. Müller & Co. in collaboration with one of Rotterdam's most distinguished shipping families, Ruys & Co.[89] This collaboration allowed Müller to execute the shipping of iron ore with ships under its own management. The Rotterdam transport branch regularly invoiced the trade department in Düsseldorf for more than 200,000 marks per month. Formally and financially, both companies were independent, but for everything else: "(. . .) the Düsseldorf and Rotterdam businesses would be harmoniously connected."[90]

By vertically integrating in sea shipping, the Rotterdam branch reinforced the Bilbao ore trade of the Düsseldorf branch considerably, especially after the sandbank at the entrance of Bilbao's port was finally removed in the early 1880s.[91] The opening of a Ruhrort branch in 1879 reinforced Müller's transhipment activities on the Rhine, while also facilitating daily contact with the industrialists in the Ruhr.[92] Nevertheless, for Müller, the superior significance of Rotterdam was clear: "The focus of our business is effectively there (. . .)," he wrote in 1878.[93] Three years later, Müller bought out his Rotterdam partner. Müller & Co. Rotterdam continued expanding and, in addition to the Düsseldorf branch, started trading ore on its own account.[94] With increasing amounts of ore transactions, one of the most important tasks would be to further control transport costs. Müller therefore built four large sea steamers that would carry the Spanish ore and also signed very beneficial contracts with the Dutch Rhenish Railway Company to transport the ore to the German hinterland. As his former companion Ruys suspected: "Müller must receive a nice drawback from the Rhenish Railways to compete the freight rates on the Rhine (. . .), because he would not pay the difference."[95]

In late 1882, Müller realised that his transport activities had become the most important element of his iron ore business. In a very short time, Rotterdam had become a vast business and it made perfect sense to consolidate all the activities within this branch. By 1883, Müller had started selling off his non-ore and non-transport subsidiaries. Düsseldorf transferred all ore trade on its own account to the Rotterdam branch, which became the company's main seat. Müller contemplated, almost to his surprise: "So, I have become here (in Düsseldorf – JS) de facto and mainly [an] agent of my Dutch enterprises (. . .)."[96] The reorganisation enabled Müller & Co. to cope with the economic crisis of 1885 and, just before Heinrich Müller died from a stroke in 1889, he secured the continuity of his business by transferring ownership and management to his son and his son-in-law.[97]

Information about the extent of Müller's iron ore trade is limited. This makes it hard to say anything about its share of the market. In 1878, Müller's total trade amounted to, by his own account, 66,000 tons, rising to about 144,000 tons in 1880. This would mean that his share of Spanish iron ore exports to West Germany was about 57 per cent in both years.[98] In 1880, Krupp imported about 100,000 tons of Spanish ore.[99] This means that, in that year, Müller and Krupp together controlled 97 per cent of the Spanish ore market in West Germany. Since Krupp imported ores strictly for his own use, it can be concluded that Müller had acquired almost a monopoly in the supply of Spanish ore in the Ruhr. This enormous achievement was largely made possible by Müller's early appraisal of combining both the ore trade and sea transport on his own account. For inland transport, Müller could play off the Dutch Rhenish Railway Company against the Rhine shippers. Müller largely owed his dominant position in the Ruhr to the fact that he could offer his clients ore at competitive all-inclusive prices, which also fluctuated less sharply over the longer term. The Rotterdam branch played a vital part in this strategy, as it enabled Müller to coordinate trade and transport in the most efficient way. However, controlling both trade and transport did not secure market dominance forever. Data on 1891 show that Müller & Co.'s market share in Spanish ore imports in West Germany fell to about 29 per cent. For Krupp and Müller together, this number was about 57 per cent.[100] The entry of new traders into the ore market explains Müller's shrinking market share, as did the company's shift to importing other ores.

With the introduction of the Thomas process in the Ruhr, the market for foreign phosphorus ores became interesting, especially when, by the end of 1894, the process became patent free.[101] Again, Müller & Co. was one of the first companies to take advantage of this opportunity; it adopted its trade and transport strategy in the Swedish ore market and became the sole-selling agent for one of the most important ore mines in the country in 1895.[102] In contrast to its business in Spain, Müller & Co.'s relationship with the mining company was of a much more dependent nature. As an agent, Müller & Co. would not trade on its own account, while it likewise did not have a free hand in the transportation of Swedish ore. Müller would organise the transport together with the mining company on a joint freight account. By means of so-called *through rates*, they standardised the transport costs from the Swedish port (Oxelösund) until the ore reached its final destination. "The proposed rates are such, that there is not much (if any) margin in the sea rates," Müller wrote to his business partner at the mining company.[103] The two companies shared the transport risk, which allowed Müller & Co. to invest in the acquisition of four large modern ore carriers.[104] The hinterland transport between Rotterdam and the Ruhr more than compensated for the losses the companies made in terms of sea transport:

> We persevered in our policy (. . .) to play out the railways against the water route and were in a position to credit the joint [freight – JS] account with

special rebates and commissions (partly secret) which resulted in a handsome profit in the joint [freight – JS] account both to the company and ourselves.[105]

By the turn of the century, Müller & Co. controlled 34 per cent of total Swedish ore exports.[106] With 400,000 tons of ore, it supplied almost all the ironworks in the Ruhr, controlling about 45 per cent of the market.[107] It also supplied ironworks in other countries with Swedish ore. Indeed, at this time, about half of Müller's sales consisted of ores from Sweden.[108]

While Müller & Co. transported and sold Spanish ore exclusively in the 1880s, by the 1890s it had become a company with a broader international reach, in which both Spanish and Swedish ores were the main focus. At the turn of the century, the company sold approximately 1.1 million tons of ore. An estimated 90 per cent of these shipments went through Rotterdam. Müller thus controlled roughly a third of the ore flow in the port.[109] The company also controlled about 36 per cent of the total ore imports in the Ruhr and supplied about one fifth of the total market there. At this time, nearly 100 per cent of the imported ores in the Ruhr were shipped via Rotterdam, meaning that about 57 per cent of the total ore consumption in the Ruhr area was supplied via that port.[110]

Controlling both trade and transport was an effective way to supply ore in standardised and stable conditions. This was important, as the scale of the consumption did not allow for large varieties in price, timing or quantities. The same can be said of the coal trade. Until the 1870s, the Ruhr mining industry had mainly tried to tackle the problem of overproduction with a strategy based on liberal market principles. They did not limit competition or production within the sector, but cooperated in marketing consortia to put pressure on the transport market and expanded their markets beyond the Ruhr by means of large-scale transport on the basis of low transport costs. The mining industry in the Ruhr had found the railways to be most reliable in these efforts since the 1860s. In fact, by 1884, more coal was sent from the Ruhr to the Netherlands by rail than by the Rhine.[111] Nonetheless, this liberal attitude changed as the result of another economic crisis in 1876. The mining industry in the Ruhr started to tackle the problem of major overproduction by means of collective production restrictions, price conventions and, most importantly, the establishment of the Rhenish-Westphalian Coal Syndicate in 1893, which was a sales cartel that, because of its unprecedented scale, had the potential to limit "unhealthy competition" in the coal market.[112] Within a couple of years, the Syndicate was the exclusive sales organisation in Germany for almost the entire mining industry in the Ruhr. What is more, it also adopted the task of organising sales abroad. Indeed, the *Ausfuhr-Verein* had been dissolved by 1894.[113] The coal Syndicate continued marketing its coal mostly via the railways, as Rhine transport was only suitable for marketing in places that were located directly along the waterway; the extra costs of rail transport to and from the river plus two transhipments weighed too heavily on sales margins. Moreover, Rhine freights fluctuated strongly during the year. As long as the Syndicate did not control Rhine freight rates, it relied on stable long-term contracts with the railway companies.[114] The Syndicate was very much aware of the significance of foreign markets, especially relying on the Netherlands and Belgium. Here, higher freight rates would certainly endanger coal distribution, as the annual report of 1899 wrote: "(. . .) an aggravation of this distribution would lead to disadvantages, which because of the current tension on the coal market, cannot be compensated for."[115] The sales in more distant markets were a valve that released the pressure on the local market and allowed the cartel members to continue developing their production and optimise their capacity utilisation.[116]

In order to stabilise prices and maintain a calm coal production increase, the Syndicate needed to improve the coordination of coal sales. In more distant markets, it managed to control wholesales by imposing stringent contracts. Merchants would only receive the Syndicate's coal sole-selling rights if they would adhere to three conditions. First, the wholesaler could only sell Syndicate coal; this eliminated competition with other coal. Second, the wholesaler was appointed a specific sales territory; this eliminated competition with other wholesalers of Syndicate coal. Third, they would purchase and pay for the coal evenly over the year; this resulted in the amalgamation of financially strong merchants into associations and limited the amount of Syndicate trading associations. By 1896, the German market was divided between several of these Syndicate wholesalers, each of them charged with the sole-selling rights for Syndicate coal in a specific territory, thereby effectively eliminating competition between them.[117]

The importance of the Dutch market is clearly illustrated by the fact that the first foreign Syndicate trading association was established in Utrecht in 1896. This was to become one of the most successful of such associations, and also enjoyed more managerial autonomy than its German counterparts. The Coal-Trading Association (*Steenkolen Handels-Vereeniging* – SHV) was a Dutch joint venture of the largest existing Syndicate coal-trading companies. They had started their loose cooperation soon after the establishment of the Syndicate in 1893. The individual traders needed the Syndicate in order to acquire the sole-selling rights of Syndicate coal that had been imported by rail for the Netherlands. The Syndicate, in turn, depended on its local market knowledge and financial resources, but most of all on its transport contracts with the railway companies. Without the discounts that were negotiated within these secret contracts, Ruhr coal could not be distributed profitably via the railways on the Dutch market. As the exclusive representative in the Netherlands, SHV found itself in a comfortable, but also dependent, position, particularly because it could not trade in anything other than Syndicate coal without the consent of the Syndicate. Furthermore, the Syndicate determined not only the volume of coal exports, but also the coal prices. Finally, the Syndicate decided on a yearly basis whether the contract with SHV should be renewed.[118]

However, SHV held a real trump card with the Dutch railway transport contracts. Indeed, in the first business year, no less than 80 per cent of SHV's total profit could be credited to the special freight discounts. Over the period

1896–1903, the profit on coal transport was as important as that on all other business activities together, including coal sales. The special freight discounts allowed SHV to charge fixed and moderate coal prices. Moreover, because the transport contracts were concluded for periods of six years, the related profits were a very important element of the enterprise's financial stability. Finally, the discounts paid the Syndicate's fee for the annual awarding of the sole-selling rights to the company.[119]

The excellent financial results that SHV achieved over the years would contribute to the continuation of the relationship with the Syndicate. In the period up to World War I, the Syndicate probably never considered terminating the contract or establishing a sales organisation of its own in the Netherlands. However, the consequence of the favourable results was that the Syndicate wanted to be more involved in the Dutch company and would go on to skim a greater share of the profits. At the turn of the century, during a period of coal shortages, the Syndicate appointed, for the first time, one of its leading men to the board of SHV and he soon tried to assert his influence.[120]

With an increasing production volume after 1880, the need for more distant markets must have been obvious in terms of growing coal sales outside the Ruhr. Studies about the precise distribution of Ruhr coal over this period of time are scarce and misleading. The main claim is that the majority of the coal was consumed within the Ruhr itself and that the ratios between the other markets were subject to very little change until 1900. Indeed, it has been argued that Ruhr coal exports became significant only after the turn of the century.[121] However, these studies did not take into account the possibility of resales, for example in the ports of Duisburg and Ruhrort, and the subsequent transportation of this coal via the Rhine to more distant markets. At that time, the Rhine was the only waterway available for long-distance coal transport starting in the Ruhr.[122] If we therefore include figures on Rhine coal transport, we get a very different and more precise picture of Ruhr coal distribution over these years.

From Figure 3.2, it becomes clear that, at least from 1880 onwards, the Ruhr was structurally unable to absorb the increasing coal production itself. Indeed, from the mid-1890s onwards, more Ruhr coal was sold for consumption outside than inside the Ruhr. Looking more closely at these figures, it becomes clear that the increase of domestic Ruhr coal sales consisted mostly of growing coal sales in territories south of the Ruhr.[123] Indeed, between 1891 and 1903, coal shipments to these areas doubled to more than 12 million tons a year. This increase was far higher than the increase of coal sales up north. Moreover, between 50 and 60 per cent of the coal sales southwards were being transported by the Rhine.[124] Indeed, between 1891 and 1902, it was the Rhine, not the railways, that was responsible for the enormous increase in domestic sales of Ruhr coal outside the Ruhr. In addition, if we look at the distribution of the coal sales, we can observe the constant, but not unimportant, share of neighbouring countries. The Netherlands had long been an important market for Ruhr coal, but Belgium was also becoming a significant consumer at the

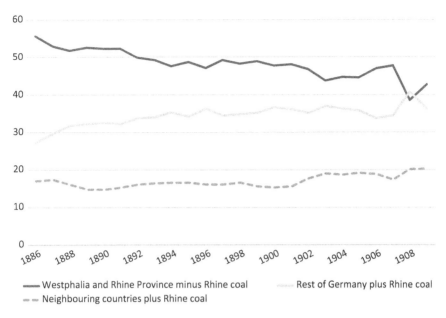

Figure 3.2 Destination Ruhr coal, cokes and briquettes, corrected for first resale on the Rhine 1880–1909 (in per cent of total sales)

Note: The data series is not complete for the initial years. This leads to minor distortions in the figure. From 1899 the coal transports on the Dortmund-Ems Canal are included in the series "Rest of Germany plus Rhine coal."

Sources: For sales over the years 1880, 1885 and 1890: Sarter, „Die syndikatsbestrebungen im niederrheinisch-westfälischen Steinkohlenbezirke," 44–45. For sales over the years 1891–1903: Gottschalk Diederich Baedeker, *Jahrbuch für den Oberbergamtsbezirk Dortmund. Ein Führer durch die rheinisch-westfälischen Berg-und Hüttenwerke und Salinen in wirtschaftlicher und finanzieller Beziehung* (Essen: XXX, 1905), table H. For sales on the Rhine over the years 1880–1900: *Die Entwickelung des niederrheinisch-westfälischen Steinkohlen-Bergbaues in der zweiten Hälfte des 19. Jahrhunderts*, Hrsg. vom *Verein für die bergbaulichen Interessen im Oberbergamtsbezirk Dortmund, part 3, book X* (Berlin: XXX, 1904), 221, table 36. For sales on the Rhine over the years 1900–1904: Baedeker, *Jahrbuch für den Oberbergamtsbezirk Dortmund*, table M. For sales on the Rhine over the years 1905–1909: „Aufzeichnungen bei der Königlich Niederländischen Zollstelle zu Lobith," *Jahres-Bericht der Zentral-Kommission für die Rheinschiffahrt* (Strasburg: XXX, 1906–1910), and Johann Kempkens, *Die Ruhrhäfen. Ihre Industrie und ihr Handel* (Bonn: XXX, 1914), 117–118. For the data on the Dortmund-Ems Canal: Kempkens, *Die Ruhrhäfen*, 8–9.

end of the 19th century. In fact, between 1885 and 1903, Ruhr coal exports to Belgium grew faster than those to the Netherlands. Partly, this growth of Belgian Ruhr coal imports was enabled by an increased use of the Rhine from barely 50,000 tons in 1885 to more than 800,000 tons in 1900. This was an average annual increase of 21 per cent, while coal distribution via the Rhine in the Netherlands was stable and even slightly declining after 1895.

The Ruhr became increasingly dependent on more distant markets, and was also able to reach these markets thanks to organising distribution, transport and production in a competitive way. At this point, it becomes clear that the mining industry in the Ruhr understood the importance of cheap waterways.

Questions then remain: why was the Rhine not used to its full potential for coal transport to the Netherlands? Why did Rotterdam not become the coal export port of the Ruhr well before 1900?

Part of the answer to these questions lies in the fact that the Rotterdam port authorities did not develop a clear modernisation strategy. It was clear to the authorities that bulk cargo constituted an increasing part of the total throughput. In order to attract these transit flows at the expense of other Western European ports, it had to invest in the modernisation of the port. Whereas up and until the turn of the century Rotterdam's port expansion was fully dedicated to facilitating Rhine transport, the mechanisation of the tranship-ments was exclusively focused on railways.[125] In 1885, and very much at the insistence of the *Ausfuhr-Verein*, the port authorities inaugurated a coal tip, i.e. a hydraulic crane installation that elevated and emptied an entire train wagon into a ship.[126] This procedure greatly accelerated the transhipment of coal and was therefore highly efficient. In the 1890s, two other tips were installed and, at the end of that decade, the Chamber of Commerce concluded: "The coal tips are exclusively used for the transhipment of German coal and cokes, and to a large extent it is certainly thanks to the presence of these tips that the export of German coal via our port increased so much lately."[127] In the same decade, the municipality approved the purchase and installation of six electric iron ore cranes, which unloaded sea steamers and loaded train wagons on three tracks simultaneously.[128] These examples illustrate that, even for those directly involved, attracting overseas bulk cargo flows seemed to have been a matter of having well-functioning train transhipment equipment until well into the 1890s. On the other hand, Rotterdam had invested hugely in the expansion of the port since the late 1880s. Indeed, with the construction of deep, spacious and permanently accessible basins, such as the *Rijnhaven* in 1895 and the *Maashaven* in 1905, the port facilitated transit trade "on stream" as well. Sea ships could efficiently unload bulky cargo directly on attached Rhine ships and sail out within only a couple of hours.[129] Possibly, the Port of Rotterdam could have accelerated the bulk cargo transit even more by taking complete advantage of its natural endowment and investing in the mechanisation of sea–Rhine, instead of sea–rail, transhipment. Nevertheless, the port acted in the spirit of the Ruhr coal mining industry, which was still very much determined by a railway paradigm. Moreover, a port can only anticipate new developments in the fore and hinterland to a limited extent.

Rotterdam and the Ruhr: a love story, 1900–1914

After the turn of the century, Rotterdam and the Ruhr became intimately intertwined, with Ruhr industrialists investing in the construction of private ports in both locations. Overseas transport was completely concentrated on the Rhine. Moreover, the Ruhr tycoons and the merchants in Rotterdam invested in transport, forwarding and transhipment companies in the city's port, facilitating the import and export of bulk cargo. Finally, the Rotterdam port authorities were also investing heavily in the expansion of a Rhine-based port. After more than 30 years, Rotterdam thus became the unchallenged seaport for bulk cargo to and from the Ruhr.

For the Ruhr tycoons, 1900–1914 was to be regarded as the most volatile period in the history of their iron ore supply. The agitation was mainly the result of a general sense of market insecurity. While the industrialists, other than Krupp, had no problem in relying on foreign ores and private ore traders before the turn of the century, by 1900 they shared a strong commitment to becoming independent in their supply. Indirectly, the market insecurity had consequences for the Rotterdam-Ruhr relationship, as it yielded new players in the field and new strategies in the coordination of the iron ore supply. "The 'iron ore crisis' is one of the most discussed economic problems of the present day," wrote Theodor Sehmer in 1911 in the introduction to his book on the European iron ore supply:

> A diminution of the ore reserves is beginning to make itself felt here and there, and the great ore consumers have been seized by a certain nervousness because they are concerned about the future arrangement of their ore supply.[130]

The increasing uncertainty about the ore supply among the Ruhr industrialists can be explained by at least two factors. On the one hand, they had seen a strong growth in ore consumption in recent years. On the other, they were confronted with the fact that there was no indication whatsoever as to the total volume of ore reserves globally.[131] In addition, the recent rising prices of Spanish ore pointed to the possible exhaustion of once promising fields. Moreover, new national policies caused anxiety. Countries had voiced their concerns about the possible exhaustion of domestic ore reserves. Instead of unrestricted exports like Spain had allowed, the Swedish parliament demanded export restrictions in order to increase the export price and to employ part of the ore reserves to develop a domestic iron industry.[132] These restrictions would be a serious blow to the iron and steel industry in the Ruhr. The German government could conclude a new trade agreement with Sweden or could threaten to reduce freight rates for Minette ore from Lorraine.[133] Nevertheless, despite governmental support, it was the Ruhr industrialists that sought to increase their collaboration in order to secure their ore supply. The first successful iron ore purchasing consortium was established in 1899. This consisted of the Dortmund steel companies Phoenix, Hoesch, Hörder Verein and Dortmunder Union and the Vereinigte Königs-und Laurahütte from Upper Silesia. Phoenix and the Dortmunder Union barely used Swedish ores in the 1890s, but they anticipated the opening of the Ofoten railway in 1903 and the subsequent large-scale ore exports via Narvik.[134]

This large-scale export had great advantages, which were not only pecuniary. The transport costs via Narvik and Rotterdam to the Ruhr were, on average, a crown per ton lower than those of the Swedish ports on the Baltic Sea to the Ruhr. Moreover, shipments in Narvik could take place throughout the year, while the ports on the Swedish east coast were frozen all winter, limiting exports to six or seven months a year.[135] The consortium acquired more than eight million tons of the finest quality North Swedish ores between 1901 and 1912. Thereafter, the consortium expanded to include Gutehoffnungshütte, Rheinische Stahlwerke, Gelsenkirchener Bergwerks, Haspe and Deutsch-Lux and the contract was extended to 1928.[136]

The success of the consortium met with encouragement among the other iron producers in the Ruhr. Cooperation between German iron and steel producers had demonstrably resulted in a stronger negotiating position. Krupp was convinced that the Swedish ore mines sold at below cost price.[137] In 1903, following the Dortmund example, large iron and steel companies around Duisburg also started to collaborate in a Swedish ore purchasing consortium. Gutehoffnungshütte and Rheinische Stahlwerke would continue this collaboration until at least 1917.[138] Even though cooperation in the steel industry in the Ruhr was not easily achieved, these examples show that consortium building was a common strategy in the early years of the 20th century. This was an important shift in the strategy of the ironworks in the Ruhr; by means of scale, they sought to construct a stronger negotiating position towards the ore mining industry directly and towards the ore traders. In addition to governmental support, consortium building was an answer from within the iron and steel sector to the increasing uncertainty in the iron ore supply.[139]

A final strategy to secure the iron ore supply was to integrate backwards in the supply chain. Consortia were again often, but not always, employed. Just after the turn of the century, the members of the Dortmund consortium, for example, founded a transport company in Rotterdam, the *Transport-Comptoir der Hüttewerke Phoenix, Hoerde & Hoesch*.[140] Their ironworks were located further away from Krupp and other competitors on the Rhine, and they therefore had an added imperative to save on transport costs. As they were, thanks to their special contract, assured of a continuous supply of large quantities of ore via the Port of Rotterdam, integrating the coordination of shipments could yield considerable benefits. Thyssen, on the other hand, expanded vertically in the ore supply chain, mostly on its own. In 1905, it constructed a private port in the Ruhr, Schwelgern. It also established a transhipment company and purchased Rhine ships. In Rotterdam, it established a trading and transport company, *Handels-en Transport Maatschappij Vulcaan*, in 1910, and before World War I started to build its own port at the Nieuwe Waterweg near Rotterdam. Thyssen also acquired ore mines within Germany and abroad.[141] In 1914, Gutehoffnungshütte followed Thyssen's example and built a private port in Duisburg, integrated Rhine transport in the company, and finally established a trading and transport firm in Rotterdam (*NV Walsum Handels-en Transport Maatschappij*). Gutehoffnungshütte would never participate in foreign mining companies without the backing of partners in a larger consortium.[142] Furthermore, Krupp still had its participation in Spain, whereas GBAG, Deutsch-Lux, Bochumer Verein, Phoenix, Hoesch en Haspe owned participations in foreign mines, most of them in French Lorraine and French Normandy.[143]

In reaction to these developments, the largest iron ore trader in the Ruhr, Müller & Co., also initiated a further integration of the ore supply chain. In addition to its shipping activities, the company started acquiring mines in Sweden, Spain and North Africa.[144] By participating in these mines, it could enforce exclusive agency contracts for Müller & Co. In this way, the company was assured of a lasting position as an intermediary between the mine and the pig iron manufacturers. This construction allowed the company to receive profits on the ore transports and minimise its trade risk, as it did not actually own the ores, but pocketed commissions for each ton sold. After 1900, Müller & Co. moved towards becoming a less Ruhr-oriented company. The iron and steel industrialists in the Ruhr were partly successful in their endeavours to become less dependent on intermediaries and started importing ores themselves, particularly from France. By 1909, Müller & Co. was exporting 40 per cent of its ores outside Germany.[145] This meant that Rotterdam also became less important for the company. Did this mean that the relationship between Rotterdam and the Ruhr weakened, too? Not really. It is true that the

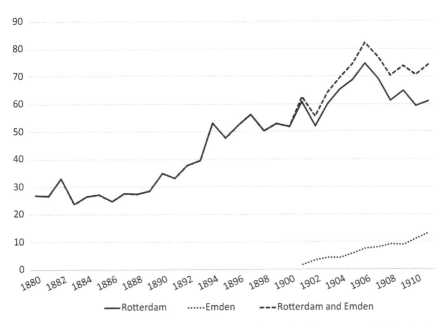

Figure 3.3 Iron ore shipped through Rotterdam as a share of total pig iron production in the Ruhr (corrected for iron value) 1880–1911 (percentage)

Source: For total pig iron production in the Ruhr 1880–1901: *Feldenkirchen, Die Eisen-und Stahlundustrie des Ruhrgebiets,* appendix, table 39. For iron ore imports in the period 1880–1897: De Goey, *Database on cargo flows in the Port of Rotterdam, 1880–2000; Goederenoverslag Rotterdamse haven, 1880–2000.* For the origins ratio: *Statistiek voor de in-, uit-en doorvoer.* "Algemene invoer ter zee," "erts," 1881–1898 and own calculations. For iron imports in the 1898–1911 period: Consul Général de Roumanie à Rotterdam (Gustav Müller), *Rapport consulaire* (Dordrecht: 1903–1914). For the iron ore transit in Emden: Kempkens, *Die Ruhrhäfen,* 8–9. For the iron value correction: Sehmer, *Die Eisenerzversorgung europas,* 226–227.

increased importation of French and German Lorraine Minette ore had a negative impact on the Rotterdam-Ruhr relationship, as these flows were organised through the French and German railways. However, the more important
Swedish ores increasingly followed the Rotterdam route. The new Ofoten
railways had opened the Norwegian Sea route up for ore exports. Moreover,
the iron and steel industry in the Ruhr anticipated this shift by integrating their
supply chain along the Rhine.

Figure 3.3 shows that the iron ore supplied via Rotterdam as a share of total
pig iron production in the Ruhr was significant in 1880. In the period to 1911,
this share more than doubled to 60 per cent. In 1906, during a short boom, the
share reached an absolute peak of nearly 75 per cent. Most of these supplies still
consisted of Spanish iron ore, but the amount of Swedish ores had increased
considerably after the opening of the Ofoten railways. During the period from
1880–1911, Rotterdam was the main transport hub for imported ores in the
Ruhr region. It is safe to say that the Ruhr would not have become the largest industrial area in Europe without Rotterdam, or at least not as quickly as it
did. Likewise, Rotterdam was also dependent on the flows of iron ore going
through its port. Indeed, as a share of the total volume in Rotterdam, iron
ore increased from about 14 per cent in 1880 to about 25 per cent just before
World War I.[146]

The increased ore imports and the growing involvement of the Ruhr industrialists in the coordination of these flows between Rotterdam and the Ruhr
also increased the interest of the Coal Syndicate in the Dutch port and the
Rhine. In 1901, the coal shortage had turned into coal abundance and the Syndicate was urgently looking for new ways to market its product. The Syndicate
used its increased influence in the SHV (which it had acquired by appointing a
board member in 1900) to press a strategic change of course, and in 1901 the
SHV board decided to establish a branch office in the Port of Rotterdam that
was instructed to outcompete English coal there, be it on the export, the bun-
kering or the local market.[147] This move should not be seen in isolation from
an important transformation of the Syndicate's organisation that occurred two
years later. In 1903, it succeeded in including the last independent coal mining
companies in the Ruhr within the structure of the sales cartel. Until then, the
coal mines and coal sales of Haniel, Stinnes, Thyssen and Krupp had competed
strongly with Syndicate coal, especially on the Dutch market.[148] In addition to
the incorporation of these mines, the Syndicate united the large-scale independent traders that were active on the Rhine in a new trading association, the
Rheinische Kohlenhandel & Rhederei Gesellschaft. The association, known as the
Kohlenkontor, incorporated all the traders' Rhine shipping companies and transhipment machinery, deposits and briquette factories in the respective Rhine
ports. What is more, the *Kohlenkontor* transported the Syndicate's coal at fixed
prices, which meant that fluctuating Rhine freight rates belonged to the past.
Consequently, the Syndicate members now finally had exclusive access to a
massive sales and distribution apparatus on the Rhine that guaranteed continuity, stability, low transport costs and the large-scale transportation of their coal.[149]

Due to their large stake in railway transport, SHV had always prevented Rhine coal from entering the Dutch market, but this would change in 1904,[150] when it concluded an arrangement with the Syndicate. In exchange for a 40 per cent share in the company, the Syndicate charged SHV with the sole-selling rights of Rhine coal. From then on, SHV was the Syndicate's exclusive sales agent in the Netherlands. Nonetheless, the Syndicate watched the activities of SHV more closely than ever before.[151] The assurance of a continuous supply of cheap Ruhr coal, obtained by the quasi-integration with the Syndicate, reduced the financial risk to SHV of scaling-up the Rotterdam branch and allowed it to invest substantially in modern transhipment facilities.[152] Rotterdam quickly became the main focus of the company. After 1907, Ruhr coal competed successfully with English coal in the Rotterdam port.[153] SHV had become the most important Syndicate trading association, with more than eight million tons of Syndicate coal, about 10 per cent of total Ruhr coal sales and about a third of total Ruhr coal exports.[154] By 1912, more than half of these shipments went to Rotterdam (Figure 3.4).[155]

This clearly shows that the Ruhr mining industry was not as dependent for its exports on Rotterdam as the iron and steel sector. For the port, however,

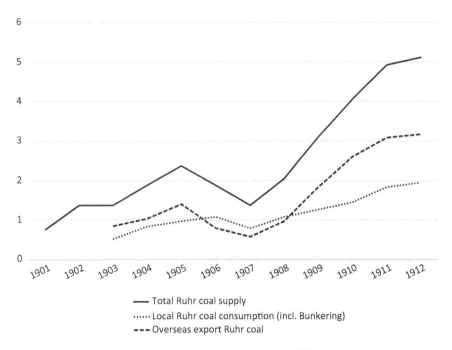

Figure 3.4 Ruhr coal supply in Rotterdam 1901–1912 (in million tons)

Source: *Annual report of the Chamber of Commerce of Rotterdam* (1905 and 1910). For 1911 and 1912: SHVBA, Verslag van den Raad van Beheer der Steenkolen Handelsvereeniging over de jaren 1911/1912 and 1912/1913.

this coal supply was of enormous importance financially, because about 17 per cent of the total throughputs consisted of coal by 1912. Yet the coal supply also had consequences of a more essential nature. The secured and continuous supply of return freight and fuel for sea ships attracted sea traffic to the Port of Rotterdam, which resulted in lower sea freights. Rotterdam finally emerged as a competitive port within the Hamburg-Le Havre range. What is more, the shift to large-scale coal traffic down the Rhine was of the greatest importance, as it complemented the upwards iron ore shipments. For 40 years, the supply and distribution functions of a large part of the coal mining industry in the Ruhr had been structured on the railways. After this supply and distribution had been restructured, the Rhine could be utilised to its full potential and the strong connections between the Port of Rotterdam and the Ruhr area could finally flourish.

Conclusion

This chapter shows that, despite favourable natural conditions, an interdependent relationship between the Ruhr and Rotterdam was not predestined. After all, for decades, railways had been a better alternative, which allowed any other sea port with a railway connection to compete for Rotterdam's hinterland. Nevertheless, even after the Rhine had gained its competitive position on the transport market, it took another decade before Rotterdam merchants and Ruhr industrialists engaged fully with the river's potential. Geographical circumstances shaped the framework within which the demand for transport and the development of transport connections came into being. However, how geographical, but also political and economic, structures were used was determined by the actors involved. National, local and port authorities all had a degree of agency within these existing structures and they certainly pursued their individual objectives. Indeed, the chapter contains several examples of such initiatives. However, it also shows that many of these initiatives, such as the mechanisation of the transhipment installations in Rotterdam, were the result of lobby activities from entrepreneurs. This chapter has explained the crucial role of entrepreneurs in the establishment of the Rotterdam-Ruhr relationship. This is a story about how, when and why (or why not) entrepreneurs could take full advantage of existing natural conditions. It reveals the activities of the entrepreneurs affected, for good or ill, as well as the scope, intensity, speed and impact of the interconnectedness between Rotterdam and the Ruhr district in the period 1860–1914.

The chapter has also assessed to what extent the development of the Ruhr depended on Rotterdam, and vice versa, by looking at the flows of raw materials, i.e. coal and iron ore, moving between the two areas over the entire period. As regards flows of goods with a low-value to volume ratio, transport costs were crucial in the formation of port-hinterland connections. Nevertheless, the Mulvany example shows that a second, crucial element in the organisation of supply chains was the predictability of the transport economy.

Entrepreneurs pursued low costs and certainty within their supply chain in at least three ways, i.e. by lobbying governments and port authorities for better transport conditions and lower tariffs, establishing relations through long-term and large-scale transport contracts and integrating transportation and transhipment activities within the organisation. It was these three strategies that ultimately created the coordination and distribution structure of the coal and iron ore supply chains.

The entrepreneurs involved in the overseas iron ore imports especially relied on a transport capacity that could cope with sudden large-scale influxes. Rotterdam provided such a transport capacity from the 1870s onwards, which consisted of a hybrid transport connection with the hinterland, using both railways and Rhine navigation. The entrepreneurs involved in the marketing of Ruhr coal, on the other hand, depended on continuity and large-scale, long-distance transportation over the long run. Starting with Mulvany, the sector focused exclusively on the most modern means of transport – the railways – for four decades. This railway paradigm informed the lobby activities of the increasingly colluding coal mining industry in the Ruhr, determined the long-term contracting relations with the railway companies and resulted in a minimal integration of Rhine shipping activities within the organisation of what was to become the largest cartel in Germany: the RWKS.

As long as the coal mining sector acted largely within the railway paradigm, geography barely played any role in the direction of the coal distribution. This conflicted with the transportation and distribution strategies of the ore importers and impeded the relationship with the Port of Rotterdam. It is remarkable that, even after the Rhine had become competitive again, the coal mining sector would still barely use it. The coal mining industry had established a structure for the distribution and marketing of its coal that, in itself, determined the room for manoeuvre of the actors involved and the course of the coal flows. An important finding of this chapter is therefore the conclusion that, besides geographical, political or economic structures, entrepreneurial agency matters when it comes to the establishment of interdependent port-hinterland connections. However, it does not necessarily matter in a positive way. Pursuing low transport costs and transport security led to the construction of transport and distribution structures that in turn did not fully exploit the Rhine's potential. Clearly, this is not a story of historical accident; the actors involved were very consciously pursuing their interests, albeit within the structures of a given geographical, political and economic environment.

It was only after the turn of the century, when the Ruhr mining sector reached an unprecedented scale of collusion, that it was able to reorganise the distribution function and upstream ore cargos on the Rhine could be complemented with downstream coal cargos. Until World War I, other sea ports like Antwerp could not match the competitive advantage that the Rhine provided to Rotterdam in terms of its position in the transit trade of bulk goods to and from the Ruhr, laying the foundations for a symbiotic relationship throughout the 20th century.

Notes

1 Hein A.M. Klemann and Friso Wielenga, "Die Niederlande und Deutschland, oder verschwindet die nationale Ökonomie? Eine Einleitung," in *Deutschland und die Niederlande. Wirtschaftsbeziehungen im 19. und 20. Jahrhundert*, ed. Hein A.M. Klemann and Friso Wielenga (Münster: Waxmann, 2009), 7–17; Hein A.M. Klemann, *Waarom bestaat Nederland eigenlijk nog? Nederland – Duitsland: Economische integratie en politieke consequenties 1860–2000* (Rotterdam: Erasmus Universiteit Rotterdam, 21 March 2006), 8, 65; André Beening, *Onder de vleugels van de adelaar. De Duitse buitenlandse politiek ten aanzien van Nederland in de periode 1870–1914* (PhD diss., Amsterdam, 1994), 16.

2 W. Abelshauser and W. Köllmann, eds., *Das Ruhrgebiet im Industriezeitalter. Geschichte und Entwicklung I* (Düsseldorf: Schwann im Patmos-Verlag, 1990); Wilfried Feldenkirchen, *Die Eisen- und Stahlindustrie des Ruhrgebiets 1879–1914. Wachstum, Finanzierung und Struktur ihrer Grossunternehmen* (Wiesbaden: Steiner, 1982), 1–8, 19–24; Stefanie Van der Kerkhof, *Von der Friedens- zur Kriegswirtschaft. Unternehmensstrategien der deutschen Eisen- und Stahlindustrie vom Kaiserreich bis zum Ende des Ersten Weltkrieges* (Essen: Klartext-Verlag, 2006), 80–89; Johannes Bähr, Ralf Banken, and Thomas Flemming, *Die MAN: eine deutsche Industriegeschichte* (München: Beck, 2008); J.R. Fear, *Organizing Control: August Thyssen and the Construction of German Corporate Management* (Cambridge, MA: Harvard University Press, 2005); Paul van de Laar, *Stad van formaat. Geschiedenis van Rotterdam in de negentiende en twintigste eeuw* (Zwolle: Waanders, 2000), 91; J. Schraver, ed., *Rotterdam. Poort van Europa. De geschiedenis van haven en handel in Rotterdam* (Rotterdam and Antwerp: Ad. Donker, 1946), 29–30; Hugo van Driel and Ferry de Goey, *Rotterdam Cargo Handling Technology 1870–2000* (Zutphen: Walburg Press, 2000); Hugo van Driel and J.W. Schot, "Het ontstaan van een gemechaniseerde massagoedhaven in Rotterdam," in *Techniek in Nederland in de Twintigste Eeuw. Part 5. Transport Communicatie*, ed. H.W. Lintzen and J.W. Schot (Zutphen: Stichting Historie der Techniek, 2002), 75–95; Hugo van Driel, "Innovation and Integration in Mineral Bulk Handling in the Port of Rotterdam 1886–1923," *Business History* 44, no. 3 (2002): 63–90; Jolke U. Brolsma, *Havens, kranen, dokken en veren. De Gemeentelijke Haveninrichtingen en het Havenbedrijf der gemeente Rotterdam, 1882–2006* (Utrecht: Stichting Matrijs, 2007); P. Serton, *Rotterdam als haven voor massale goederen. Een bijdrage tot de geografie van het verkeer* (Nijmegen: Ten Hoet, 1919). A more internationally oriented study, albeit mostly quantitative and comparative: R. Loyen, E. Buyst, and G. Devos, eds., *Struggling for Leadership: Antwerp-Rotterdam Port Competition between 1870 and 2000* (Heidelberg and New York: Physica-Verlag, 2002); Ferry de Goey, ed., *Comparative Port History of Rotterdam and Antwerp 1880–2000: Competition, Cargo and Costs* (Amsterdam: Aksant, 2004). Older, although still valuable studies, are: Fritz Krieger, *Die wirtschaftliche Verflechtung des Unterruhrgebietes mit den Niederlanden im 19. Jahrhundert* (PhD diss., Cologne, 1935); J. Lülsdorfs, *Die Bedeutung Rotterdams für die rheinische Wirtschaft, insbesondere für die deutsche Rheinschiffahrt* (Cologne: Orthen, 1940); Renate Laspeyres, *Rotterdam und das Ruhrgebiet* (PhD diss., Marburg, 1969).

3 David Held uses the same variables in the analysis of globalisation. It is arguable to see the increasing interconnectedness between Rotterdam and the Ruhr since the end of the 19th century as part of a process of globalisation. Held defines globalisation as: "a process (or set of processes) which embodies a transformation in the spatial organization of social relations and transactions, expressed in transcontinental or *interregional flows* and networks of activity, interaction and power." Italics Joep Schenk. D. Held, A. McGrew, D. Goldblatt, and J. Perraton, *Global Transformations: Politics, Economics and Culture* (Cambridge: Polity Press, 1999), 16.

4 The Commission concluded that there was no need for the government to intervene, although the individual companies should show a more transparent pricing policy. Philip S. Bagwell, *The Transport Revolution 1770–1985* (London: Routledge, 1988), 165–166.

5 Royal Commission on Railways, *Evidence and Papers Relating to Railways in Ireland* (London: Pr. for H.M.S.O, 1866), 52; Bagwell, *The Transport Revolution*, 157–166; Evelyn Kroker, "Mulvany, William Thomas," in *Neue deutsche Biographie* 18 (1997): 577–578. www. deutsche-biographie.de/sfz67270.html, retrieved on 30 January 2014.

6 Abelshauser, *Das Ruhrgebiet, 263. Die Entwickelung des niederrheinisch-westfälischen Steinkohlen-Bergbaues in der zweiten Hälfte des 19. Jahrhunderts, hrsg. vom Verein für die bergbaulichen Interessen im Oberbergamtsbezirk Dortmund, Part 3, book X* (Berlin: Springer-Verlag, 1904), 190–193.

7 *Die Gutehoffnungshütte Oberhausen, Rheinland: zur Erinnerung an das 100 jährige Bestehen 1810–1910* (Oberhausen: August Bagel, 1910), 25.

8 Dieter Ziegler, *Eisenbahnen und Staat im Zeitalter der Industrialisierung* (Stuttgart: Franz Steiner Verlag, 1996), 16–17; G. Gebhardt, *Ruhrbergbau, Geschichte, Aufbau und Verflechtung seiner Gesellschaften und Organisationen. Unter Mitw. Der Gesellschaften des Ruhrbergbaus zusammengestellt* (Essen: Verlag Glückauf, 1957), 19; Rainer Fremdling, "Railroads and German Economic Growth: A Leading Sector Analysis with a Comparison to the United States and Great Britain," *Journal of Economic History* 37, no. 3 (1977): 601.

9 Gebhardt, *Ruhrbergbau*, 19; Feldenkirchen, *Die Eisen- und Stahlundustrie*, 22.

10 Kroker, "Mulvany."

11 Gebhardt, *Ruhrbergbau*, 20; *Entwickelung des niederrheinisch-westfälischen Steinkohlen-Bergbaues*, 194–195.

12 Abelshauser, *Das Ruhrgebiet im Industriezeitalter*, 230–232.

13 *Royal Commission on Railways*, 52.

14 Measured from the centre of the Ruhr district.

15 *Royal Commission on Railways*, 52.

16 Rainer Fremdling, "Anglo-German Rivalry on Coal Markets in France, the Netherlands and Germany, 1850–1913," *Groningen Growth and Development Centre Research Memorandum 199521* (Groningen: Groningen Growth and Development Centre, 1995), 14. https://www.rug.nl/research/portal/publications/pub(8c2dcd1d-fd9b-42cf-92c4-3214bb68dfaa).html. Retrieved 29 April 2019.

Wolfgang Köllmann, "Heydt, August Freiherr von der," in *Neue deutsche Biographie* 9 (1972): 74–76. www.deutsche-biographie.de/sfz32097.html, retrieved on 30 September 2014.

17 Both Fremdling and Ziegler claim that the *Einpfennigtarif* imposed in Upper Silesia stood at the base of Mulvany's special freight rates. However, it is more convincing to argue that both Von der Heydt and Mulvany based their rates on the calculations of the British railway companies that were determined by the logic of profitability. Nonetheless, Mulvany tried to convince the German railways of the viability of this logic, whereas Von der Heydt seems to have taken the freight rate as an arbitrary maximum. Fremdling, *Anglo-German rivalry on coal markets*, 14; Ziegler, *Eisenbahnen und Staat*, 26. Also: *Entwickelung des niederrheinisch-westfälischen Steinkohlen-Bergbaues*, 122–124; *Royal Commission*, 52; W. Klee, *Preusische Eisenbahngeschichte* (Stuttgart: Kohlhammer, 1982), 126 ff.

18 Joseph von Renauld, *Der Bergbau und die Hüttenindustrie von Oberschlesien 1884–1897. Eine Untersuchung über die Wirkungen der staatlichen Eisenbahntarifpolitik und des Wasserverkehrs. Mit einem Anhang graphischer Darstellungen und einer Karte der Provinz Schlesien* (Stuttgart: Cotta, 1900), 212. Also: Boris Gehlen, "Zwischen Wettbewerbsideal und Staatsräson: Die Diskussionen im Deutschen Handelstag über Regulierung und Verstaatlichung der Eisenbahnen (1861–1879)," in *Jahrbuch für Wirtschaftsgeschichte/Economic History Yearbook* 52 (2011): 124, note 24; Volker Then, *Eisenbahnen und Eisenbahnunternehmer in der Industriellen Revolution: ein preussisch/deutsch-englischer Vergleich* (Göttingen: Vandenhoeck & Ruprecht, 1997), 365; *Royal Commission on Railways*, 52.

19 "The Coal Traffic of Railways," *Hunt's Merchants' Magazine and Commercial Review* 27 (1852): 379–380.

20 Jan Luiten van Zanden and Arthur van Riel, *Nederland 1780–1914. Staat, instituties en economische ontwikkeling* (Amsterdam: Balans, 2000), 218, 261–265.

21 Charles Welch, "Forbes, James Staats (1823–1904)," in *Oxford Dictionary of National Biography*, rev. Ralph Harrington (Oxford, 2004. www.oxforddnb.com/view/article/33192, retrieved on 31 October 2012.

22 Willem van den Broeke and Elise van Nederveen Meerkerk, "Spoorlijnen en geldstromen. Een onderzoek naar de financiers van de Nederlandsche Rhijnspoorweg-Maatschappij 1845–1890," *NEHA – Jaarboek voor Economische, bedrijfs- en techniekgeschiedenis* 64 (2001): 154–177. Utrechts Archief, Utrecht (UA), 901, Nr. 62, Vergadering van de Raad van Commissarissen, 24 October 1857. E.A. Pratt, *Railways and Their Rates, with an Appendix on the British Canal Problem* (London: J. Murray, 1905), 265–271; Van Zanden, *Nederland 1780–1914*, 233.

23 Pratt, *Railways and Their Rates*, xi en 274.

24 Ibid., 276.

25 *Royal Commission on Railways*, 52.

26 UA, 901, Nr. 65, Kwartaalverslagen van de Directie aan de Raad van Commissarissen, 20 October 1859.

27 *Royal Commission on Railways*, 52–53; *Algemeen Handelsblad*, 2 November 1859, Dag, 5.

28 "Uitvoer van Hibernia-Steenkolen uit Nederlandsche havens," *Nieuw Amsterdamsch handels-en effectenblad*, 3 August 1860, 3. https://resolver.kb.nl/resolve?urn=ddd:01013 1889:mpeg21:a0034, retrieved from Delpher on 29 April 2019.

29 UA, 901, Nr. 65, Kwartaalverslagen van de Directie aan de Raad van Commissarissen, 7 March 1860.

30 Pratt, *Railways and Their Rates*, 277; Piet 't Hart, *H.A. van Beuningen. 'Een van Utrechts beste burgers'* (unpublished, 2006), 65.

31 UA, 901, Nr. 65, Kwartaalverslagen van de Directie aan de Raad van Commissarissen, 9 May 1859; Pratt, *Railways and Their Rates*, 277; Z.W. Sneller, *Geschiedenis van den steenkolenhandel van Rotterdam* (Groningen and Batavia: Wolters, 1946), 179.

32 Pratt, *Railways and Their Rates*, 279; Sneller, *Geschiedenis van den steenkolenhandel*, 171–173.

33 Total production of the Hibernia mine (in 1000 tons) between 1859 and 1861: 98.5, 148.8 and 162. Olaf Schmidt-Rutsch, *William Thomas Mulvany. Ein irischer Pragmatiker und Visionär im Ruhrgebiet 1806–1885* (Cologne: Stiftung Rheinisch-Westfälisches Wirtschaftsarchiv, 2003), 125. Dutch imports by railway (in 1000 tons) for those years: 13.7, 33.2 and 69.6. *Staatkundig en staathuishoudkundig jaarboekje* (Amsterdam 1858–1862). Until 1861, all coal Germany imported via the railways was Hibernia coal.

34 Sneller, *Geschiedenis van den steenkolenhandel*, 171.

35 UA, 901, Nr. 66, Kwartaalverslagen van de Directie aan de Raad van Commissarissen, 17 October 1863. *Nederlandse Staatscourant*, 26 September 1862, 4. *Algemeen Handelsblad*, 13 October 1862, 3. *Algemeen Handelsblad*, 29 October 1867, Dag, 10. 't Hart, *H.A. van Beuningen*, 63, 66.

36 *Entwickelung des niederrheinisch-westfälischen Steinkohlen-Bergbaues*, 122–124.

37 Fritz Krönig, *Die Differential-Tarife der Eisenbahnen* (Berlin: F. Vahlen, 1877), 127, appendix 1. *Entwickelung des niederrheinisch-westfälischen Steinkohlen-Bergbaues*, 123; *Royal Commission on Railways*, 53.

38 See Article 45, par. 2 *Reichsverfassung*, 16 April 1871.

39 *Royal Commission on Railways*, 53.

40 See Chapter 2, this book.

41 H.P.H. Nusteling, *De Rijnvaart in het tijdperk van stoom en steenkool 1831–1914: een studie van het goederenvervoer en de verkeerspolitiek in de Rijndelta en het achterland, mede in verband met de opkomst van de spoorwegen en de concurrentie van vreemde zeehavens* (Amsterdam: Holland University Press, 1974), 213.

42 S.P. Lipman, "Regeling van de belangen der Nederlandsche scheepvaart," *Algemeen Handelsblad*, 22 April 1850, Dag.

43 Kamer van Koophandel en Fabrieken, *Rotterdam, Jaarverslagen* (Rotterdam: Kamer van Koophandel en Fabrieken, 1858–1862).

44 *Handelingen Tweede Kamer 1859–1860*, 8 November 1859, 115.
45 "Ingezonden stukken. De lijn Rotterdam-Dordrecht-Moerdijk-Breda," *Nieuwe Rotterdamsche courant: staats-, handels-, nieuws- en advertentieblad*, 19 July 1860, Dag. *Handelingen Tweede Kamer*, 1859–1860, 8 November 1859, 115–118. By comparison, Dutch DGP was seven times this amount: *Tweehonderd jaar statistiek in tijdreeksen 1800–1999* (Voorburg and Heerlen: CBS, 2001), 77, table 9.
46 *Handelingen Tweede Kamer 1859–1860*, 8 November 1859, 116–118.
47 See Chapter 2, this book.
48 Nusteling, *De Rijnvaart*, 109. As cited by Wouter Van Stiphout, *Maak een stad: Rotterdam en de architectuur van J.H. van den Broek* (PhD diss., Groningen, 2005), 65.
49 Pratt, *Railways and Their Rates*, 279; Van den Broeke, "Spoorlijnen," 68–69; "Beschouwingen over spoorwegen in Nederland," *De Economist* 23 (1874): 412–413.
50 Abelshauser, *Das Ruhrgebiet im Industriezeitalter*, 269. Feldenkirchen, *Die Eisen- und Stahlindustrie*, 1–8, 19–28, 58–64; Van der Kerkhof, *Von der Friedens- zur Kriegswirtschaft*, 80–89; Theodor Sehmer, *Die Eisenerzversorgung europas. Probleme der Weltwirtschaft 2* (Jena: G. Fischer, 1911), 213–224, 233; Ulrich Wengenroth, *Enterprise and Technology: The German and British Steel Industries, 1865–1895* (Cambridge and New York: Cambridge University Press, 1994), 24.
51 Feldenkirchen, *Die Eisen- und Stahlindustrie*, 35.
52 Both Goldstein and Sehmer complained about this deficit at the beginning of the 20th century. G. Goldstein, *Die Entwicklung der deutschen Roheisenindustrie seit 1879* (PhD diss., Halle, 1908), 418; Sehmer, *Eisenerzversorgung*, 348.
53 Feldenkirchen, *Die Eisen- und Stahlindustrie*, 43, 59.
54 *Statistik des Deutschen Reiches*, 1871, 1881. Calculated as follows: (import) / (production – export + import) * 100 = total share of foreign ores in total consumption. 1870: (300) / (3.839–84 + 300) * 100, and 1880: (607) / (7.239–1.263 + 607) * 100.
55 From which the English "ore" originates, www.oxforddictionaries.com.
56 *Leeuwarder courant*, 18 February 1872, Dag, 2.
57 Nusteling, *De Rijnvaart*, appendix 13 C. Nusteling must have intended 'Noord Afrika' when he wrote 'Noord-Amerika'; Die Gutehoffnungshütte Oberhausen, Rheinland: *zur Erinnerung an das 100jährige Bestehen – 1810–1910*, tafel A.
58 Ulrich Wengenroth, *Auslandsinvestitionen der deutschen Schwerindustrie zur Sicherung ihrer Erzversorgung zwischen Gründerjahren und Weltwirtschaftskrise*, München Zentrum für Wissenschafts- und Technikgeschichte Working Paper (München, 1998), 3; *Krupp'sche Gussstahlfabrik, Krupp: A Century's History of the Krupp Works, 1812–1912* (Essen: np, 1912), 137–138, 153–115; Edoardo Jorge Glas, *Bilbao's Modern Business Elite* (Reno: University of Nevada Press, 1997), 57–72; Javier Loscertales, *Deutsche Investitionen in Spanien 1870–1920* (Stuttgart: Steiner, 2002), 94–99.
59 Hein A.M. Klemann, "Vlissingen als haven voor het Duitse achterland," in *Zeeland en de wijde wereld. Liber Amicorum voor Willem van den Broeke*, ed. Tobias van Gent and Pieter Ippel (Middelburg: De Drvkkery, 2012), 27–47.
60 Loscertales, *Deutsche Investitionen*, 94–95; Bert Altena, *Een broeinest der anarchie: arbeiders, arbeidersbeweging en maatschappelijke ontwikkeling: Vlissingen 1875–1929 (1940)* (PhD diss., Amsterdam, 1989), 37–42.
61 Loscertales, *Deutsche Investitionen*, 98–99, 320.
62 Rheinisch-Westfälisches Wirtschaftsarchiv, Cologne (RWWA), 130, 30006/0, Letter G. Müller to Wormstall, 18 January 1896. Loscertales, *Deutsche Investitionen*, 87; *A Century's History of the Krupp Works*, 137–138, 153–155; Wengenroth, *Auslandsinvestitionen der deutschen Schwerindustrie*, 1–5.
63 Jesús María Valdaliso, "La exportación de hierro Español. 1850–1914. Una primera eproximación al tráfico marítimo y sus beneficios," *Areas: Revista internacional de ciencias sociales* 16 (1994): 131–164; William Gill, "Der Eisenerz-District von Bilbao," *Stahl und Eisen* 8 (1882): 344. Revised by W(ilhelm)H(einrich)M(üller).
64 "Der Eisenerz-District von Bilbao," *Stahl und Eisen*, 337–345.

65 Abelshauser, *Das Ruhrgebiet*, 233–234; *Entwickelung des niederrheinisch-westfälischen Steinkohlen-Bergbaues*, 196–197; Klaus Tenfelde, *Sozialgeschichte der Bergarbeiterschaft and der Ruhr im 19. Jahrhundert* (Bonn: Verlag Neue Gesellschaft, 1977), 201–202.

66 *Entwickelung des niederrheinisch-westfälischen Steinkohlen-Bergbaues*, 196–198; Kurt Wiedenfeld, *Das Rheinisch-Westfälische Kohlensyndikat* (Bonn: A. Marous und E. Weber, 1912), 2, 12–17; Horst Schleuning, *Der deutsche Kohlenhandel: ein Weg von der freizügigen zur gebundenen Marktversorgung* (Berlin etc.: De Gruyter, 1936), 19–25; Sneller, *Geschiedenis van den steenkolenhandel*, 197.

67 Fremdling, *Anglo-German rivalry*, 15–18.

68 These are the average transport costs for loaded 400-ton trains with closed wagons. The measures have been recalculated from the Taler per German mile, as: one Taler is three marks. One German mile is approximately 7.5 kilometres.

69 Haniel Archiv, Ruhrort (HA), 954, Memorandum, H. Haniel and W.T. Mulvany, *Deutschlands Nordseehäfen und ihrer Eisenbahn Verbindung* (27 December 1874); Schmidt-Rutsch, *William Thomas Mulvany*, 200–206; Fremdling, *Anglo-German rivalry*, 15–17.

70 HA, 954, W.T. Mulvany, Memorandum. Export of Westphalian coal (Düsseldorf) 12 April 1876; Haniel Archiv, Ruhrort (HA), access number 954, C. Kunst, *Ausfuhr westfälischer Kohle und Kokes nach überseeischen Ländern. Practische Beweise ihrer Ausfuhrbarkeit* (Brake, 1 September 1876).

71 G.J. Rive, "Antwerpen, als uitvoerhaven voor steenkolen," *De Economist* (1876): 670–672; A. Beaujon, "Een tolverbond met België?," *De Economist* (1877): 732; G.J. Rive, "De tegenwoordige steenkool-handel," *De Economist* (1878): 588–600; Schmidt-Rutsch, *William Thomas Mulvany*, 200–202, 206–211; W.O. Henderson, *William Thomas Mulvany. Ein irischer Unternehmer im Ruhrgebiet 1806–1885* (Cologne: Universität zu Köln, 1970), 12–13; Paul Schachert, *Die überseeische Kohlenausfuhr Deutschlands* (Cologne: np, 1885), 24; *Annual Report Chamber of Commerce Rotterdam*, 1882, 10; Also cited by Sneller, *Geschiedenis van den steenkolenhandel*, 184–185, 223.

72 Hugo Van Driel, *Rotterdam Cargo Handling Technology*; Technische Universiteit Eindhoven, "De overslag van kolen en erts," *Techniek in Nederland in de Twintigste eeuw*. www.techniekinnederland.nl/nl/index.php?title=De_overslag_van_kolen_en_erts, retrieved on 12 August 2012; Rive, "De tegenwoordige steenkool-handel," 587–600. Bergbau Archiv, Bochum (BBA), 32/751, Protokoll über ein Konferenz vom Westfälischen Kohlen-Ausfuhrverein, 9 February 1878. Stellungnahmen Mulvanys zu Export- u. Verkehrsfragen (1864–1885). Schmidt-Rutsch, *William Thomas Mulvany*, 210. *De Standaard*, 7 February 1878.

73 Rive, "De tegenwoordige steenkool-handel," 586–590.

74 Schachert, *Die überseeische Kohlenausfuhr*, 21; Paul Neubaur, *Mathias Stinnes und sein Haus. Ein Jahrhundert der entwickelung 1808–1908* (Mülheim an der Ruhr: Bagel, 1909), 273–274.

75 Schachert, *Die überseeische Kohlenausfuhr*, 19–21.

76 "The Coal Trade of Great Britain," *The Times* (London) (16 June 1879), 5.

77 Wengenroth, *Enterprise and technology*, 157ff. Abelshauser, *Das Ruhrgebiet im Industriezeitalter*, 279–285.

78 Wilfried Plücker, *Der schwedische Eisenerzbergbau und seine Beziehungen zur westdeutschen Eisenhüttenindustrie 1880–1965* (Cologne: Gouder & Hansen, 1968), 15; Feldenkirchen, *Die Eisen- und Stahlindustrie*, 7; Van der Kerkhof, *Von der Friedens- zur Kriegswirtschaft*, 141.

79 As cited by: Goldstein, *Die Entwicklung*, 315.

80 Sehmer, *Eisenerzversorgung*, 250.

81 Goldstein, *Die Entwicklung*, 318–322, 427.

82 Wengenroth, *Enterprise and Technology*, 157–165, 171; Goldstein, *Die Entwicklung*, 317.

83 Feldenkirchen, *Die Eisen- und Stahlindustrie*, 34–39; Steven B. Webb, "Tariffs, Cartels, Technology, and Growth in the German Steel Industry, 1879 to 1914," *The Journal of Economic History* 40 (1980): 309–330, there 310–311.

84 Feldenkirchen, *Die Eisen- und Stahlindustrie*, 137; Goldstein, *Die Entwicklung*, 317.
85 Archiv des Landschaftsverbandes Rheinland, Pulheim (ALVR), Bestand 9 RH, 397, Anna Müller, *Wm. H. Müller. Nach Briefen und nach eigenen Erinnerungen von seiner Schwester Anna, unpublished manuscript* (Hannover, 1924), 20–91, 104–106, 127–135, 168–177, 191–198. Stadsarchief Rotterdam, Rotterdam (SAR), 1256, 1731: *Entwurf. Aufzeichnungen über Gründung und Entwicklung der Firma Wm. H. Müller & Co. aus der Perspektive von Düsseldorf und des Erzgeschäftes aus gesehen* (zt zp +/- > 1960) 1–11, there 1. *Beknopte geschiedenis van Wm. H. Müller & Co.* (zt zp +/- 1946) 1–13, there 1. John M. Kleeberg, *The Disconto-Gesellschaft and German Industrialization: A Critical Examination of the Career of a German Universal Bank, 1851–1914* (Oxford: np, 1988), 275–276; "Müller, Wilhelm Heinrich," *Deutsche Biographie*. www.deutsche-biographie. de/sfz66838.html, retrieved on 5 August 2013.
86 ALVR, 9 RH, 397, Müller, *Wm. H. Müller*, 206. In 1878, Müller claims to have transported 100,000 to 120,000 Centener of iron ore per month, i.e. 5,500 tons per month, and 66,000 tons per year. Total exports of Spanish ore to the Netherlands in 1878 amounted to 113,000 tons. Valdaliso, "La exportación de hierro Español," appendix 2.
87 ALVR, 9 RH, 397, Müller, *Wm. H. Müller*, 206.
88 SAR, 325, 57, Letter Wm. H. Müller to Ruys & Co., Düsseldorf, 10 April 1878.
89 SAR, 615, 61 Statutes Firma Wm. H. Müller & Co, *Overeenkomst van oprichting 3 juni 1878*. SAR, 1256, 1731, *Beknopte geschiedenis van Wm. H. Müller & Co.* (zt zp +/- 1946) 1–13, there 1.
90 SAR, 325, 57, Letter Wm. H. Müller to Ruys & Co., Düsseldorf, April, 1878.
91 ALVR, 9 RH, 397, Müller, *Wm. H. Müller*, 206–208.
92 Ibid., 214–216, 219–220.
93 Ibid., 212.
94 ALVR, 9 RH, 397, Müller, *Wm. H. Müller*, 219–226. SAR, 1256, 881–882: Manuscript geschiedenis Müller, G.A. Appeldoorn, *Historie* (np nt), 8. The Commanditaire Vennootschap with Ruys & Co. was liquidated on 31 December 1880. On 22 November 1880, Wm. H. Müller and W.N.A. Kröller established Wm. H. Müller & Co. The company's goal was to "(. . .) het uitoefenen van cargadoors-, expeditie-, en reederij-zaken in den uitgebreidsten zin, benevens den goederen-handel (. . .)." Also there, 615, nr. 61 Statutes, Firma Wm. H. Müller & Co, *Bericht van oprichting en (overeenkomstige oprichtingsakte)* 22 November 1880. Also there, 1256, 1731, *Beknopte geschiedenis van Wm. H. Müller & Co.* (nt np +/- 1946) 1–13, there 1.
95 ALVR, 9 RH, 397, Müller, *Wm. H. Müller*, 247–248. UA, 901, 67, Kwartaalverslagen van de Directie aan de Raad van Commissarissen, March, 24, 1880. SAR, 325, 68, Letter, Willem Ruys to Daan Ruys, 19 July 1881.
96 ALVR, 9 RH, 397, Müller, *Wm. H. Müller*, 258.
97 Ibid., 315, 329–330, 351–355, 364–367, 375–378, 383; Eva Rovers, *De eeuwigheid verzameld. Helene Kröller-Müller 1869–1939* (Amsterdam: Prometheus Bert Bakker, 2012), 1–30.
98 Total exports of Spanish iron ore to the Netherlands in these years were 113,666 tons and 251,212 tons, respectively. Valdaliso, "La exportación de hierro Español," 131–164, appendix 2.
99 Loscertales, *Deutsche Investitionen*, 320, table 65.
100 Riksarkivet, Stockholm (RA), GGAB, F1, Nr. 7, Sammandrag af Rotterdams Jernmalms-Import 1891. Valdaliso mentions the export of Spanish iron ore to Germany, via the Netherlands, of 715,000 tons. Valdaliso, "La exportación de hierro Español," 131–164, appendix 2. Loscertales, *Deutsche Investitionen*, 320, table 65.
101 RA, GGAB, F1, Nr. 7, Letter Wm. H. Müller & Co. to G.D. Frænckel, 13 October 1892.
102 SAR, 325, 50, Ruys & Co., Reisbeschrijving Berlijn, 24–25 juni 1891. RA, Trafikaktiebolaget Grängesberg – Oxelösund (TGO), Handlingar rörande bolaget F1, Nr. 42, 2, Agenturkontrakt af 5/7 1893 med Wm. H. Müller & Co. och G.D. Frænkel. RA,

TGO, F1, Nr. 42, 2, Agenturkontrakt af 7/5 1895 gällande intill slutet af 1899. Also: Agenturkontrakt af 2/5 1898 gällande för åren 1900–1904 (Stockholm and Rotterdam), and: Agenturkontrakt 27/2 1905 gällande för åren 1908–1912 (Stockholm and Rotterdam). RA, GBAG, F1, Nr. 5, Jarnmalms Afslutningars. GGAB, F1, Nr. 1, C.H. Byström, *Klotens Aktiebolag och Grängesbergs Grufveaktiebolag 1872–1920* (July 1911 and November 1920): 62. Martin Fritz, *Svensk järnmalmexport, 1883–1913* (Göteborg: np, 1967), 43, there diagram 4, 47–48. Plücker, *Der schwedische Eisenerzbergbau*, 46–48.

103 RA, TGO, F1, Nr. 30, Wm H. Müller & Co. aan Grängesberg, 23 February 1898.

104 GRT of Maud Cassel (1897), Skandia (1899), Grängesberg (1903) and Blötberg (1907) together was almost 20,000 tons. www.shipsnostalgia.com/showthread.php?t=43772, retrieved on 18 September 2013.

105 RA, TGO, F1, Nr. 30, Letter Müller to Grängesberg, 23 February 1898.

106 Fritz, *Svensk järnmalmexport*, 53, 109–110; Martin Fritz, *Järnmalmsproduktion och järnmalmsmarknad 1883–1913* (Göteborg: np, 1967), 28–33.

107 Fritz, *Järnmalmsproduktion och järnmalmsmarknad*, 42, table 158; Fritz, *Järnmalmsproduktion och järnmalmsmarknad*, 28, 35, table 135 and 151.

108 In 1900, Müller & Co. supplied a total of 525,000 tons of Gränges ore. Fritz, *Järnmalmsproduktion och järnmalmsmarknad*, 28, table 135. Müller & Co.'s total ore sales amounted to 1.1 million tons. S.F. van Oss, *Van Oss' effectenboek* (Groningen: P. Noordhoff, 1911), 746.

109 Other important ore importers in Rotterdam were Krupp, Ruys & Co. and Jos. de Poorter. Ore transports were also executed by shipping and forwarding companies like Phs. van Ommeren, P.A. van Es & Co., Hudig & Blockhuyzen, etc. For Krupps Spanish ore imports: Loscertales, *Deutsche Investitionen*, 320, table 65. See, for Rotterdam ore imports in 1891: RA, GGAB, f1,7, Sammandrag af Rotterdams Jernmalms-Import 1891. See, for Rotterdam ore imports 1891–1895: *De Hollandsche Revue* 1 (1896): 363.

110 Müller & Co.'s archives do not contain import statistics. See, for relevant statistics regarding Swedish ore: Fritz, *Järnmalmsproduktion och järnmalmsmarknad*, 28–29, 35, table 135, 136, 151. See, for Müller & Co.'s total ore sales (1898–1907 and 1909): *Van Oss' effectenboek* (1911): 746, 1668, (1888 en 1908): SAR, 1256, 881–882, *Historie*, 15. See, for Müller & Co.'s ore supply in Rotterdam (1891–1895): *De Hollandsche Revue* 1 (1896): 363. See, for the total iron ore supply in Rotterdam (1898–1914): Consul Général de Roumanie à Rotterdam (Gustav Müller), *Rapport consulaire sur l'année . . .* (Rotterdam 1903–1915). See, for the total ore supply and ore imports in the Ruhr (1901–1914): Feldenkirchen, *Die Eisen- und Stahlindustrie*, bijlagen, tables 12 and 13.

111 Nusteling, *De Rijnvaart*, 171–179, 274–283; Sneller, *Geschiedenis van den kolenhandel*, 164–165.

112 Gebhardt, *Ruhrbergbau*, 27–28, 306–309, 330–332; Wilhelm Goetzke, *Das Rheinish-Westfärlische-Kohlen-Syndikat und seine wirstschaftliche Bedeutung* (Essen: Baedecker, 1905), 19–28; Franz Sarter, "Die Syndikatsbestrebungen im niederrheinisch-westfälischen Steinkohlenbezirke. Eine geschichtlich-kritische Studie," in *Jahrbücher für Nationalökonomie und Statistik. Dritte Folge. Siebente Band* (Jena: G. Fischer, 1894), 19–21, 42; Feldenkirchen, *Die Eisen- und Stahlindustrie*, 110–112; Evelyn Kroker, *Rheinisch-Westfälisches Kohlensyndikat 1893–1945. Findbuch zum bestand 33* (Bochum: Deutscher Bergbau-Museum Bochum, 1979), viii–ix.

113 Neubaur, *Mathias Stinnes und sein Haus*, 273–274.

114 BBA, 33, 318/2, Geschäftsberichte (1893–1920), 1901.

115 BBA, 33, 318/2, Geschäftsberichte (1893–1920), 1899.

116 Maryan Glowacki, *Die Ausfuhrunterstützungspolitik der Kartelle* (PhD diss., Leipzig, 1909), 37–38, 74–75. Eva-Maria Roelevink and Joep Schenk, "Challenging Times: The Renewal of a Transnational Business Relationship: The Rhenish-Westphalian Coal Syndicate and the Coal Trade Association, 1918 to 1925," *Zeitschrift für Unternehmensgeschichte* 57, no. 2 (2012): 164; Eva-Maria Roelevink, *Organisierte Intransparenz*:

Das Kohlensyndikat und der Niederländische Markt, 1915–1932 (PhD diss., Bochum, 2014), 70–85; Goetzke, *Das Rheinish-Westfärlische-Kohlen-Syndikat*, 38.

117 Schleuning, *Der deutsche Kohlenhandel*, 84; Wiedenfeld, *Das Rheinisch-Westfälische Kohlensyndikat*, 30. Steenkolen Handelsvereeniging Bedrijfsarchief, Utrecht (SHVBA), (no signature); Z.W. Sneller, *De geschiedenis van de Steenkolen Handelsvereeniging* (unpublished manuscript +/-, 1946), 30–31, 43–46; Wiedenfeld, *Das Rheinisch-Westfälische Kohlensyndikat*, 30–31; R.W.J.M. Bos, *Brits-Nederlandse handel en scheepvaart, 1870–1914. Een analyse van machtsafbrokkeling op een markt* (PhD diss., Wageningen, 1978), 135.

118 SHVBA, Sneller, *De geschiedenis van de Steenkolen Handelsvereeniging*, 30–31, 43–46; 't Hart, *H.A. van Beuningen*, 78–79. SHVBA, 1603: *Voorgeschiedenis SHV, Bescheiden en notulen*. See, for the transport contracts: BBA, 1005, Kohlenhandelsgesellschaften – Ausland (1900–1909), Abschrift, Vertrag der Steenkolen Handelsvereeniging Utrecht, mit der Maatschappij tot Exploitatie van Staatsspoorwegen Utrecht, 30 and 31 March 1900. SHVBA, 586, 3057, Vergaderingen van de Raad van Beheer 1896–1904, 24 November 1899: Also: Roelevink, *Organizierte intransparenz*, 100–101.

119 SHVBA, 556, Verslag van den Raad van Beheer der Steenkolen Handelsvereeniging over de jaren 1896/1897 tot en met 1902/1903.

120 SHVBA, 556, Verslag van den Raad van Beheer der Steenkolen Handelsvereeniging over de jaren 1897–1899. SHVBA, 586, 3057, Vergaderingen van de Raad van Beheer, 24 November 1899, 30 May and 5 October 1900; 't Hardt, *H.A. van Beuningen*, 95–97.

121 Gebhardt, *Ruhrbergbau*, 37.

122 *Entwickelung des niederrheinisch-westfälischen Steinkohlen-Bergbaues*, 63. The Lippe and the Ruhr had been insignificant for coal transport for decades. The Dortmund-Ems-canal only transported 50,000, 100,000, 150,000 and 250,000 tons of coal in the years 1900, 1901, 1902 and 1903, respectively. *Entwickelung des niederrheinisch-westfälischen Steinkohlen-Bergbaues*, 86. BBA, 33, 318/2, Geschäftsbericht RWKS, 1900.

123 These territories were: Frankfurt am Main, Hessen-Nassau, Bavaria, Baden, Württemberg and Alsace-Lorraine.

124 Joep Schenk, *Havenbaronnen en Ruhrbonzen. Oorsprong van een wederzijdse afhankelijkheidsrelatie tussen Rotterdam en het Ruhrgebied 1870–1914* (PhD diss., Rotterdam, 2015), 204.

125 Van Driel, *Rotterdam Cargo Handling Technology*, 20.

126 Sneller, *Geschiedenis van den steenkolenhandel*, 184–185, 223–225.

127 Kamer van Koophandel Rotterdam, *Jaarverslagen*, 1893, 1896 and 1898; Sneller, *Geschiedenis van den steenkolenhandel*, 226–227.

128 Kamer van Koophandel Rotterdam, *Jaarverslagen*, 1895 and 1896; Van de Laar, *Stad van formaat*, 92; Van Driel, *Rotterdam Cargo Handling Technology*, 22–23.

129 Van de Laar, *Stad van formaat*, 105–117; Van Driel, *Rotterdam Cargo Handling Technology*, 13–14; Len de Klerk, Paul van de Laar, and Herman Moscoviter, *G.J. De Jongh. Havenbouwer en stadsontwikkelaar in Rotterdam* (Hilversum: Thoth, 2008), 96–97. Nationaal Archief, Den Haag (NA), 2.21.183.69, 144, Stukken betreffende een stoomvaartdienst van Roemenië op een onzer Noordzeehavens (Amsterdam of Rotterdam) unsigned, undated (1897). I am grateful to Ariëtte Dekker, who told me about this file.

130 Sehmer, *Die Eisenerzversorgung*, 1.

131 Until the publication of *The iron ore resources of the world* in 1910, the industry was in the dark when it came to the exact scale and distribution of the world's ore reserves. Johan Gunnar Andersson, *The Iron Ore Resources of the World: An Inquiry Made Upon the Initiative of the Executive Committee of the XI International Geological Congress, Stockholm, 1910 with the Assistance of Geological Surveys and Mining Geologists of Different Countries* (Stockholm: Generalstabens litografiska anstalt, 1910).

132 Ibid., 43–44, 76.

133 Plücker, *Der schwedische Eisenerzbergbau*, 180–194; Salmon, *Scandinavia and the Great Powers*, 39–40. Also: "Der Schwedische Staat und die lappländische Eisenerzgruben,"

Stahl und Eisen, 1907/48 (Sonderabdruck) Sehmer, *Die Eisenerzversorgung*, 234–242; RA, TGO, F1: 7, "Schwedische erze, eisen, stahl"; RA, TGO, F1, Nr. 7, 2, (Afschrift) Rapport nr. 15, 1907, Kungl. Svenska vice Konsulatet, Hugo Appeltoft, Duisburg am Rhein, 2 July 1907; Fritz, *Järnmalmsproduktion och järnmalmsmarknad*, table 157.

134 Plücker, *Der schwedische Eisenerzbergbau*, 77, 89, 206.

135 Ibid.

136 Ibid., 114–115, 151–152: Also: Salzgitter Konzern Archiv (SKA), P. 4.25.50.1, book 1, passim; Lutz Hatzfeld, "Wilhelm Beukenberg," in *Rheinisch-Westfälische Wirtschaftsbiographien*, Vol. 10 (Münster: Aschendorff Verlag, 1974), 202–203; Klaus-Dieter Walter Pomiluek, *Heinrich Wilhelm Beukenberg. Ein Montanindustrieller seiner Zeit* (PhD diss., Düsseldorf, 2002), 132–136.

137 Pomiluek, *Heinrich Wilhelm Beukenberg*, 132.

138 RWWA, 130, 30006/3. Passim, especially the correspondence in the period between 27 July 1903 and 21 May 1904, and a copy of the contract between Grängesberg and Gutehoffnungshütte, 24 May 1904.

139 Serton notes a collaboration between mining companies and iron ore traders, but ignores the collaboration between the iron and steel companies, Serton, *Rotterdam als haven voor massale goederen*, 75–76.

140 SKA, P. 4.25.50.1, book 1, passim.

141 Fear, *Organizing control*, 91–92, 195, 235, 261–263, 288–290, 322; Vera Schmidt, Mafred Rasch, and Gerald D. Feldman, *August Thyssen und Hugo Stinnes: ein Briefwechsel 1898–1922. Schriftenreihe zur Zeitschrift für Unternehmensgeschichte*, Band 10 (München: C.H. Beck, 2003), 39, 52–62; Carl Strikwerda, "The Troubled Origins of European Economic Integration: International Iron and Steel and Labor Migration in the Era of World War I," *American Historical Review* 98, no. 4 (1993): 1113–1114; Klaus Wilsberg, "'Terrible ami – aimable ennemi,' Kooperation und Konflikt in den deutsch-französischen Beziehungen 1911–1914," *Pariser historische Studien* 49 (1998): 227–233; Wilhelm Treue, *Die Feuer verlöschen nie. August Thyssen-Hütte 1890–1926* (Düsseldorf: Econ-Verlag, 1969), 82–89; Lutz Hatzfeld, "Zur Erzversorgung deutschlands vor dem ersten Weltkriege," *Tradition: Zeitschrift für Firmengeschichte und Unternehmerbiographie* 9, no. 5 (1964): 235–240; Manfred Rasch, "Unternehmungen des Thyssen-Kozerns im zarischen Rußland," in *". . . das einzige Land in Europa, das eine große Zukunft vor sich hat." Deutsche Unternehmen und Unternehmer im Russischen Reich im 19. und 20. Jahrhundert*, ed. Dittmar Dahlmann and Carmen Scheide (Essen: Klartext-Verlag, 1998), 225–271.

142 Haniel Archiv, Ruhrort (HA), JWW, 26, "Expose über die Niederlassung in Rotterdam 20–02–1914, Vereinigte Frankfurter Rhedereien." Erich Maschke, *Es entsteht ein Konzern. Paul Reusch und die GHH* (Tübingen: Rainer Wunderlich, 1969), 81; Bähr, *Die MAN*, 118–119.

143 'Het economisch doordringen van Duitschland in Frankrijk naar Louis Bruneau', *Tijdschrift voor economische geographie* 6 (1915): 72–78.

144 SAR, 1256, 1731, *Beknopte geschiedenis van Wm. H. Müller & Co.* (zt zp +/- 1946), 1–13, there 2. Also, 1256, 859, Notities uit de Jaarverslagen 1899–1925 van Wm. H. Müller & Co.'s Algemeene Scheepvaart Maatschappij; Also: 1256, 881–882, G.A. Apeldoorn, *Over het erts- en mijnbouwbedrijf* (Unpublished manuscript: np, nt), 1–8; Also: 615, 959, letter Nederlands Beheersinstituut to Nederlandsche Bank, 12 May 1949. Also: 1256, 615, Balansboek, Afdeling Rotterdam, Boekjaar 1899 en 1900; *Van Oss' effectenboek* (1904–1909). RA, TGO, F1, Nr. 7 and Nr. 49, Promemoria, no date, no author (+/- January 1927), and: unreadable author, *Reseberättelse från resa i Algeriet och Tunis 1925. Also see: Nordafrika. Sammandrag av min reseberättelse över de Nord-Afrikanska järnmalmförekomsterna. Forüt överlämnad, med uppgift över de firmor och personer, som hava ett kontrollerande intresse i den Nordafrikanska malmindustrien* (Stockholm, 1922) unreadable author. Wilhelm Pothman, "Zur Frage der Eisen- und Manganerzversorgung der deutsche Industrie," in *Probleme der Weltwirtschaft. Schriften des Instituts für*

Seeverkehr und Weltwirtschaft an der Universität Kiel, ed. Bernhard Harms (Jena: Fischer, 1920), 89; Wengenroth, *Auslandsinvestitionen*, 11–12, nt. 62; Ariëtte Dekker, *Leven op krediet. Anton Kröller (1862–1941)* (Amsterdam: Prometheus Bert Bakker, 2015).

145 Schenk, *Havenbaronnen en Ruhrbonze*, table 5.2.
146 For ore imports in the 1880–1897 period: F. de Goey and H. van Driel, *Database on Cargo Flows in the Port of Rotterdam, 1880–2000: Goederenoverslag Rotterdamse Haven, 1880–2000*. For ore imports in the 1898–1911 period: Consul Général de Roumanie à Rotterdam (Gustav Müller), Rapport consulaire (Dordrecht, 1903–1914). For total throughput: Paul Th. van de Laar, "Port Traffic in Rotterdam: The Competitive Edge of a Rhine-Port (1880–1914)," in *Struggling for leadership: Antwerp-Rotterdam port competition between 1870 en 2000*, ed. R. Loyen, E. Buyst, and G. Devos (Heidelberg and New York: Physica-Verlag, 2003), 66–73. (I am grateful to Paul van de Laar for sharing his data with me.)
147 SHVBA, 586, 3057, Vergaderingen van de Raad van Beheer, 4 October 1901.
148 SHVBA, 556, Verslag van den Raad van Beheer der Steenkolen Handelsvereeniging over het jaar 1901/1902, 1902/1903, 1903/1904.
149 SHVB, Sneller, De geschiedenis van de Steenkolen Handelsvereeniging, 79–81. Idem, Geschiedenis van den steenkolenhandel, 212. Neubaur, Mathias Stinnes und sein Haus, 291–299.
150 SHVBA, 556, Verslag van den Raad van Beheer der Steenkolen Handelsvereeniging over het jaar 1903/1904.
151 Extensively: Roelevink and Schenk, "Challenging Times," 154–180. Also: Roelevink, *Organisierte Intransparenz*, 91–112.
152 SHVBA, 556, Verslag van de NV Steenkolen Handelsvereeniging over het boek-jaar 1905/1906, 1906/1907, 1907/1908. Also, 723, Verslag van de NV Steenkolen Handelsvereeniging over het boekjaar 1911/1912. Also: Sneller, *De geschiedenis van de Steenkolen Handelsvereeniging*, 113–115; Harry van Wijnen, *Grootvorst aan de Maas. D.G. van Beuningen 1877–1955* (Amsterdam: Balans, 2004), 116–120; Van Driel, "Innovation and Integration in Mineral Bulk Handling," 77–80.
153 Bos, *Brits-Nederlandse handel en scheepvaart*, 146.
154 Schenk, *Havenbaronnen*, 250–252, afb. 8–5.
155 Ibid., 255, Table 8.2.

Bibliography

Abelshauser, Werner, and Wolfgang Köllmann (1990), *Das Ruhrgebiet im Industriezeitalter. Geschichte und Entwicklung* (Düsseldorf: Schwann).

Altena, Bert (1989), *Een broeinest der anarchie: arbeiders, arbeidersbeweging en maatschappelijke ontwikkeling: Vlissingen 1875–1929* (1940) (PhD diss., Amsterdam).

Bagwell, Philip S. (1988), *The Transport Revolution 1770–1985* (London: Routledge).

Bähr, Johannes, Ralf Banken and Thomas Flemming (2008), *Die MAN: eine deutsche Industriegeschichte* (München: C.H. Beck).

Beening, André (1994), *Onder de vleugels van de adelaar. De Duitse buitenlandse politiek ten aanzien van Nederland in de periode 1890–1914* (PhD diss., Amsterdam).

Bos, Roeland W.J.M. (1978), *Brits-Nederlandse handel en scheepvaart, 1870–1914. Een analyse van machtsafbrokkeling op een markt* (PhD diss., Wageningen).

Brolsma, Jolke U. (20907), *Havens, kranen, dokken en veren. De Gemeentelijke Haveninrichtingen en het Havenbedrijf der gemeente Rotterdam, 1882–2006* (Utrecht: Stichting Matrijs).

Brough, Bennett H., ed. (1903–1905), *The Journal of the Iron and Steel Institute 2*, Vol. 50 (London and New York: 1897).

Centraal Bureau voor de Statistiek (2001), *Tweehonderd jaar statistiek in tijdreeksen* (Voorburg: CBS).

Consul Général de Roumanie à Rotterdam (Gustav Müller), *Rapport consulaire sur l'année . . .* (Rotterdam 1903–1915).

De Goey, Ferry, ed. (2004), *Comparative Port History of Rotterdam and Antwerp 1880–2000: Competition, Cargo and Costs* (Amsterdam: Aksant).

De Klerk, Len, Paul van de Laar, and Herman Moscoviter (2008), *G.J. De Jongh. Havenbouwer en stadsontwikkelaar in Rotterdam* (Hilversum: Thoth).

Dekker, Ariëtte (2015), *Leven op krediet. Anton Kröller (1862–1941)* (Amsterdam: Prometheus Bert Bakker).

Entwickelung, Die, des niederrheinisch-westfälischen Steinkohlen-Bergbaues in der zweiten Hälfte des 19. Jahrhunderts (1904), Hrsg. vom Verein für die bergbaulichen Interessen im Oberbergamtsbezirk Dortmund, Part 3, book X (Berlin: Springer-Verlag).

Fear, Jeffrey R. (2005), *Organizing Control: August Thyssen and the Construction of German Corporate Management* (Cambridge, MA and London: Harvard University Press).

Feldenkirchen, Wilfried (1982), *Die Eisen- und Stahlindustrie des Ruhrgebiets 1879–1914. Wachstum, Finanzierung und Struktur ihrer Grossunternehmen* (Wiesbaden: Steiner).

Fremdling, Rainer (1977), "Railroads and German economic growth: A leading sector analysis with a comparison to the United States and Great Britain." *Journal of Economic History* 37, no. 3: 583–604.

Fremdling, Rainer (1995), *Anglo-German Rivalry on Coal Markets in France, the Netherlands and Germany, 1850–1913,* Groningen Growth and Development Centre Research Memorandum 199521 (Groningen).

Fritz, Martin (1967a), *Järnmalmsproduktion och järnmalmsmarknad 1883–1913* (Gothenburg: np).

Fritz, Martin (1967b), *Svensk järnmalmexport, 1883–1913* (Gothenburg: np).

Gebhardt, G. (1957), *Ruhrbergbau, Geschichte, Aufbau und Verflechtung seiner Gesellschaften und Organisationen. Unter Mitw. Der Gesellschaften des Ruhrbergbaus zusammengestellt* (Essen: Verlag Glückauf).

Gehlen, Boris (2011), "Zwischen Wettbewerbsideal und Staatsräson: Die Diskussionen im Deutschen Handelstag über Regulierung und Verstaatlichung der Eisenbahnen (1861–1879)." *Jahrbuch für Wirtschaftsgeschichte/Economic History Yearbook* 52.

Gill, William (1882), "Der Eisenerz-District von Bilbao." *Stahl und Eisen* 8: 337–345.

Glas, Edoardo Jorge (1997), *Bilbao's modern business elite* (Reno: University of Nevada Press).

Glowacki, Maryan (1909), *Die Ausfuhrunterstützungspolitik der Kartelle* (PhD diss., Leipzig).

Goetzke, Wilhelm, *Das Rheinish-Westfärlische-Kohlen-Syndikat und seine wirstschaftliche Bedeutung* (Essen: Baedecker, 1905).

Goldstein, G. (1908), *Die Entwicklung der deutschen Roheisenindustrie seit 1879* (PhD diss., Halle).

Gutehoffnungshütte Oberhausen, Rheinland, Die (1910): *zur Erinnerung an das 100 jährige Bestehen 1810–1910* (Oberhausen: August Bagel).

Hatzfeld, Lutz (1964), "Zur Erzversorgung deutschlands vor dem ersten Weltkriege." *Tradition: Zeitschrift für Firmengeschichte und Unternehmerbiographie* 9, no. 4: 235–240.

Hatzfeld, Lutz (1974), "Wilhelm Beukenberg." *Rheinisch-Westfälische Wirtschaftsbiographien* 10: 202–203.

Held, David, and Andrew McGrew (1999), *Global Transformations: Politics, Economics and Culture* (Cambridge: Polity Press).

Henderson, William O. (1970), *William Thomas Mulvany. Ein irischer Unternehmer im Ruhrgebiet 1806–1885* (Cologne: Universität zu Köln).

Kamer van Koophandel en Fabrieken Rotterdam (1858–1862), *Jaarverslag van de Kamer van Koophandel en Fabrieken Rotterdam* (Rotterdam: Kamer van Koophandel).

Klee, Wolfgang (1982), *Preußische Eisenbahngeschichte* (Stuttgart: Kohlhammer).

Kleeberg, John M. (1988), *The Disconto-Gesellschaft and German industrialization: A Critical Examination of the Career of a German Universal Bank, 1851–1914* (Oxford: np).

Klemann, Hein A.M. (2006), *Waarom bestaat Nederland eigenlijk nog? Nederland-Duitsland: Economische integratie en politieke consequenties 1860–2000* (Rotterdam: Erasmus Universiteit).

Klemann, Hein A.M. (2012), "Vlissingen als haven voor het Duitse achterland." In *Zeeland en de wijde wereld*, edited by Tobias van Gent and Pieter van Ippel: 27–47 (Middelburg: De Drukkery).

Klemann, Hein A.M., and Friso Wielenga (2009), "Die Niederlande und Deutschland, oder verschwindet die nationale Ökonomie? Eine Einleitung." In *Deutschland und die Niederlande. Wirtschaftsbeziehungen im 19. und 20. Jahrhundert*, edited by Hein A.M. Klemann and Friso Wielenga: 7–17 (Münster: Waxmann).

Krieger, Fritz (1935), *Die wirtschaftliche Verflechtung des Unterruhrgebietes mit den Niederlanden im 19. Jahrhundert* (PhD diss., Cologne).

Kroker, Evelyn (1979), *Rheinisch-Westfälisches Kohlensyndikat 1893–1945. Findbuch zum bestand 33* (Bochum: Deutscher Bergbau-Museum Bochum).

Krönig, Fritz (1877), *Die Differential-Tarife der Eisenbahnen* (Berlin: F. Vahlen).

Krupp'sche Gussstahlfabrik (1912), *Krupp. A century's history of the Krupp works, 1812–1912* (Essen: np).

Laspeyres, Renate (1969), *Rotterdam und das Ruhrgebiet* (PhD diss., Marburg).

Loscertales, Javier (2002), *Deutsche Investitionen in Spanien 1870–1920* (Stuttgart: Steiner).

Loyen, Reginald, Erik Buyst, and Greta Devos, eds. (2002), *Struggling for Leadership: Antwerp-Rotterdam Port Competition between 1870 and 2000* (Heidelberg and New York: Physica-Verlag).

Lülsdorfs, Josef (1940), *Die Bedeutung Rotterdams für die rheinische Wirtschaft, insbesondere für die deutsche Rheinschiffahrt* (Cologne: Orthen).

Maschke, Erich (1969), *Es entsteht ein Konzern. Paul Reusch und die GHH* (Tübingen: Rainer Wunderlich).

Neubaur, Paul (1909), *Mathias Stinnes und sein Haus. Ein Jahrhundert der entwickelung 1808–1908* (Mülheim an der Ruhr: Bagel).

Nusteling, Hubertus P.H. (1974), *De Rijnvaart in het tijdperk van stoom en steenkool 1831–1914: een studie van het goederenvervoer en de verkeerspolitiek in de Rijndelta en het achterland, mede in verband met de opkomst van de spoorwegen en de concurrentie van vreemde zeehavens* (Amsterdam: Holland Universiteits Pers).

Plücker, Wilfried (1968), *Der schwedische Eisenerzbergbau und seine Beziehungen zur westdeutschen Eisenhüttenindustrie 1880–1965* (Cologne: Gouder & Hansen).

Pomiluek, Klaus-Dieter Walter (2002), *Heinrich Wilhelm Beukenberg. Ein Montanindustrieller seiner Zeit* (PhD diss., Düsseldorf).

Pothman, Wilhelm (1920), "Zur Frage der Eisen- und Manganerzversorgung der deutsche Industrie." In *Probleme der Weltwirtschaft. Schriften des Instituts für Seeverkehr und Weltwirtschaft an der Universität Kiel*, edited by Bernhard Harms (Jena: Fischer).

Pratt, Edwin A. (1905), *Railways and Their Rates, with an Appendix on the British Canal Problem* (London: J. Murray).

Rasch, Manfred (1998), "Unternehmungen des Thyssen-Kozerns im zarischen Rußland." In *". . . das einzige Land in Europa, das eine große Zukunft vor sich hat." Deutsche Unternehmen und Unternehmer im Russischen Reich im 19. und 20. Jahrhundert*, edited by Dittmar Dahlmann and Carmen Scheide (Essen: Klartext-Verlag).

Renauld, Joseph von (1900), *Der Bergbau und die Hüttenindustrie von Oberschlesien 1884–1897. Eine Untersuchung über die Wirkungen der staatlichen Eisenbahntarifpolitik und des Wasserverkehrs.*

Mit einem Anhang graphischer Darstellungen und einer Karte der Provinz Schlesien (Stuttgart: Cotta).

Roelevink, Eva-Maria (2014), *Organisierte Intransparenz: Das Kohlensyndikat und der Niederländische Markt, 1915–1932* (PhD diss., Bochum).

Roelevink, Eva-Maria, and Joep Schenk (2012), "Challenging times: The renewal of a transnational business relationship: The Rhenish-Westphalian Coal Syndicate and the Coal Trade Association, 1918 to 1925." *Zeitschrift für Unternehmensgeschichte*, 57, no. 2: 154–180.

Roosevelt, Theodore (2013), "Natural resources: Their wise use or their waste." In *Selected Speeches and Writings of Theodore Roosevelt*, edited by Gordon Hutner (New York: Vintage) no page numbers.

Rovers, Eva (2012), *De eeuwigheid verzameld. Helene Kröller-Müller 1869–1939* (Amsterdam: Prometheus Bert Bakker).

Royal Commission on Railways (1866), *Evidence and Papers Relating to Railways in Ireland* (London: Pr. for H.M.S.O).

Salmon, Patrick (2002), *Scandinavia and the Great Powers* (Cambridge: Cambridge University Press).

Sarter, Franz (1894), "Die Syndikatsbestrebungen im niederrheinisch-westfälischen Steinkohlenbezirke. Eine geschichtlich-kritische Studie." *Jahrbücher für Nationalökonomie und Statistik. Dritte Folge 7* (Jena: G. Fischer).

Schachert, Paul (1885), *Die überseeische Kohlenausfuhr Deutschlands* (Cologne: np).

Schenk, Joep (2015), *Havenbaronnen en Ruhrbonzen. Oorsprong van een wederzijdse afhankelijkheidsrelatie tussen Rotterdam en het Ruhrgebied 1870–1914* (PhD diss., Rotterdam).

Schleuning, Horst (1936), *Der deutsche Kohlenhandel: ein Weg von der freizügigen zur gebundenen Marktversorgung* (Berlin: De Gruyter).

Schmidt, Vera, Manfred Rasch en Gerald D. Feldman (2003), *August Thyssen und Hugo Stinnes: ein Briefwechsel 1898–1922. Schriftenreihe zur Zeitschrift für Unternehmensgeschichte, Band 10* (München: C.H. Beck).

Schmidt-Rutsch, Olaf (2003), *William Thomas Mulvany. Ein irischer Pragmatiker und Visionär im Ruhrgebiet 1806–1885* (Cologne: Stiftung Rheinisch-Westfälisches Wirtschaftsarchiv).

Schraver, Jan, ed. (1946), *Rotterdam. Poort van Europa. De geschiedenis van haven en handel in Rotterdam* (Rotterdam and Antwerp: Ad. Donker).

Sehmer, Theodor (1911), *Die Eisenerzversorgung Europas. Probleme der Weltwirtschaft 2* (Jena: G. Fischer).

Serton, Petrus (1919), *Rotterdam als haven voor massale goederen. Een bijdrage tot de geografie van het verkeer* (Nijmegen: Ten Hoet).

Sneller, Zeger W. (1946), *Geschiedenis van den steenkolenhandel van Rotterdam* (Groningen and Batavia (Jakarta): Wolters).

Staatkundig en staathuishoudkundig jaarboekje 1858–1862 (Amsterdam: De Vereeniging voor de Statistiek in Nederland).

Strikwerda, Carl (1993), "The troubled origins of European economic integration: International iron and steel and labor migration in the era of World War I." *American Historical Review*, 98, no. 4: 1106–1129.

Sundquist, Björn, and Christer Nordlund (2004), "Science and honour: The 11th international geological congress in Stockholm 1910." *Episodes*, 44, no. 27: 284–292.

Tenfelde, Klaus (1977), *Sozialgeschichte der Bergarbeiterschaft and der Ruhr im 19. Jahrhundert* (Bonn-Bad: Verlag Neue Gesellschaft).

't Hart, Piet D. (2006), *H.A. van Beuningen. 'Een van Utrechts beste burgers'* (np).

Then, Volker (1997), *Eisenbahnen und Eisenbahnunternehmer in der Industriellen Revolution: ein preussisch/deutsch-englischer Vergleich* (Göttingen: Vandenhoeck & Ruprecht).

Treue, Wilhelm (1969), *Die Feuer verlöschen nie. August Thyssen-Hütte 1890–1926* (Düsseldorf: Econ-Verlag).

Valdaliso, Jesús María (1994), "La exportación de hierro Español. 1850–1914. Una primera eproximación al tráfico marítimo y sus beneficios." *Areas: Revista internacional de ciencias sociales* 16: 131–164.

Van de Laar, Paul, "Port traffic in Rotterdam: the competitive edge of a Rhine-port (1880–1914)." In *Struggling for Leadership: Antwerp-Rotterdam Port Competition between 1870 and 2000*, edited by R. Loyen, E. Buyst and G. Devos: 66–73 (Heidelberg and New York: Physica-Verlag, 2003).

Van de Laar, Paul (2000), *Stad van formaat. Geschiedenis van Rotterdam in de negentiende en twintigste eeuw* (Zwolle: Waanders).

Van den Broeke, Willem, and Elise van Nederveen Meerkerk (2001), "Spoorlijnen en geldstromen. Een onderzoek naar de financiers van de Nederlandsche Rhijnspoorweg-Maatschappij 1845–1890." *NEHA-Jaarboek voor Economische, bedrijfs- en techniekgeschiedenis* 64: 154–177.

Van der Kerkhof, Stefanie (2006), *Von der Friedens- zur Kriegswirtschaft. Unternehmensstrategien der deutschen Eisen- und Stahlindustrie vom Kaiserreich bis zum Ende des Ersten Weltkrieges* (Essen: Klartext-Verlag).

Van Driel, Hugo (2000), "Innovation and integration in mineral bulk handling in the Pof Rotterdam 1886–1923." *Business History* 44, no. 3: 63–90.

Van Driel, Hugo, and Ferry de Goey (2000), *Rotterdam Cargo Handling Technology 1870–2000* (Zutphen: Walburg Pers, 2000).

Van Driel, Hugo, and J.W. Schot (2002), "Het ontstaan van een gemechaniseerde massagoedhaven in Rotterdam." In *Techniek in Nederland in de Twintigste Eeuw. Part 5. Transport Communicatie*, edited by J.W. Schot etc. (Zutphen: Stichting Historie der Techniek).

Van Oss, S.F. (1911), *Van Oss' effectenboek* (Groningen: P. Noordhoff).

Van Stiphout, Wouter (2005), *Maak een stad: Rotterdam en de architectuur van J.H. van den Broek* (Rotterdam: 010).

Van Wijnen, Harry (2004), *Grootvorst aan de Maas. D.G. van Beuningen 1877–1955* (Amsterdam: Balans).

Van Zanden, Jan Luiten, and Arthur van Riel (2000), *Nederland 1780–1914. Staat, instituties en economische ontwikkeling* (Amsterdam: Balans).

Webb, Steven, B. (1980), "Tariffs, cartels, technology, and growth in the German steel industry, 1879 to 1914." *Journal of Economic History* 40, no. 2: 309–330.

Wengenroth, Ulrich (1994), *Enterprise and Technology: The German and British Steel Industries, 1865–1895* (Cambridge and New York: Cambridge University Press).

Wengenroth, Ulrich (1998), *Auslandsinvestitionen der deutschen Schwerindustrie zur Sicherung ihrer Erzversorgung zwischen Gründerjahren und Weltwirtschaftskrise*, working paper (München).

Wiedenfeld, Kurt (1912), *Das Rheinisch-Westfälische Kohlensyndikat* (Bonn: A. Marous und E. Weber).

Wilsberg, Klaus (1998), "'Terrible ami – aimable ennemi,' Kooperation und Konflikt in den deutsch-französischen Beziehungen 1911–1914." *Pariser historische Studien*, 49: 227–233.

Ziegler, Dieter (1996), *Eisenbahnen und Staat im Zeitalter der Industrialisierung* (Stuttgart: Franz Steiner Verlag).

Archives

Archiv des Landschaftsverbandes Rheinland, Pulheim' (ALVR).

Bergbau Archiv, Bochum (BBA).

Haniel Archiv, Ruhrort (HA).

Nationaal Archief, Den Haag (NA).
Rheinisch-Westfälisches Wirtschaftsarchiv, Cologne (RWWA).
Salzgitter Konzern Archiv (SKA).
Stadsarchief Rotterdam, Rotterdam (SAR).
Steenkolen Handelsvereeniging Bedrijfsarchief, Utrecht (SHVBA).
Utrechts Archief, Utrecht (UA).

4 Tensions within the Lower Rhine economy

AKU versus VGF, 1929–1969

Ben Wubs

Introduction

The manufacture of artificial silk (later called rayon) started at the end of the 19th century. Fabrics had long been made from "natural fibres," including cotton, wool, silk and flax. In the 20th century, however, there was a synthetic revolution, with a new sector emerging in Europe and North America: the artificial silk (rayon) industry. Companies like the Dutch AKU, the German Glanzstoff and the Italian SNIA created a new fibre that was based on wood pulp. In a way, rayon could therefore still be called a natural fibre. At the end of the 1930s, however, the US firm DuPont produced nylon, the first man-made fibre based on petrochemicals.[1] Many new synthetic fibres were then developed after World War II. The Nazi autarkic system also gave a boost to the development of such fibres, with the output of staple fibres, such as those used in car tyres, increasing rapidly. The 1950–1970s period can nonetheless be regarded as the golden years of the man-made fibre industry, which showed unprecedented growth in Europe, the US and Japan. This was a period of extensive investment by both new and existing chemical companies in the manufacture of new fibres like acryl, polyester and Lycra, which were completely based on oil.[2] Polyether was the most famous example and is still the most dominant synthetic fibre globally.[3]

During the 1930s, two of the world's leading rayon manufacturers were the Dutch *Algemeene Kunstzijde Unie NV* (AKU) in Arnhem and its German subsidiary *Vereinigte Glanzstoff Fabriken AG* (VGF) in Wuppertal. After their merger in 1929, the group produced around 27 per cent of the world's rayon.[4] AKU had its headquarters in Arnhem, located on the banks of the Rhine (*Nederrijn*) in the east of the Netherlands, not far from the German border. VGF's headquarters, meanwhile, were located in Wuppertal, a city in the Rhine-Ruhr region, now North Rhine Westphalia. Its most important subsidiary plants in Germany were also located close to the Rhine. This multinational conglomerate of Dutch and German artificial-fibre firms, which had merged in 1929 and became part of AKU, was thus a good example of transnational amalgamations within the Rhine region. The two sides had been multinationals before the merger, with affiliates in the UK, Italy and the US. Nevertheless, ownership and management relations after the merger were not always clear; indeed, there were significant problems and many changes during the turbulent years between the 1930s and the late 1960s. As a result, after World War II, the British and, in particular, the US occupation authorities questioned the national ownership of AKU and VGF and whether these different parts should be treated as Allied or enemy companies. The Dutch government had excluded enemy stockholders and transferred the stock held by German citizens and priority shares to the State of the Netherlands after the war. Meanwhile, the Allies had appointed the former VGF chairman as custodian. AKU therefore demanded a majority for the Dutch on the Advisory Board and an overriding influence on the Executive Board. A long-lasting conflict between the Dutch and German sides thus began. Indeed, it was not until 1969, when the two companies completely merged and soon became part of Akzo (now AkzoNobel), that the disagreements about management and ownership issues came to an end.

This chapter addresses the tensions and conflicts within this Dutch-German multinational in the first 40 years of its existence, and looks closely at the historical background of the strife that existed between the management of the Dutch parent company (AKU) and its German subsidiary (VGF). How was VGF managed in these years, and what did the parent company do to influence the decisions of the German management team? What role did nationality play and what was the role of the two national governments? Although this book clearly shows that a long-term transnational economic region existed that was made possible by its geographical location and natural conditions, the AKU-VGF case clearly shows that the role of agency also was very important. Multinational companies and governments created the economic reality and shaped the Lower Rhine economy, but this was frequently against the odds and was often accompanied with conflicts and discontent. The chapter also explores political risk and the role that its most extreme form – war – has played in the formation of this transnational region.

The rise of Dutch multinationals in Germany

Dutch direct investment in Germany originated in the context of integrated economic relations between the Netherlands and its large neighbour from the end of the 19th century onwards. Their geographical locations, connected by the Rhine and several railways, led to cross-border economic cooperation. The Ruhr area developed into Europe's most important industrial centre from the 1870s onwards, an expansion that would not have been possible without the Rhine. The same can be said of the development of Rotterdam's port into the continent's most important deep-sea port.[5] Transit traffic had become the source of extensive trade connections. At the same time, mutual trade between Germany and the Netherlands was greatly stimulated, with the latter becoming an important market for German industrial products, while the former became the principal buyer of Dutch agrarian goods.

As a consequence of the rapidly improving economic relations between the two nations, Dutch capital began to flow into German industry. At the same time, Dutch entrepreneurs in these rising industries often sought out opportunities to contact highly developed German companies. Dutch industrialists were keen on German technology.[6] In addition, Germany's protectionist policy stimulated Dutch cross-border investments: in order to maintain their market position in Germany, Dutch firms had to establish subsidiaries there.[7] The direct investments of Unilever's forerunners in Germany, Van den Bergh and Jurgens, for instance, date back to the late 19th century. In 1888, Jurgens set up a margarine plant just across the border in Germany (Goch) after the Bismarck administration levied a tariff on the product.[8] Demand for the cheap butter substitute by the working masses had been significant in the country's growing industrial regions, such as the Ruhr district.[9] Around the same time, Van den Bergh, Jurgens' main competitor in the margarine business, also set up a plant in Cleves in Germany, also just across the Dutch border and near Goch. The two companies were subsequently able to build large edible fat empires in Germany from these locations.

Dutch investments in Germany grew again after World War I, as Dutch companies had become increasingly dependent on their relations with the country and quickly resumed their capital investments there. Good financial results during and right after the war allowed major Dutch firms to expand internationally. In addition, the strong Dutch guilder had a great advantage over the weak mark at the start of the 1920s, with the Dutch taking over numerous German companies after its depreciation.[10] The major Dutch firms also had access to cheaper capital than their local rivals via the Amsterdam and London stock exchanges and the expansion of the Dutch banking system in the 1920s. Acquisitions of German firms were mostly financed through the Dutch capital market. Van den Bergh and Jurgens bought oil mills and other margarine factories, but also expanded the production column in other directions in Germany in this period.[11] Philips was able to acquire an important X-ray equipment manufacturer and a radio-valves factory that was, technologically, a huge leap forward for this Dutch electronics firm.[12] Along with these acquisitions, Dutch companies also expanded in Germany by way of cross-border mergers, with an important example being the Dutch-German merger between Enka and Vereinigte Glanzstoff Fabriken AG (VGF).

Enka, Glanzstoff and AKU

In 1911, the chemist J.C. Hartogs set up the *Nederlandsche Kunstzijdefabriek* (Enka) in Arnhem.[13] The second founder and major financier of Enka was the coal merchant F.H. Fentener van Vlissingen, who was chairman of the board of *Steenkolenhandelsvereeniging* (SHV).[14] Another financier was van Vlissingen's companion in the coal business, the German J. Balthazar, who had also been involved with the establishment of VGF.[15] The two men had been interested in the manufacture of artificial silk, because its production process was based on large quantities of energy, i.e. coal. During World War I, Enka profited from a huge demand for artificial silk (later called rayon) and exported it to Germany in particular. At the end of the war, Enka's financial position was so strong that it could pay a dividend of 92.5 per cent. It also built a new plant in Ede, which was one of the most modern rayon factories in Europe. Rayon was a booming and expanding business internationally and the Dutch were part of this.[16] After the war, Enka and VGF reached an agreement on the exchange of patents and set up a small holding company in the Netherlands. Along with the big players on the world market for rayon – the British Courtaulds, the German VGF and the American Viscose Company – the smaller Dutch Enka was able to increase its production, mainly for exports, during the first half of the 1920s. As rising tariffs in various export markets threatened Enka's position, it set up an international holding company called Maekubee (a Dutch abbreviation for Society for the Exploitation of Artificial Silk Factories Abroad).[17] This company took over two factories in Italy and set up new ones in Britain and Germany.[18] The latter was a joint venture with VGF and was established in Breslau (now Wroclow in Poland) in 1927.[19] In 1929, after the US patents of Viscose Company had expired, Enka also set up an important factory in the US, namely the American Enka Corporation.[20]

At the end of the 1920s, Enka started negotiations with IG Farben about a merger. Director Hartogs was in favour of such a move. In contrast, however, Fentener van Vlissingen, chairman of Enka's Advisory Board, favoured an amalgamation with VGF. Although VGF's strength in Germany had been interrupted by the implementation of the Treaty of Versailles, whereby it had lost foreign assets and its position in foreign markets, it had been able to regain its strong position in Germany and rebuild its foreign relations and even take over other foreign companies.[21] In 1925, VGF had formed Glanzstoff-Courtaulds GmbH in Cologne. This was a joint venture with the British Courtaulds, which was one of the strongest players on the world market for viscose. The two companies contributed each 50 per cent of the capital.[22]

In 1929, VGF, which was nonetheless one of the largest viscose manufacturers in the world, got into major financial trouble. This meant that the smaller, but financially much stronger, Enka, which actually lagged behind in terms of technology, could now acquire all the shares of the dynamic, but highly indebted, VGF. Deutsche Bank played a major role in the establishment of a new holding company under the Dutch name *Algemeene Kunstzijde Unie* (AKU). The joint German-Dutch company that controlled both Enka and VGF was formed through an exchange of shares. The AKU board consisted of four delegates from the Dutch group, four from the German group and one neutral member. In addition, each group received 22 priority shares, while Courtaulds, which also had a stake in the new merger on the basis of its joint venture with VGF, received four priority shares. During the 1930s, however, the German side of the company became highly indebted to its Dutch counterpart. As a result, an ever-greater part of the company fell into Dutch hands.[23] Nevertheless, most of AKU's production was still located in Germany. Prior to

World War II, the viscose industry was clearly part of the transnational Rhine economy: not only were Enka's main plants in Arnhem on the border of the Rhine and Ede not far from the Rhine, but the VGF plants were also located in the Rhine delta, near the rivers Rhine, Wupper or Main, as the manufacture of viscose relied heavily on the cheap transport of coal. The manufacture of rayon was an energy intensive industry, based on coal and wood pulp, both of which were supplied by barges via the Rhine or its tributaries. VGF's plants were located in Wuppertal-Elberfeld, Oberbruch and Obernburg and in Kelsterbach in Essen, all of which were located in the German state now known as North Rhine Westfalia.

Currency restrictions imposed from 1931 onwards by the government of Reich Chancellor Heinz Brüning, and reinforced by Hjalmar Schacht's New Plan in 1934, seriously affected the Dutch investors' position in Nazi Germany. The normal transfer of interest, profits and dividends was no longer allowed, and there were far fewer facilities for transferring the capital itself. As a result, Dutch companies were in no sense free in terms of their decisions to withdraw from or retain their investments in Germany. It even became essential to identify new investment opportunities in that country in order to use non-transferable accounts.[24] During the 1930s, the Nazi regime's autarkic policy, currency restrictions and increasing control over the economy created huge difficulties and challenges for all major Dutch multinationals. At the same time, the economic boom that had resulted from Germany's anti-cyclical economic policy and the ensuing war preparations created many opportunities for new investments. As a result, Dutch FDI, like other international investments in Nazi Germany, increased in this period. At times, these investments were the result of German government pressure, and sometimes they were due to Dutch multinationals' autonomous business strategies; at other times the interests merged. In all cases, however, the measures of exchange control were paramount.[25]

During the 1930s, VGF became a more important artificial-fibre manufacturer than its competitor IG Farben. In 1930, its market share amounted to almost 64 per cent of Germany's total viscose sales. As a result of the crisis, the autarkic policy of the Nazi regime and monetary problems, production in the Dutch plants in Arnhem and Ede was cut back and employment figures fell dramatically. The total number of Enka staff in the Netherlands shrunk from 8,000 in 1929 to only 2,000 in 1936, while at the same time employment in Germany increased spectacularly, from almost 12,000 in 1931 to 25,000 in 1938.[26] The German National Fibre Programme of 1934 led to huge increases in the German output of artificial fibre, but not by as much as the Nazi regime had hoped for.[27] Total outputs of rayon and tyre-corduroy in German factories between 1933 and 1941 increased six-fold. Synthetic fibre manufacturers benefitted from import restrictions on cotton and wool under Schacht's New Plan.[28] Indeed, by 1939, Germany was the world's leading producer of staple fibre.[29]

As soon as the Nazis had come to power, they began to ask questions about the multinational nature of the company and the Dutch ownership. In 1937,

Göring's Four Year Plan asked the German side whether plans existed to nationalise the company. The German board members responded that it would be tactically wrong to do so at the time. The firm had to appear to be non-German-owned with a majority Dutch participation to avoid retaliation on its US subsidiaries. Göring and his Four Year Plan organisation were not, however, convinced and replaced all four German delegates, despite protests from their Dutch colleagues, with four new, more politically reliable, Supervisory Board members, including Hermann Abs of Deutsche Bank[30] and Ernst Helmutt Vits of the *reichseigenen Treuhandgesellschaft Treuarbeit* – the Reich-owned Trust Company *Treuarbeit*.[31] In this way, the German Reich had widened its influence in the largest artificial-fibre manufacturer. In April 1940, a month before the German occupation of the Netherlands, Vits was appointed VGF's general director, which was a decision supported by the all-powerful Dutch chairman of AKU's Supervisory Board, Fentener van Vlissingen. Simultaneously, the Dutch and German sides signed a contract to reduce foreign influence in the German business. The German priority delegates on AKU's board would be responsible for the German firms, while the Dutch delegates would focus on subsidiaries outside Germany.[32]

After the outbreak of war in September 1939, the contract was suspended for as long as the war lasted to avoid the risk of the sequestration of assets on behalf of the Trading with Enemy regulation in Allied countries. According to van Vlissingen:

> Therefore, it is of utmost importance for AKU that, as long as the war lasts, the neutral, i.e., Dutch character of the company, should be highlighted. The importation of raw materials, as well as the export of our products, would be seriously damaged.[33]

It was decided that all the German members of the Advisory and Executive boards of AKU, and all the Dutchmen on VGF's Advisory Board, would withdraw during the war. Abs made an offer to the Dutch to appoint a German trustee to the German boards to represent the Dutch. As a result, Stephan Karl Henkell, van Vlissingen's son-in-law and the brother-in-law of Hitler's Foreign Minister von Ribbentrop, was appointed in Germany. After his death as an army officer in June 1940, he was succeeded by Werner Carp on VGF's Advisory Board.

As soon as the German army occupied the Netherlands, the German members of AKU's Advisory and Executive boards returned to their positions. Furthermore, during the entire war, Ludwig Vaubel was appointed in Arnhem as a permanent deputy to Schmekel the German AKU executive.[34] As a result, the German Reich did not appoint a state supervisor (*Verwalter*) in Arnhem, as it had done in the case of, for example, Philips.[35] In fact, AKU continued manufacturing until 1944, building two new factories in the Netherlands, one to process straw to produce raw materials for rayon yarns, and the other to make rayon fibre a replacement for wool and cotton (*Zellwolle*). The investment of 10 million guilders in German machines was paid for by Dutch AKU shares. These were bought by Deutsche Bank, which paid the bill in Germany, although the guilders used for this transaction came from the Dutch Central Bank that obtained worthless German banknotes in exchange.

This was just one of the methods used by the Reich to repatriate AKU shares back to Germany during the war. Directly after the merger in 1929, 60 per cent of AKU shares had been in the hands of the Germans. However, after the currency restrictions of the Brüning government in 1931 and their tightening by Schacht after 1934, German shareholders sold their AKU shares on the Berlin stock market. With the permission of the Reich Bank, AKU had acquired its own shares with its German profits, which were transferred in this way to the Netherlands. Consequently, at the end of the 1930s, the balance of ownership had shifted to the Dutch side, which now owned 70 per cent of AKU's shares. As a result, during the German occupation, the German Reich endeavoured to shift the balance of property back to the German side. Its main tool was the German Golddiscontobank, which acquired a large amount of AKU shares on the Amsterdam stock exchange, but used German banknotes to get guilders. The Dutch Central Bank was obliged to exchange these into guilders.[36] Accordingly, by the end of the war, around 60 per cent of all issued shares had come into German hands. One way to incorporate the occupied economies was the penetration (*Verflechtung*) of German (private) capital into large companies in the occupied nations. Penetration thus succeeded in the case of AKU.[37] However, the largest Dutch multinationals – Unilever, Royal Dutch and Philips – were able to frustrate German plans for capital penetration.[38] During the war, they were controlled by either a *Verwalter* or *Reichskommissar*. Ultimately, this did not work out unfavourably for the Dutch companies, as these German officials had to defend their interests against major German competitors. Moreover, the other Dutch multinationals had made complicated legal provisions in the UK, US and South Africa, which made it impossible to acquire a significant stake in these companies.[39]

AKU-VGF in the post-war period

Compared to the other three Dutch multinationals, AKU and its German subsidiary, VGF, probably faced the most complicated post-war situation. The company had lost control over three plants in the Soviet Zone: Elsterberg, Sydowsaue and Breslau. The former was nationalised and transformed into a VEB (*volkseigener Betrieb*, a state-owned company), while the latter two were partly dismantled by the Soviets and then handed over to the Polish state. A plant in Lobositz was nationalised by the Czechoslovakian government without compensation.[40] Nevertheless, VGF's most important plants were located in the British and American occupation zones. Obernburg and Kelsterbach restarted rayon production at the end of 1945, but AKU's biggest plant, in Oberbruch near Aachen, was only able to resume production in 1947.[41]

The Allies' deconcentration plans posed another serious threat to the company. In 1939, the VGF group, including its subsidiaries in Germany – Spinnfaser, Kuag, Glanzstoff-Courtaulds and Bemberg – had over 26,000 staff. Although it had lost its production capacity in the east, VGF once again employed around 21,000 people by 1949.[42] This meant that it was regarded as too large and had to be deconcentrated. To the British and US occupation authorities, however, it was unclear whether AKU and VGF were Dutch or German companies and whether they should be treated as Allied firms or not. This also applied to AKU and VGF's subsidiaries in Britain and the US (the North American Rayon Corp., the US Bemberg Corp., and the US Enka Corp). If they were determined to be German, they would be treated as enemy property; if not, they had to be returned to their Dutch owner, i.e. AKU. The Dutch government had been in discussions with the US Alien Property Custodian and the State Department over the issue from 1943 onwards. The Dutch government contended that "at no time since 1934 had the German interest in the common stock of the A.K.U. exceeded thirty percent" and "that for years the daily management of the corporation had been exclusively in Dutch hands . . ."[43] In reality, however, the property relations were much more complicated than that. During the 1930s, a changing minority of ordinary AKU stock, which had also been traded on the Berlin stock exchange, had been in the hands of German citizens. During the German occupation, much more AKU stock had been bought by Germans on the Amsterdam stock exchange. Moreover, according to agreements in 1929 and 1939, German citizens representing the VGF group also held 50 per cent of the priority shares, which gave them the right to nominate AKU's Executive Board and Advisory Board members. Directly after the war, however, the Dutch government removed enemy stockholders on the basis of the Decree on Enemy Property and transferred the stock held by German citizens, ordinary as well as priority, to the State of the Netherlands.[44]

Meanwhile, VGF in West Germany had been placed under Allied control and its former chairman, Ernst Vits, had been appointed custodian. The Dutch sent E. Wittert van Hoogland from Arnhem to Wuppertal to be resident manager, and he demanded a majority for the Dutch on VGF's Advisory Board and an overriding influence on the Executive Board. A long-lasting conflict between the Dutch and German sides thus began, with each of them backed by their respective governments. The German side claimed that its shareholder legislation should be followed and that VGF had the right to an independent board.[45] In 1947, AKU board member Johannes Meynen, who had been Defence Minister in the first post-war Dutch cabinet, which had lasted only a year, and VGF's Vits had a meeting in which their different opinions regarding VGF's management clashed. Meynen, who would become AKU's chairman in 1948, proposed letting Wittert van Hoogland represent VGF, at least to the outside world, and in particular to the Allies. Vits agreed that van Hoogland could pretend to be the Dutch director, but maintained that no one on VGF's board would take any orders from him.[46] Furthermore, he told Meynen that:

> We will accept only those measures which work in favour of the continuation of the group, because we at Glanzstoff believe that survival of the group is in our own interest. We hope, in the future, to gain the gateway to abroad again via AKU.[47]

In conclusion, VGF did not want to destroy the unity of the group, but did not accept Dutch management control in Germany. VGF had needed the Dutch side for its relations with the rest of the world during the 1930s, and it certainly did not want to give up this advantage. The Dutch, on the other hand, thought they could control VGF once they owned the German subsidiary completely. This appeared, however, to be a major miscalculation.

As a consequence, VGF pursued its own business strategy. In the late 1940s, the German company decided to develop completely synthetic fibres and to build a perlon plant in Oberbruch in 1950. The German board had taken this direction in the immediate post-war years, largely inspired by DuPont's successes with nylon in the US. In addition, IG Farben's dismantling offered VGF the opportunity to develop IG's patent further and bring it to the market. VGF's top managers and engineers travelled to the US several times to study the large-scale production of man-made fibres.[48] AKU's board in Arnhem was nevertheless opposed to the German plans because they were deemed to be too risky financially. The market proved, however, that the German management had been right: by 1955, 50 per cent of VGF's profits came from perlon. Notably, the perlon plant was financed by several German insurance companies, the state of North Rhine Westphalia and the Economics Ministry of the Federal Republic of Germany (FRG) without any financial or managerial interference by the Dutch parent company.[49]

In 1953, AKU and VGF reached an understanding, with AKU offering 20 million *Deutsch Mark (DM)* of VGF stock via a German bank consortium to former AKU shareholders, who had lost their shares after the war. These stocks were offered at *DM* 102, even though they had a market value on the stock exchange of *DM* 160. As a result, AKU's participation in its German subsidiary fell from 99 to 76 per cent. In addition, all former German shareholders received *DM* 300 in cash. According to the AKU board, this gesture was made to create "fruitful relations in the future."[50] In exchange, however, AKU received half of the seats on VGF's Advisory Board, one seat on the Executive Board, and a renewal of all technical cooperation and cross-licensing contracts. Their sales organisation, however, which had been split up at the start of the war, remained separated. The corporate sales organisation had been in the Netherlands before the war, but now VGF would serve the large German market itself and AKU would export to the rest of the world.[51]

In 1955, VGF decided to build a nylon-corduroy factory after observing the US car-tyre market, where demand for nylon-corduroy had increased rapidly.

German car manufacturers had also begun to use tyres made with nylon fibres, which proved to be stronger than perlon or rayon. Consequently, by the end of the 1950s, VGF was the largest producer of tyre-corduroy in Germany. The company started the production of polyester fibres (*diolen*) in the same period, and also became number one in the Federal Republic with these synthetic fibres. Indeed, between 1953 and 1968, VGF's synthetic fibre production increased from 2,906 to 117,043 tons. Table 4.1 shows that VGF had become the largest manufacturer of synthetic fibres in the Federal Republic of Germany by 1968.

In the meantime, AKU in the Netherlands had also started the production of synthetic fibres like nylon (enkalon) and polyester-based fibres (terlenka). In part, they were using the technical cooperation and cross-licensing contracts with VGF, but were also partly experimenting in their own research laboratory in Arnhem. Output expanded rapidly during the 1950s and employment rose spectacularly. However, AKU faced major competition. Indeed, the global production capacity of synthetic fibres rocketed during the 1950s and 1960s, as many chemical firms entered the global market (Table 4.2).[52]

Table 4.1 The five largest chemical fibres companies in FRG in 1968, ranked by production (in 1,000 tons)

Company	Production in Germany	Foreign participation
1. Glanzstoff (VGF)	102 (28.2%)	(76%) AKU (Netherlands)
2. Hoechst	100 (27.7%)	
3. Bayer	90 (24.9%)	
4. DuPont	45 (12.5%)	E.I. du Pont de Nemoers&Company, Inc. (US)
5. ICI	25 (6.9%)	Imperial Chemical Industries (UK)
Total FRG	361	

Source: Winfried Schmitz-Esser, *Auslandkapital in der deutschen Wirtschaft* (Bonn: Möller 1969) 50–95.

Table 4.2 Break-down of manufacturing of synthetic fibres in the world, 1910–1970 (in 1,000 tons)

	West-Europe	USA	Japan	Rest	Total
1910	4	1	0	0	5
1920	10	4	1	0	15
1930	121	58	17	12	208
1940	607	214	228	83	1,132
1950	687	618	116	260	1,681
1960	1,223	823	551	770	3,367
1970	2,685	2,302	1,417	1,999	8,403

Source: Ludwig Vaubel, *Glanzstoff, Enka, Aku, Akzo. Unternehmungsleitung im nationalen Spannungsfeld 1929 bis 1978* (Wuppertal: Enka AG, 1986), 220.

The final merger

Ever since January 1959, AKU and VGF had discussed in joint board meetings how they could collaborate more commercially and take advantage of the group's structure, without the latter losing its managerial independence. It was not only the growing competition from old and new competitors globally, but also the rise of an internal European market and the EEC's endeavours to break down tariff-walls that forced both sides to rethink their former strategies. A break-down of tariff-walls would mean that Germany and the Netherlands would be part of the same tariff-system, but also that Italy and France would become contested markets for the two companies. Simultaneously, the Treaty of Rome and its cartel paragraphs meant that it was not permitted to pursue a joint price policy.[53] In addition, the home market conditions of AKU and VGF differed greatly: AKU exported an average of 65 per cent of its output, while for VGF this figure was only 15 to 20 per cent of its much larger yield.[54]

When the two companies were discussing closer collaboration, the technological basis, and with it the industrial structure, changed rapidly. Chemical companies like DuPont, Monsanto, ICI, Bayer and Hoechst had entered the European synthetic fibre market during the 1950s. Then, during the 1960s, new fibres were developed on a petrochemical basis and major integrated chemical firms could use their own raw feedstock in their own fibre plants, while simultaneously selling their side products. In conclusion, it became increasingly obvious that AKU and VGF had become too small and were not integrated enough to be competitive on the world fibre market.[55] A memorandum from February 1966 reveals that VGF's board was discussing the issue of closer collaboration with AKU concerning raw materials, manufacturing and sales:

> The development of international competition in the field of chemical fibres, increasingly from the dominant position of the big chemical firms like DuPont, ICI, Monsanto, as well as Bayer and Hoechst, is the inducement to explore once more the possibilities of a closer collaboration between AKU and Glanzstoff.[56]

A few months later, Meynen was pensioned off as AKU's chairman. This ended the personal rivalry between Meynen and Vits, which had played a role since 1945. His successor, Klaas Soesbeek, showed more tact towards the German side. He was able to renew the 1953 contract for five more years and intensify the collaboration between the two sides. In the same year, AKU and VGF presented a consolidated annual report for the first time. Prior to the presentation of the report, Vits and Soesbeek met and agreed that:

> . . . the confinement towards chemical fibre production is difficult. Mr. Soesbeek also emphasized that in his view the AKU/Glanzstoff group has no attraction to capital. On the other hand, from a broad perspective, both

AKU and Glanzstoff need an increase of capital. The question is therefore whether we should collaborate with a different and larger group.[57]

In this respect, Soesbeek informed Vits that leading players from Bayer had visited AKU in Arnhem and proposed a collaboration between the two companies. AKU had, however, refused. Talks with Royal Dutch Shell had also failed.

In 1966 and 1967, the economic tide for the international synthetic fibre industry completely changed. Rayon prices plummeted as a result of overproduction. Collaboration and mergers were no longer theoretical issues, but became inevitable solutions. Clearly VGF and AKU had to rationalise the group structure, coordinate and concentrate production, cut raw material costs and improve their marketing. Simultaneously, the group had to change its monoculture and diversify in other directions in the chemical industry. However, it was deemed too late to enter the raw material sector, and the group therefore had to look for partners. On the VGF side, Vaubel wanted to finish the merger process by the middle of 1969 before Vits' period as chairman of the board came to an end and Abs had left the Advisory Board. A merger contract was therefore signed in May 1969. It included the following agreements:

1   AKU N.V. was transformed into a holding company, which was responsible for coordination in the group.
2   Enka N.V. was set up in Arnhem and took over AKU's assets in the Netherlands, Belgium, Austria and Switzerland.
3   Glanzstoff and Enka merged into one company, with joint Dutch and German management.
4   Enka International N.V. was set up to manage all foreign participations, particularly in South and North America.[58]

Diversification ambitions were nonetheless not yet satisfied. A merger with Dutch State Mines (DSM), which would be a perfect partner, including for VGF, failed in March 1969 because DSM was a state-owned chemical company that could not be privatised in the left-wing political climate in the Netherlands at the time. A solution was identified rather quickly: in July 1969, a Letter of Intent was signed with *Koninklijke Zout-Organon* N.V. (KZO), which had itself been formed by a merger of several smaller chemical firms a few years previously. The AKU/VGF agreement that had only been concluded several months earlier continued to exist. However, the new holding company, AKU N.V., merged with KZO into Akzo N.V. The Executive Board of Akzo consisted of eight KZO and seven AKU members. The new Advisory Board, meanwhile, had 16 members. Abs returned as chairman of Glanzstoff's Advisory Board after Vits died in 1970. Glanzstoff-operating companies had now become part of Akzo's new multidivisional structure.[59]

Conclusions

In order to explain the deep-rooted conflict within the AKU-VGF conglomerate after the war, one has to return to the genesis of the Dutch–German merger and its evolution during the extremely difficult years for international business in the Rhine economy during the 1930s and 1940s. The big Dutch multinationals followed a historical path in Germany, which was a move that had begun long before World War II. The strong economic position they had built had been the result of the close economic integration of the two neighbouring countries since the end of the 19th century and the locational advantages that Germany offered to Dutch companies at the time. This was reinforced by the competitive advantages Germany offered them after World War I. The so-called nearby factor – the Netherlands was very close to Germany geographically and culturally – therefore seems to be an attractive explanation for the massive Dutch presence in Germany. One should, however, bear in mind that the two countries diverged significantly both politically and economically during the 1930s and 1940s. However, in the late 1940s, the Dutch realised that they needed their large neighbour's market for their own recovery.

Compared to other Dutch multinationals in Germany, the artificial (or man-made) fibre manufacturer AKU, and its German subsidiary VGF, probably faced a very complicated post-war situation. VGF's most important plants were located in West Germany, near the Rhine in the British and US occupation zone. It was unclear to these occupation authorities whether AKU and VGF were Dutch or German companies and whether they should be treated as Allied businesses or not. During the 1930s, a changing minority of ordinary AKU stock, which had also been traded on the Berlin stock exchange, had been in the hands of German citizens. During the German occupation, many more AKU stocks had been bought by Germans on the Amsterdam stock exchange using money confiscated in the Netherlands. Moreover, according to the agreements of 1929 and 1939, German citizens representing the VGF group also held 50 per cent of the priority shares, which gave them the right to nominate members of AKU's Executive and Advisory boards.

Directly after the war, the Dutch government used the Decree on Enemy Property to remove enemy stockholders and transferred the ordinary and priority stock held by German citizens to the State of the Netherlands. VGF did not, however, recognise the sequestration of all German AKU stocks in Germany by the Dutch government. Moreover, the Western Allies doubted the complete Dutch ownership of VGF and sequestrated its US and British subsidiaries. Meanwhile, VGF in West Germany had been placed under Allied control and its former chairman (Vits) had been appointed custodian. As a result, the Dutch sent a resident manager from Arnhem to Wuppertal who demanded a majority for the Dutch on the Advisory Board and an overriding influence on the Executive Board. The Germans accepted that having a Dutch director might look better to the occupying forces, but they would never follow his orders. A long-lasting conflict between the Dutch and German sides thus began, with each of them supported by their respective governments. The German side claimed that its own shareholder legislation had to be followed and that VGF had the right to an independent board, as agreed upon in 1929 and 1939. Obviously, national background mattered a great deal in these years.

As a consequence, during the 1950s, VGF pursued its own strategy and, for example, successfully set up a new synthetic fibre plant without any financial support from its Dutch parent company. In 1953, AKU had to compromise to regain some control over its profitable subsidiary in the Federal Republic. It therefore returned part of its VGF shares to Germany and thereby reduced its stake in the German subsidiary from 99 to 76 per cent. AKU received half of the seats on VGF's Advisory Board, but only one on the Executive Board. All the technological cooperation and licensing contracts were renewed, but the two sales organisations remained separate. The German company did not get back its priority shares, which would have given it the right to return to AKU's boards in Arnhem. As a result, during the 1950s, the two companies operated, practically speaking, as two independent firms with some exchanges of information.

At the end of the 1950s, the two sides were forced to rethink their positions. After the war, numerous large integrated chemical companies had entered the market with newly developed synthetic fibres mainly based on petrochemicals. As a result, AKU and VGF became less competitive and needed to rethink and rationalise their group structure. Furthermore, during the 1960s, they began to realise that diversification and a possible merger with different chemical firms, in particular those active on the raw materials side, was the only solution in the highly competitive market. When rayon prices plummeted in 1966, these solutions became prerequisites for the group's survival. However, it was not until 1969 that the two companies merged completely and became part of Akzo. It was only then that the disagreements about management issues were completely resolved.

The post-war AKU-VGF case clearly shows that property relations, in particular between parent company and subsidiary, do not always determine management control. If one side decides not to follow the instructions of its headquarters and is thereby supported by the local government, foreign companies can do very little about it, particularly if they come from relatively small countries like the Netherlands. The decentralisation strategy pursued by Dutch multinationals after World War II was therefore probably more a result of the institutional conditions created by the national governments of larger states than a deliberate policy of these companies. This case also clearly shows that, despite the close economic relations in the Rhine economy, different national interests also played a role in the final development of company structures in that cross-border region. It also shows that while economic and geographical structures are a prerequisite for the creation of an economic region, political relations and historical exogenous shocks are equally important for the final outcome.

Notes

1 Geoffrey Owen, *The Rise and the Fall of Great Companies: Courtaulds and the Reshaping of the Man-Made Fibres Industry* (Oxford: Oxford University Press, 2010), 12.
2 Ibid., 35.
3 "Man-Made Fibers Continue to Grow," *Textile World*, www.textileworld.com/textile-world/fiber-world/2015/02/man-made-fibers-continue-to-grow/, retrieved on 2 November 2018.
4 Theodor Langenbruch, *Glanzstoff 1899–1949* (Wuppertal: Enka AG, 1985), 72.

5 Renate Laspeyres, *Rotterdam und das Ruhrgebiet* (Marburg: Marburger geographische Schriften, 1969); Paul Th. van der Laar, "Port Traffic in Rottterdam: The Competitive Edge of a Rhine-Port (1880–1914)," in *Struggling for Leadership: Antwerp-Rotterdam Port Competition between 1870–2000*, ed. Reginald Loyen, Erik Buyst, and Greta Devos (Heidelberg and New York: Physica-Verlag, 2003), 63–86; Hein A.M. Klemann and Friso Wielenga, "Die Niederlande und Deutschland, oder verschwindet die nationale Ökonomie? Eine Einleitung," in *Deutschland und die Niederlande. Wirtschaftsbeziehungen im 19. und 20. Jahrhundert*, ed. Hein A.M. Klemann and Friso Wielenga (Münster: Waxmann, 2009), 7–17; Hein A.M. Klemann and Ben Wubs, "River Dependence: Creating a Transnational Rhine Economy, 1850s–2000," in *Perspectives on European Economic and Social History / Perspektiven der Europäischen Wirtschafts- und Sozialgeschichte*, ed. Jan-Otmar Hesse, Christian Kleinschmidt, Alfred Reckendrees, and Ray Stokes (Baden-Baden: Nomos, 2014), 219–246; Ferry de Goey, ed., *Comparative Port History Rotterdam-Antwerp, 1880–2000: Competition, Cargo, and Costs* (Amsterdam: Aksant, 2004); Ralf Banken and Ben Wubs, eds., *A Transnational Economic History* (Baden-Baden: Nomos, 2017), 13–29.

6 Ernst Homburg and Arjan van Rooij, "Die Vor- und Nachteile enger Nachbarschaft. Der Transfer deutscher chemischer Technologie in die Niederlande," in *Technologietransfer aus der deutschen Chemieindustrie (1925–1960)*, ed. Rolf Petri (Berlin: Duncker & Humblot, 2004), 201–251.

7 AkzoNobel Historical Archive (ANHA), 552, Participations Duitsland 1948, Netherlands Interests in Germany, 2.

8 Charles Wilson, *The History of Unilever: A Study in Economic Growth and Social Change* (London: Cassell, 1954) 190.

9 G. Busch, *Der Unilevertrust und seine Stellung in der deutschen Volkswirtschaft* (PhD diss., Berlin, 1937), 21.

10 Keetie Sluyterman and Ben Wubs, *Over Grenzen. Multinationals en de Nederlandse markteconomie* (Amsterdam: Boom, 2009), 94.

11 Ben Wubs, *International Business and National War Interests: Unilever between Reich and Empire* (Abingdon and New York: Routledge, 2008), 37–40.

12 Kees Boersma, "Tensions within an Industrial Research Laboratory: The Philips Laboratory's X-Ray Department between the Wars," *Enterprise & Society* 4 (2003): 82–83.

13 B.P.A. Gales and K.E. Sluyterman, "Outward Bound: The Rise of Dutch Multinationals," in *The Rise of Multinationals in Continental Europe*, ed. G. Jones and H.G. Schröter (Aldershot: Edward Elgar, 1993), 65–98.

14 H.A. Van Wijnen, *D.G. van Beuningen, 1877–1955. Grootvorst aan de Maas* (Amsterdam: Balans, 2004).

15 Johan de Vries, "Fentener van Vlissingen, Frederik Hendrik (1882–1962)," in *Biografisch Woordenboek van Nederland*. http://resources.huygens.knaw.nl/bwn/BWN/lemmata/bwn5/fentener, retrieved on 15 December 2018.

16 Max Dendermonde, *Nieuwe tijden. Nieuwe schakels. De eerste vijftig jaar van de AKU* (Wormerveer: Meijer's Industriële Uitgeverij, 1961), 34–40.

17 Maekubee means Maatschappij tot Exploitatie van Kunstzijdefabrieken in het Buitenland.

18 Dendermonde, *Nieuwe tijden*, 64–67.

19 Paul Heinz Boeddinghaus, *Die Konzentration in der Kunstseidenindustrie unter besonderer Berücksichtigung des Zusammenschlusses von "Glanzstoff" und "Enka" zur "Aku"* (Elberfeld: Gummersbach, 1931), 53.

20 Sluyterman and Wubs, *Over Grenzen*, 105–107.

21 Christian Kleinschmidt, "An Americanised Company in Germany: The Vereinigte Glanzstoff Fabriken AG in the 1950s," in *The Americanisation of European Business*, ed. Matthias Kipping and Ove Bjarnar (London and New York: Routledge, 1998), 172–173.

22 Geoffrey Jones, "Courtaulds in Continental Europe, 1920–1945," in *British Multinationals: Origins, Management and Performance*, ed. Geoffrey Jones (Aldershot: Gower, 1986), 122.

23 Lothar Gall, Gerald D. Feldman, Harold James, Carl-Ludwig Holtfrerich, and Hans E. Büschgen, *The Deutsche Bank, 1870–1995* (München: C.H. Beck, 1995), 361–364.

24 Wubs, *International Business*, 47–49.
25 Ben Wubs, "A Dutch Multinational's Miracle in Post-War Germany," *Economic History Yearbook: International Economic and Business Relations* 1 (2012): 20.
26 Langenbruch, *Glanzstoff*, 126–127.
27 Christoph Bucheim and Jonas Scherner, "The Role of Private Property in the Nazi Economy: The Case of Industry," *The Journal of Economic History* 66, no. 2 (June 2006): 399.
28 Kleinschmidt, "The Vereinigte Glanzstoff Fabriken," 172–174.
29 Jeffrey Harrop, "The Growth of the Rayon Industry in the Inter War Years," *Bulletin of Economic Research* 20, no. 2 (1969): 79.
30 Gall, Feldman, James, Holtfrerich, and Büschgen, *Die Deutsche Bank*, 317–318.
31 Langenbruch, *Glanzstoff*, 81–82.
32 Ibid., 83.
33 Fentener van Vlissingen in the meeting of Delegates, 29 September 1939. Langenbruch, *Glanzstoff*, 83.
34 Ludwig Vaubel, *Glanzstoff, Enka, Aku, Akzo. Unternehmungsleitung im nationalen Spannungsfeld 1929 bis 1978* (Wuppertal: Enka AG, 1986).
35 Yvo Blanken, *The History of Philips Electronics N.V. Volume 4: Under German Rule* (Zaltbommel: European Library, 1999), 138–144.
36 Hein A.M. Klemann, *Nederland 1938–1948 Economie en samenleving in jaren van oorlog en bezetting* (Amsterdam: Boom, 2002), 140 et seq.
37 Gall, Feldman, James, Holtfrerich, and Büschgen, *The Deutsche Bank*, 315–318.
38 Adam Tooze, *The Wages of Destruction: The Making and Breaking of the Nazi Economy* (London: Allen Lane, 2006), 383–390.
39 Wubs, *International Business*, 62–65.
40 Langenbruch, *Glanzstoff*, 88–93.
41 Kleinschmidt, "An Americanised Company in Germany," 176.
42 Langenbruch, *Glanzstoff*, 125.
43 Netherlands Institute for War Documentation (NIOD), 212e, 179, Bregstein, Algemene Kunstzijde Unie N.V., Memorandum.
44 NIOD, 212e, 179, Bregstein, Algemene Kunstzijde Unie N.V., Memorandum, 18–19.
45 Langenbruch, *Glanzstoff*, 106–107.
46 Vaubel, *Glanzstoff, Enka, Aku, Akzo*, 84.
47 Ibid.
48 Kleinschmidt, "An Americanised Company in Germany," 178–180.
49 Langenbruch, *Glanzstoff*, 109–113.
50 ANHA, 318, Allied Enemy Property: Aufsichtsratssitzung VGF, 24 March 1953.
51 Langenbruch, *Glanzstoff*, 113.
52 Jonathan Steffen, *AkzoNobel, Tomorrow's Answers Today: The History of AkzoNobel since 1646* (Amsterdam: AkzoNobel, 2008), 44–45.
53 Susan Sugar Nathan, "Antitrust Law of the European Economic Community: An Interpretation of Articles 85 and 86 of the Treaty of Rome," *Maryland Journal of International Law* 4, no. 2 (1979): 253–255.
54 Vaubel, *Glanzstoff, Enka, Aku, Akzo*, 116–119.
55 Ibid., 119.
56 Ibid., 132.
57 Ibid., 138–139.
58 Ibid., 155–157.
59 Ibid., 167–177.

Bibliography

Banken, Ralf, and Ben Wubs, eds. (2017), *A Transnational Economic History* (Baden-Baden: Nomos).

Blanken, Yvo (1999), *The History of Philips Electronics N.V. Volume 4. Under German Rule* (Zaltbommel: European Library).

Boeddinghaus, Paul Heinz (1931), *Die Konzentration in der Kunstseidenindustrie unter besonderer Berücksichtigung des Zusammenschlusses von "Glanzstoff" und "Enka" zur "Aku".* Inaugural-Dissertation zur Erlangung der Doktorwürde der Universität Köln* (Elberfeld: Gummersbach).

Boersma, Kees (2003), "Tensions within an industrial research laboratory: The Philips laboratory's X-Ray 1department between the wars." *Enterprise & Society* 4, no. 1: 65–98.

Bucheim, Christoph and Jonas Scherner (2006), "The role of private property in the Nazi economy: The case of industry." *The Journal of Economic History* 66, no. 2: 390–416.

Busch, G. (1937), *Der Unilevertrust und seine Stellung in der deutschen Volkswirtschaft* (PhD diss., Berlin).

Christian Kleinschmidt (1998), "An Americanised company in Germany: The Vereinigte Glanzstoff Fabriken AG in the 1950s." In *The Americanisation of European Business,* edited by Matthias Kipping and Ove Bjarnar, 171–189 (London, New York: Routledge).

De Goey, Ferry, ed. (2004), *Comparative Port History Rotterdam-Antwerp, 1880–2000: Competition, Cargo, and Costs* (Amsterdam: Aksant).

Dendermonde, Max (1961), *Nieuwe tijden. Nieuwe schakels. De eerste vijftig jaar van de AKU* (Wormerveer: Meijer's Industriële Uitgeverij).

De Vries, Joh. (2018), "Fentener van Vlissingen, Frederik Hendrik (1882–1962)." In *Biografisch Woordenboek van Nederland.* Accessed 15 December 2018. http://resources.huygens.knaw.nl/bwn/BWN/lemmata/bwn5/fentener

Gales, Ben P.A., and Keetie E. Sluyterman (1993), "Outward bound: The rise of Dutch multinationals." In *The Rise of Multinationals in Continental Europe,* edited by Geoffrey Jones and Harm Schröter, 65–98 (Alderschot: Edward Elgar Publishing).

Harrop, Jeffrey (1969), "The growth of the Rayon industry in the inter war years." *Bulletin of Economic Research* 20, no. 2: 71–84.

Homburg, Ernst and Arjan van Rooij (2004), "Die Vor- und Nachteile enger Nachbarschaft. Der Transfer deutscher chemischer Technologie in die Niederlande." In *Technologietransfer aus der deutschen Chemieindustrie (1925–1960),* edited by Rolf Petri, 201–251 (Berlin: Duncker & Humblot).

James, Harold (1995), "The Deutsche Bank and the Dictatorship 1933–1945." In *The Deutsche Bank 1870–1995,* edited by Lothar Gall, Gerald D. Feldman, Harold James, Carl-Ludwig Holtfrerich and Hans E. Büschgen, 277–356 (London: Weidenfeld & Nicolson).

Jones, Geoffrey (1986), "Courtaulds in continental Europe, 1920–1945." In *British Multinationals: Origins, Management and Performance,* edited by Geoffrey Jones, 119–136 (Alderschot: Gower).

Jones, Geoffrey (2006), "The end of nationality? Global firms and 'borderless worlds'." *Zeitschrift für Unternehmensgeschichte* 51, no. 2: 149–166.

Klemann, Hein A.M. (2002), *Nederland 1938–1948. Economie en samenleving in jaren van oorlog en bezetting* (Amsterdam: Boom).

Klemann, Hein A.M., and Friso Wielenga (2009), "Die Niederlande und Deutschland, oder verschwindet die nationale Ökonomie? Eine Einleitung." In *Deutschland und die Niederlande. Wirtschaftsbeziehungen im 19. und 20. Jahrhundert,* edsited by Hein A.M. Klemann and Friso Wielenga, 7–17 (Münster: Waxmann).

Klemann, Hein A.M., and Ben Wubs (2014), "River dependence: Creating a transnational Rhine economy, 1850s-2000." In *Perspectives on European Economic and Social History / Perspektiven der Europäischen Wirtschafts- und Sozialgeschichte,* edited by Jan-Otmar Hesse, Christian Kleinschmidt, Alfred Reckendrees and Ray Stokes, 219–246 (Baden-Baden: Nomos).

Langenbruch, Theodor (1985), *Glanzstoff 1899–1949* (Wuppertal: Enka AG).

Laspeyres, Renate (1969), *Rotterdam und das Ruhrgebiet* (Marburg: Marburger geographische Schriften).

Lindner, Stephan H. (2001), *Den Faden verloren. Die westdeutsche und die französische Textilindustrie auf dem Rückzug (1930/45–1990)* (München: Beck).

Nathan, Susan Sugar (1979), "Antitrust law of the European economic community: An interpretation of articles 85 and 86 of the treaty of Rome." *Maryland Journal of International Law* 4, no. 2: 251–273.

Owen, Geoffrey (2010), *The Rise and the Fall of Great Companies: Courtaulds and the Reshaping of the Man-Made Fibres Industry* (Oxford: Oxford University Press).

Schmitz-Esser, Winfried (1969), *Auslandkapital in der deutsche Wirtschaft* (Bonn: Möller).

Sluyterman, Keetie and Ben Wubs (2009), *Over Grenzen. Multinationals en de Nederlandse Markteconomie* (Amsterdam: Boom).

Steffen, Jonathan, ed. (2008), *Tomorrow's Answers Today: The History of AkzoNobel since 1646* (Amsterdam: AkzoNobel).

Tooze, Adam (2006), *The Wages of Destruction: The Making and Breaking of the Nazi Economy* (London: Allen Lane).

Van der Laar, Paul. Th. (2003), "Port traffic in Rottterdam: The competitive edge of a Rhineport (1880–1914)." In *Struggling for Leadership: Antwerp-Rotterdam Port Competition between 1870-2000*, edited by Reginald Loyen, Erik Buyst and Greta Devos, 63–86 (Heidelberg and New York: Physica-Verlag).

Van Wijnen, Harry. A. (2004), *D.G. van Beuningen, 1877–1955. Grootvorst aan de Maas* (Amsterdam: Balans).

Vaubel, Ludwig (1986a), *Glanzstoff, Enka, AKU, Akzo. Unternehmensleitung im nationalen und internationalen Spannungsfeld 1929 bis 1978. Band 1* (Wuppertal: Enka AG).

Vaubel, Ludwig (1986b), *Glanzstoff, Enka, AKU, Akzo. Unternehmensleitung im nationalen und internationalen Spannungsfeld 1929 bis 1978. Band 2* (Wuppertal: Enka AG).

Wicht, Wolfgang E. (1992), *Glanzstoff. Zur Geschichte der Chemiefaser, eines Unternehmens und seiner Arbeiterschaft* (Neustadt an der Aisch: Schmidt).

Wilson, Charles (1954), *The History of Unilever: A Study in Economic Growth and Social Change* (London: Cassell).

Wubs, Ben (2008), *International Business and National War Interests: Unilever between Reich and Empire, 1939–1945* (London: Routledge).

Wubs, Ben (2012), "A Dutch multinational's miracle in post-war Germany." *Jahrbuch für Wirtschaftsgeschichte/Yearbook for Economic History* 53, no. 1: 15–41.

Archives

AkzoNobel Historical Archive (ANHA).
Netherlands Institute for War Documentation, Amsterdam (NIOD).

5 Coal to oil and the post-war expansion of port and hinterland, 1945–1973

Marten Boon

Introduction

World War II caused a major rupture in the Rhine region's history and economy, leaving the Rhine-Ruhr area, with its huge resource-bound coal, steel and chemical industries, shaken to its core. The subsequent occupation by Allied forces and the simultaneous discovery of huge oil reserves in the Middle East set in motion a major transition from the area's abundant coal resources to a dependence on imported oil. This transition of the fuel base of West German and other Western European economies caused a long-term decline of the coal industry and a rapid growth of the oil and petrochemical sector. Massive investments in plants and infrastructure were required to utilise the economies of scale in the transportation and processing of oil. The logistical demands of the expanding oil and petrochemical clusters in the Rhine basin fostered the emergence of new transnational business and infrastructural networks that strengthened cross-border relations in the Rhine region, in particular the Lower and Middle Rhine. That this was to happen was far from clear at the outset.

At the end of World War II, the oil industry in Western Europe was still small, with a limited refinery capacity, and was mostly geared towards the marketing of oil products. Oil refining was typically conducted near the source, not near the market. When from the mid-1950s onwards, oil consumption in West Germany and more general in Western Europe started rising rapidly, oil companies and national governments scrambled to plan the oil supply infrastructure required to facilitate the build-up of a European refining sector. The outcome of that process and its consequences for the transnational economic connections in the Rhine basin were uncertain and depended on the interplay between corporate and governmental actors and their local, national and transnational interests. This chapter presents an analysis of that process by questioning how and why the transition from coal to oil affected transnational connections in the Rhine basin.

In building the West European refining industry in the 1950s and 1960s, the choice of a landing port for oil imports was a particularly consequential decision, with long-term implications for the extent of transnational regional integration in the Rhine basin. A seaport is the link between the maritime and overland parts of the supply chain, and this is of particular significance in the case of oil, where pipelines are the preferred means of transportation. Pipelines are immovable once constructed and tend to concentrate and fix the flow of oil. As a consequence, a key question concerns to what extent the oil companies' logistical requirements or the efforts of port managers valourising their port's location and facilities determined the choice of the landing port. At a port level, the port authority and the oil companies are therefore key actors. However, local and national governments are also highly relevant, not only because ports were communal in that period, but also because large parts of the oil transport infrastructure crossed one or several borders. The policies and regulations in the various West European oil importing countries were therefore also highly relevant to the outcome of the infrastructural decision-making. This is somewhat underplayed in the recent port-hinterland literature, but this and other chapters in this book highlight that, until the 1990s, national transport and infrastructure policies were rarely coordinated among the member states of the European Economic Community (see, in particular, Chapter 6). National governments and the various national regulatory frameworks were therefore influential factors in building the West European refining industry.

This chapter is structured according to the layers of our port-hinterland model. To unravel the effect of the transition on transnational economic relations in the Rhine basin, it is important to start with the factors that gave rise to the transition in the first place. The first section, therefore, starts with the macro-economic hinterland and discusses the origins of the transition from coal to oil and its consequences for the localisation of the investments in refineries in the Rhine basin. The second section considers the physical hinterland and looks at the theoretical implications of the new pipeline infrastructure, which was needed to supply the growing number of inland refineries in Western Europe. The third section discusses the actual decision-making process relating to the new crude oil pipeline infrastructure. Finally, the fourth part of the chapter considers how these decisions affected the logistics of crude oil imports in the 1950s and 1960s and their implications for transnational integration in the Rhine basin.

Energy transition: the growth of oil and petrochemical clusters in the Rhine basin

The transition from coal to oil fundamentally changed the West German economy, providing one of the foundations of the West German post-war economic miracle.[1] The transition had its roots in the Allied occupation of Germany after World War II on the one hand and the liberal economic policies of the Adenauer cabinets in the 1950s on the other. By 1947, Europe was being threatened by a severe energy shortage, with Germany, the most important pre-war continental source of coal, only producing 40 per cent of its pre-World War II level.[2] Being starved of the necessary investments during the Nazi period and the faltering Allied management of the sector during the post-war occupation hampered German coal production, and it never recovered.[3] Shortages of coal disrupted industrial production and household heating, but Europe lacked the financial and natural resources to avert the crisis on its own. Resolving the energy crisis of 1947 was one of the goals of the Marshall Plan, which, according to a contemporary American report, could not have succeeded without oil.[4] Oil was indeed the single largest part of the plan's aid package: 10 per cent of the dollars allocated under the plan were used to enable the dollar-starved Western European countries to import dollar-oil from the Middle East.[5] The Economic Cooperation Administration (ECA), which was managing the allocation of Marshall Plan dollars, directed oil from the Middle East to Europe to resolve the energy crisis and to secure the American oil supply from its own domestic sources. This also helped the US oil companies to retain their European markets.[6] The low extraction costs of Middle Eastern oil, the increasing size of its production, and the structural rise in the cost of labour, which strongly affected the cost price of the coal production in Europe, caused oil to become much cheaper than coal, ultimately setting in motion the transition from coal to oil as the primary source of fuel in most European economies.[7]

The second part of the solution to Europe's energy shortage was the expansion of the refining capacity in Western Europe. This would save dollar outlays for oil product imports and would thus be beneficial with respect to the effectiveness of the Marshall Plan for a European recovery.[8] The creation of the Bizone in 1947, in which the American and British occupation zones in Germany were combined following their policy pivot regarding the importance of an economically strong Germany, and the launch of the Bizonal Oil Refinery Plan in the same year provided for the expansion of crude oil imports and refining capacity in Germany.[9] The economic necessity of solving the energy shortage caused a shift in Allied policy with regard to Germany's war-associated sectors, in particular the synthetic fuels and chemicals industry. The Rhine–Ruhr area especially inherited a number of synthetic fuel plants from the Nazi period that were designed to produce motor and aviation fuels through the hydrogenation of coal, but they could also be used to produce high-quality motor fuels from crude or residual oil. These plants could switch between coal and oil because they were essentially oil refineries; they produced hydrocarbons out of coal and hydrogen and then refined those hydrocarbons into fuels. As war-related installations, these hydrogenation plants were slated for dismantling. However, the acuteness of the energy situation in 1947 halted this and, in 1948, the hydrogenation plants were added to the Bizonal Oil Refinery Plan, cementing a US policy shift that increasingly prioritised a strong West Germany as a buffer against the perceived Soviet threat to European security.[10] The reactivation of the hydrogenation plants in the Rhine–Ruhr region transformed the area into one of Germany's largest oil refining regions at a stroke.[11] However, in contrast to the easy access to seaborne crude oil supplies of Hamburg's refining cluster, the Rhine–Ruhr lacked a ready source of crude oil. As a result, Royal Dutch Shell (RDS), Standard Oil of New Jersey (SO), Socony-Vacuum (Standard Oil of New York, from 1955 Mobil) and British Petroleum (BP) closed processing deals with these plants over the course of 1949 and 1950.

During the 1950s, the former hydrogenation plants would form the basis of the emergence of West Germany's largest concentration of oil and petrochemical activity in the Rhine-Ruhr area. However, this would not have happened without the economic policy choices of consecutive Adenauer cabinets in response to further energy crises in the early 1950s. In 1950–51, West Germany suffered a crippling shortage of coal. An immediate response was the increased importation of US coal, which, with continuously rising coal prices in West Germany, emerged as a serious competitor to the German product.[12] A more consequential effect of the crisis was its influence on federal government thinking regarding the long-term security of the energy supply to West German industry and economic growth. Indeed, from an energy policy heavily dependent on coal, consecutive Adenauer cabinets shifted to a strategy of competition between energy sources. The federal minister of economics, Ludwig Erhard (CDU), argued: "[t]he competition between energy sources that we pursue will result in a more efficient energy supply in the long run."[13] Between 1953 and 1956, Erhard gradually opened up the West German market for energy imports, in particular fuel oil.[14] At the time, fuel oil was particularly used in industry, and, because energy costs in the German industry were the principal concern of Erhard, his import liberalising policies particularly benefitted the oil industry that was competing for industrial clients with the coal producers in the Rhine-Ruhr area. While prices for German coal kept rising throughout the 1950s, in particular after price controls were lifted in 1956, fuel oil prices started falling after the Suez crisis subsided in early 1957.[15] The widening gap between coal and fuel oil prices fuelled a strong growth of fuel oil imports, which, together with an economic slowdown in 1957–1958, contributed to a glut in Ruhr coal production, triggering what became known as the coal crisis of 1958 and the irreversible decline of the German coal industry.

As between 1955 and 1960 German industries switched fuels, oil companies grasped the emerging growth market by strongly expanding refining capacity in West Germany. The vast majority of this expansion was realised in North Rhine Westphalia, and in particular the Rhine-Ruhr area, as West Germany's biggest consumer of fuel oil.[16] More than 80 per cent of the new capacity planned in 1957 consisted of green-field investments in new refineries by Royal Dutch, Standard Oil, BP and Petrofina.[17] Although the former hydrogenation plants undertook only 17 per cent of the planned expansions, the green-field projects were designed to replace the processing deals the major companies had with those plants, as well as adding to the local supply of petrochemical feedstock in the Rhine-Ruhr area.[18] When the hydrogenation plants were finally safe from the threat of dismantling in 1949, it was not only the foreign oil companies that were interested in cooperating with them. Indeed, from the early 1950s, the heirs of Germany's giant chemical conglomerate, IG Farben – chiefly BASF, Bayer, Hoechst, Agfa and CW Hülst – were very interested in using the gaseous and liquid by-products from refining as petrochemical feedstock for the production of chemicals, rubber, plastics and fibres.[19] Although these companies almost exclusively engaged in coal-based chemistry at the time, they clearly understood the cost and material benefits of using oil-based feedstock and were on the lookout for domestic sources.[20] This effort was part of a fundamental feedstock shift of the entire West German chemical sector, and was one that ensured its international competitiveness in the long run.[21] The Rheinische Olefinwerke, a joint venture between BASF and Deutsche Shell located near Cologne, was established in 1953 and was West Germany's first dedicated petrochemical plant. The plant used the gaseous by-products from Union Kraftstoff, a former hydrogenation plant near Cologne that processed crude oil on behalf of Deutsche Shell. As such, it was the Shell group that was responsible for the delivery of feedstock to the joint venture. When production at the Olefinwerke expanded, the additional need for feedstock required Deutsche Shell to expand its production of feedstock and so its refining capacity in the area. Other joint ventures between foreign oil and German chemical companies followed a similar pattern of growth and development. This reinforcing feedback loop of back- and forwards linkages between oil refining and the production of petrochemicals was a major driver of the Rhine-Ruhr area's economic development during the years of West Germany's economic miracle.

The growth of the West German refining sector was part of a concerted drive of the major oil companies to develop West European markets through major capital investments in mid- and downstream assets.[22] The expansion of refinery capacity in Western Europe, planned to start between 1955 and 1975, required the expansion of port, terminal, pipeline and storage infrastructure. The growth of West European oil imports drove economies of scale in oil transportation, particularly in maritime tankers, which grew rapidly in size especially after the 1956 Suez Crisis had highlighted the strategic risk of depending on the Suez Canal for European supply security.[23] While a rise in the size of tankers was a major driver of port investments and growth on the maritime side, the biggest driver of infrastructural investment was the expansion of inland refining locations to serve local and regional markets. Inland refinery capacity grew from just 18 million tons per annum in 1955 to 271 million tons in 1975, a 15-fold increase or double the growth of the total refining capacity in the same period.[24] The expansion of the inland refining capacity was particularly apparent in West Germany and France, with Germany leading the way in the late 1950s and growth in France taking off in the early 1960s.[25] Refinery expansion in West Germany first developed in the Rhine-Ruhr area in the 1950s before moving south along the Rhine and into Baden-Württemberg and Bavaria in the 1960s.

The transition from coal to oil in Western Europe required massive infrastructural investment to answer the logistical needs of transporting the growing quantities of imported oil and regional and local exchanges of fuels, feedstock and base chemicals. These infrastructural investments heavily affected local communities, as well as regional connections and as such fundamentally altered transnational relations in the Rhine basin, forging new cross-border networks of companies and infrastructures.

The implications of the pipeline infrastructure

The transition from coal to oil and the refining of oil close to regional markets had a transformational impact on transport and trade relations in the Rhine basin. First, countries in Western Europe increasingly substituted oil product imports for crude oil imports, putting a strain on the existing transport capacity and infrastructures of rail and inland navigation, which were insufficient to secure a constant flow of crude oil to inland refineries. Whereas oil product imports before World War II made for a fine-grained network of storage and distribution between seaports and inland markets, the much larger-scale transport, storage and processing of crude oil that developed from the 1950s onwards, created a supply chain of large port terminals, pipelines running inland, expanding refinery complexes and large regional storage facilities.[26] The fine-grained logistics of distribution shifted from seaports to inland markets, leading to a reduced number of storage facilities and shorter hauls between refinery or tank farms and the final customer. This stimulated the domestic trucking sectors, but introduced tough times for the international inland tank-shipping fleet on the Rhine, which was built entirely on the expanding oil product imports into Germany, France and Switzerland before and shortly after World War II.[27] As the expansions of refinery capacity during the late 1940s and 1950s were based on domestic self-sufficiency, the Rhine import trade of oil products into the Rhine border-states was reduced in relative terms. Pipelines were to take over as the main transport arteries of the oil industry and, as such, reshaped transnational transport relations in the Rhine basin. However, whereas governmental public spending facilitated the infrastructures of rails, roads and inland navigation, pipelines were mostly private investments, putting the cargo, the means of transportation and the infrastructure in the control of private firms. In that respect, the multinational oil companies were at the apex of their control over every stage of the oil industry in the 1950s and 1960s. Nevertheless, reconfiguring the infrastructure and logistics of the oil supply chain in Western Europe was far from easy. The outcome was as much shaped by economics as by the political and regulatory framework.

In the mid-1950s, oil pipelines were virtually non-existent on the West European continent, thus requiring a massive investment effort by the oil industry to build a dedicated pipeline infrastructure. Pipelines are large sunk capital investments that require a complex process of planning, coordination and regulatory compliance. Planning for pipelines was therefore undertaken simultaneously with the planning of new refinery projects. However, while refineries are typically wholly owned by a single company, pipelines are usually owned by consortia. The decision-making regarding the capacity, routeing and operation of pipelines is complex and time consuming, and pipeline economics, the regulatory framework and political considerations all play into this. As a result, pipeline decision-making processes are a window into transnational economic regions. The same barriers and constraints generally affect them. Once constructed, pipelines are a physical representation of the region, which extends as far as the interplay of transport economics and institutional, political and geographical barriers allow it to reach.

Given concentrated flows of oil, pipelines are by far the cheapest overland mode of transportation; only maritime oil tankers can be cheaper. Consequently, the structure of the supply chain of Middle Eastern crude oil to the Rhine region depended in part on the relative costs per ton-kilometre of pipelines and tankers.[28] As long as tankers remained small, pipelines offered the largest relative transport cost reductions in the supply chain. Short sea routes between the Middle East and Western Europe and long pipelines across the European continent were favoured. However, when tankers became larger and unit transport costs for sea transport lower, long sea routes no longer mattered and could even become an advantage in combination with short pipelines. This trade-off between the relative advantages of pipelines and tankers was a decisive factor in reshaping the oil transport infrastructure in the Rhine region.

Pipeline economics differ considerably from other modes of transportation because, in the case of pipelines, the transported goods move and the means of transport remain immobile. This means that pipelines can be highly efficient, but are also very inflexible. Decisions where to construct a pipeline involve a careful process of planning, in which several issues are at stake. In general, the capital costs and amortisation make up 65 per cent of the total operating costs of a pipeline.[29] The longer the pipeline, the higher the capital outlay for its construction. Due to the high share of fixed costs in a pipeline's cost structure, ton-kilometre costs do not fall with distance, unlike the position with most other transport modalities.[30] Indeed, the capacity of a pipeline is the only variable that can lower its ton-kilometre costs substantially. Increased capital costs derived from distance can be offset by increasing the diameter of a pipe, because capacity increases exponentially while the capital costs rise linearly, causing the ton-kilometre costs to fall as the capacity increases.[31] However, because fixed costs are relatively high, pipelines require a stable and continuous payload in order to be competitive and efficient. A key factor is the question of whether there is sufficient demand to warrant a continuous payload on or near the full capacity of a pipeline over the long term.[32]

As capacity and payload are the largest determinants of ton-kilometre costs, it is generally more efficient to serve a region or market with one large-diameter pipeline than with several pipelines with a smaller capacity.[33] In theory, the capacity of a pipeline is unlimited as long as there are pumps capable to increase the speed of the flow through the pipe. However, adding pumps inflates operating costs, at some point raising them faster than the amount of oil pumped through the pipe, causing ton-kilometre costs to rise again.[34] The effect of adding horsepower to the pumping capacity is higher in larger diameter pipelines than in smaller ones. The main economic problem with pipeline planning is therefore finding the optimal configuration of diameter and pumping power at the expected throughput in order to ensure the lowest possible ton-kilometre cost.[35] An additional problem is planning for sufficient spare capacity in a pipeline to allow for future growth while maintaining sufficiently low ton-kilometre costs in the first few years of its operations. This means that if a pipe from, for instance, Marseille could operate a sufficiently higher capacity pipeline to the Rhine-Ruhr area than a pipe from Rotterdam, it could be cheaper to supply crude oil from Marseille, even though the distance from Marseille to Cologne is four times longer than from Rotterdam to Cologne.

Pure pipeline economics were, however, not the only determining factor of pipeline planning. Institutional issues are just as important when it comes to understanding how and why such planning evolved historically.[36] Pipelines have a high degree of asset specificity, meaning that they are geographically fixed and dedicated to serving a limited number of users in a limited space. Beyond transporting oil from A to B, they are useless. As the capital invested in pipelines is sunk, the routeing, operation and transport tariffs need to be concluded and fixed before the pipes are actually built, especially when private capital is involved. Privately funded pipelines therefore tend to be part of vertically integrated oil companies as a way of dealing with the potentially high transaction, coordination and contracting costs.[37] However, because of the capital outlay and the efficiency of larger capacity pipelines, pipeline ownership tends to be spread among a consortium of companies.

Besides the difficulties of forming a stable and committed consortium, another source of uncertainty is government legislation and regulation. Although oil and gas pipelines are technically similar the world over, their operations, governance and regulation differ from country to country.[38] In contrast to the US, where pipeline legislation and regulation was already in place – an inheritance from the Standard Oil Trust era – in the 1950s, no pipeline legislation existed in Western Europe, let alone legislation for cross-border pipelines. The oil companies considering pipelines in Western Europe in the 1950s were therefore planning in a regulatory void, which made for considerable uncertainty. Due to the lack of legislation and regulation, it was unclear what the technical and safety requirements would be, what taxes would apply, whether transport tariffs were to be regulated or whether future legislation could impose a common carrier regime, i.e. the obligation to allow companies outside of the consortium access to the pipeline and to set non-discriminatory tariffs.

Consequently, the three main factors affecting pipeline planning in Western Europe in the 1950s emerge. The first is timing. The growth of oil consumption in the 1950s and 1960s defied the expectations of contemporaries. Indeed, the need for a larger oil processing capacity increased each consecutive year. This made it difficult to predict the optimal size and capacity of the pipeline network to balance manageable capital and transport costs in the short run with the maximum capacity and efficiency of the pipeline in the longer term. The projected refineries in the Rhine-Ruhr area were the first to start operating and therefore the first to require a pipeline connection. This could be achieved either by a limited capacity pipe that would only allow the servicing of future growth in the Rhine-Ruhr area, or by a larger diameter pipe that could be connected to other areas that were projected to expand at a later stage. The larger pipeline would ultimately have lower tariffs, but only after additional demand outside the Rhine-Ruhr area raised the load factor. This would require large capital outlays up front, while transport efficiencies would only be realised in the medium or long term, creating considerable uncertainty over tariffs and the pay-out time. Such uncertainty could draw out the planning process or lead to a delay, for which some companies might have time, while others might not, depending on their own refinery expansion schedule.

The second factor was the question of how the transport cost economies of pipelines would compare to tankers over time. Pipeline planners in the major oil companies were well aware that the trend of expanding maritime tankers could significantly alter the future pay-out and tariffs of pipelines. Moreover, the choice of a port for a pipeline's terminal was important, because a port's inability to accommodate larger tankers would severely impair the ability to set competitive tariffs and undermine the ability to realise low overall transport costs between the oil field and the refinery. The questions of how the relative transport economics of pipelines and tankers would play out and the future capacity of ports added to the uncertainty involving the timing of refinery expansions.

Legal and regulatory uncertainty because of the lack of pipeline legislation and regulation posed the third major uncertainty factor. Given the importance of stable political and legal conditions for the optimal economic functioning of pipelines, it is no surprise that the legal void and diverse political interests of governments in pre-integration Cold War Western Europe were perceived by oil companies as hurdles when it came to effective pipeline planning. It is difficult to overcome the economic uncertainties of timing and transport economies if one is uncertain that private contractual arrangements will be honoured and facilitated by politics and regulations that still had to take shape at the time.

Pipeline planning in the 1950s: reshaping the Rhine region

Pipeline plans emerged first as nationally oriented projects initiated by domestic oil companies or subsidiaries of multinational oil firms. In 1955, a consortium of West German oil companies – among them the former hydrogenation plants in the Rhine-Ruhr area – and subsidiaries of the major oil firms revealed a plan to construct a pipeline from a North Sea port to the Rhine-Ruhr area.[39] Esso AG, the German subsidiary of Standard Oil, took the lead, because its new refinery near Cologne was to be the first of the four newly planned refineries to start operating in the area in 1959. The consortium considered the North German Port of Wilhelmshaven and the Port of Rotterdam to be two possible candidates to host the pipeline terminal. Its decision-making was guided by the three constraining factors identified above. The consortium started out from the premise of selecting the seaport with the greatest potential for deep-sea expansion combined with the shortest pipeline route. Both Rotterdam and Wilhelmshaven had the potential to accommodate future tanker growth, with the former offering the shorter route. The subsidiaries of Royal Dutch Shell and BP favoured Rotterdam, because it was the shorter route and it was much more of an oil port than Wilhelmshaven, which was basically a deserted Navy port. Esso AG, which had the tightest schedule, favoured Wilhelmshaven, because it could offer the required facilities earlier than Rotterdam. Moreover, the West German federal government was interested in steering the consortium towards choosing Wilhelmshaven, because such a decision would bring economic development to this depressed area of North Germany, and because it favoured a pipeline on German soil from an economic and strategic perspective. The Federal Republic was willing to make financial and fiscal concessions in return for a decision in favour of Wilhelmshaven. Given timing and political constraints, the consortium opted for Wilhelmshaven in November 195. This was much to the dismay of Royal Dutch Shell, which had already ordered its German subsidiary out of the consortium in July 1956, and BP, which had attempted to delay the decision-making to study alternatives before committing capital to the Wilhelmshaven pipeline.

The Wilhelmshaven pipeline was one that suited the interests of the German-owned oil companies in the consortium, as they were only active on the West German market. Standard Oil had a highly decentralised organisational structure, leaving Esso AG to choose its own best solution. Royal Dutch and BP were relatively less decentralised and applied a more European perspective to pipeline planning. However, because alternatives in 1956 were at a very immature stage, BP, albeit grudgingly, chose to go along with the Wilhelmshaven consortium to ensure a pipeline connection to its Rhine-Ruhr refinery, which was due to open in 1960. Out of the majors involved, Royal Dutch Shell was in arguably the best position when it came to securing alternatives. Having established itself in the Port of Rotterdam in 1902, it had long-standing and excellent relations with Rotterdam's city council and its communal port authority. Moreover, in its attempt to convince the German consortium to choose the Rotterdam option, the company had secured the full cooperation of the Dutch government when it came to facilitating the construction of the pipeline from Rotterdam.

Having retreated from the German consortium, Royal Dutch was forced to develop alternatives, of which Rotterdam was one, although the company considered it to be the less efficient solution. Economically, a large capacity, integrated West European crude oil pipeline system made much more sense than a collection of smallish domestic pipelines. Accordingly, in mid-1956, Royal Dutch Shell established a company (Sappeur BV) to study the available options. Sappeur latched on to a French plan that had emerged in early 1956, which proposed constructing a pipeline from the Port of Marseille to Northeast France, in particular the area around Strasbourg.[40] The plan was originally launched by the Pechelbronn/Antar group, a French oil company that traced its origins to oil fields in the Alsace, which were depleted by 1956. The pipeline was to reinvigorate its operations by constructing a modern refinery that could supply Northeast France and Southwest Germany. To circumvent the high transportation costs of supplying crude oil to the new refinery over the Rhine, Pechelbronn came up with the idea of a pipeline from Marseille. Although the French plan was domestically oriented at first, Royal Dutch proposed combining it and its own Trans-European pipeline, inviting all interested oil companies to join. Marseille was a growing oil port in the Mediterranean, and Western Europe received the vast majority of its oil from the Middle East, with most of it flowing through the Mediterranean via the Suez Canal and the Trans-Arabian and Iraq Petroleum Company pipelines.[41] Moreover, exploration activities in North Africa held further promise of crude oil being available for importation into Western Europe. At the time, tankers were relatively small. In 1956, 78 per cent of the world tanker fleet consisted of vessels with a 25,000-ton carrying capacity.[42] The German pipeline consortium, however, required vessels of 45,000 tons, while ships of up to 70,000 tons had already been ordered. However, the world tanker fleet comprised just 1 per cent of ships larger than 45,000 tons, a far cry from the 165,000-ton vessels that would sail the seas a decade later.

A short sea haul combined with a single large-diameter pipeline to distribute crude oil throughout Western Europe appeared to make sense in 1956. After the Wilhelmshaven pipeline, the Marseille pipe would transform transport and trade relations in the Rhine basin. Instead of Rotterdam as its main seaport, the burgeoning oil and petrochemical clusters along the German and French Rhine would no longer be supplied from a Rhine delta port, severing an important and rapidly growing part of the existing relations between the Rhine basin and the ports in its delta.

After Royal Dutch Shell had first attempted to frustrate the decision-making in the German consortium, the company understood by November 1956 that it needed to move on with the Trans-European plan. Haste was necessary, because the pipeline depended for the first phase of its operations on the part of the demand in the Rhine-Ruhr area that was not yet committed to the Wilhelmshaven pipeline. Demand in South Germany and Northeast France was not expected to be present in earnest before 1963. Accordingly, to make the plan viable in the short run, it also required a connection to the refineries in the ports of Rotterdam and Antwerp to secure a sufficient payload for the pipeline to cover its operations between 1960 and 1963. For Royal Dutch, it was no option to delay the pipeline until 1963, because it required a pipe to its new Rhine-Ruhr refinery by 1960. It was thus operating under a clear time constraint. However, with 14 companies participating in the consortium, decision-making was highly problematic. Moreover, the lack of any legal or regulatory framework controlling pipelines, on both the national and the international level, created uncertainty over the security and vulnerability of such a transnational venture. The geopolitical situation was equally fraught, with France diverting from the transatlantic alliance and seeking its own security of supply in its North African dominions, while Italy's state-owned ENI flirted with the Soviets to capture a market share from the major oil companies in Western Europe.[43] An integrated pipeline with complete freedom of operation and fully controlled by the major oil companies could therefore also function as a formidable barrier to entry for emerging competitors such as ENI or the Soviets. In short, Royal Dutch Shell was in a hurry, but the conditions did not facilitate swift decision-making, which was further impaired by the consortium taking considerable time to devise a contractual arrangement under international law that would bind the countries along the pipeline's trajectory to respect the private character and freedom of operation of the consortium and the pipeline. Royal Dutch Shell was especially wary of potential French interference born out of its national security of supply policy and the French regional interests that were at the origin of the Marseille pipeline plan. France had a tradition of statism, also in petroleum matters, and with the petroleum law of 1928 had the legal tools to intervene in the national oil market in a major way.[44]

Economically, the Trans-European pipeline was quite clearly superior in terms of capital and operational costs than several pipelines serving the various inland markets separately, even with the Wilhelmshaven pipeline competing for custom in the Rhine-Ruhr area. However, this was a static picture. Larger tankers would reduce the difference in the unit transport costs of the sea routes to Marseille compared to the North Sea ports. This was especially so when shipments were forced around the Cape of Good Hope, for instance in the periods the Suez Canal was blocked, such as during the 1956–1957 Suez Crisis and between 1967 and 1975, or in case a tanker exceeded the Canal's capacity. Larger tankers thus offered the opportunity for more crude oil pipelines to run north to south instead of south to north. Moreover, if the Trans-European pipeline needed a branch to Rotterdam to secure a sufficient payload in the first few years, the pipe would be competing against increasingly lower tanker freight rates in the Port of Rotterdam. This would require competitive tariffs for crude oil pumped from Marseille to Rotterdam, which then needed to be offset by relatively higher tariffs between Marseille and inland destinations. This caused much concern among the smaller West German companies which, unlike Royal Dutch Shell and BP (from 1960), could not offset their higher transport costs with the lower ones enjoyed by the major operating refineries in Rotterdam. The interests and schedules of the 14 members of the consortium thus diverged considerably, while the delays and Royal Dutch's own time constraints made matters worse.

By mid-1957, it was clear that the Trans-European pipeline would not be ready by 1960, and so Royal Dutch Shell reverted to the option of building a pipe from Rotterdam to the Rhine-Ruhr area. As this pipeline would gobble up the remaining untapped demand for crude oil in the Rhine-Ruhr region, the basis for a Trans-European pipeline disappeared and, by mid-1958, the plan was dead and buried. Along with Royal Dutch Shell, the consortium continued to plan and construct the South European Pipeline (SEPL), a slimmed-down version running from Marseille to Karlsruhe in Baden-Württemberg. The failure to produce an integrated Western European pipeline system reoriented the outlook for the development of an oil infrastructure and the logistics of oil transportation in the Rhine basin. The Upper Rhine fell to the South European Pipeline PL, while a large chunk of supplies to the Rhine-Ruhr area were shipped via Wilhelmshaven. The case for a Rotterdam pipeline to the

Rhine-Ruhr thus seemed limited. Close cooperation between Royal Dutch Shell's Dutch directors and the Rotterdam Port Authority ensured, however, that the Rotterdam port's long-term development and expansion was in step with Shell's own extensive investments in the port area. The directors of Royal Dutch signalled that Rotterdam would have a major role to play in oil logistics by developing swaths of land for refineries and petrochemical plants and maintaining and expanding the facilities to receive ever-larger tankers to feed the pipeline.

In Rotterdam, the news of the decision of Royal Dutch to go through with the Rotterdam-Rhine Pipeline was received with great relief. The port authority and the municipal government had been gravely concerned that Rotterdam would lose its Rhine basin gateway function in the oil supply chain, threatening the ambitious port expansion plan, Europoort (named after its envisioned role as the gateway to Europe), which was launched in 1955. The oil and petrochemical sectors had been identified as the two biggest growth industries in both the Dutch national industrialisation plans and the port's central position within this plan. Royal Dutch had already invested heavily in the port by upgrading its Rotterdam refinery into a regional balancing plant, which was, in effect, the largest and most flexible and efficient refinery of the Shell group, and putting it at the heart of one of its largest petrochemical production facilities. The Rotterdam-Rhine Pipeline promised to add a logistical function to the port's developing industrial function, which would bring significant ship movements, and therefore revenues to the port and the city.

Nonetheless, although it abandoned the Trans-European pipeline plan in 1958, the consortium still maintained the idea of integrating the separate pipelines at a later stage. Although the Rotterdam-Rhine Pipeline secured a portion of the crude oil import flow for Rotterdam, the vision of this integrated pipeline system and competition from Marseille continued to threaten its position. However, integration never materialised. In the 1960s, crude oil pipelines to Southern Germany were constructed from the ports of Marseille, Genoa and Trieste, but none of these lines extended past Karlsruhe (Figure 5.1). The crude oil pipelines into West Germany therefore consisted of a northern and a southern system. Analogous to the term water-shed in hydrology, the divide between the northern and southern pipeline systems has been called the *oil-shed*.[45] Part of the explanation for this oil-shed is that the South European Pipeline had been constructed with a smaller diameter than envisioned for the Trans-European pipeline, reducing viability when it came to offsetting the capital costs of extending and integrating the pipeline by expanding the capacity through extra pumps. The pipeline's optimal capacity utilisation was too low to allow for competitive tariffs to Northwest Europe. This was reinforced by the growing size of tankers in the 1960s, causing unit transport costs for tankers to drop relative to those for pipelines, decreasing the spread between freight costs to Mediterranean and North Sea ports.

In addition, The Federal Republic Germany diversified its crude oil sources in the same period.[46] Until 1960, 80 per cent of its oil came from the Middle

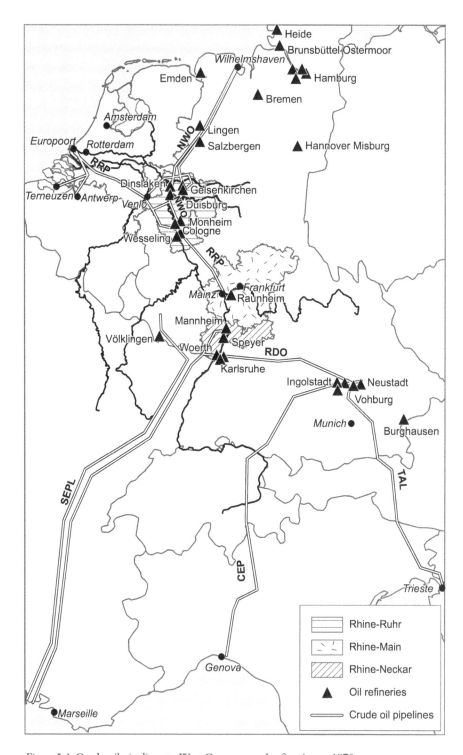

Figure 5.1 Crude oil pipelines to West Germany and refineries, c. 1970

Source: W. Molle and E. Wever, *Oil refineries and petrochemical industries in Western Europe: Buoyant past, uncertain future* (Aldershot 1984) 53, 164–168.

East. Within a decade, the Middle Eastern share had fallen to 34 per cent, as African crude oil became available from the early 1960s onwards, comprising as much as 59 per cent of West German imports in 1970. The rapid growth of North African production particularly added to the economics of expanding refinery capacity in Bavaria and other Central European regions. The oil-shed largely represented the transport economics of West Germany's crude oil import sources. In 1968, the North Sea pipelines received 46 per cent of their imports from North Africa, 37 per cent from the Middle East, 9 per cent from the Soviet Union and 4 per cent from West Africa.[47] In contrast, the Mediterranean pipelines received imports from just two sources: the Middle East (25 per cent) and North Africa (75 per cent).

The oil-shed comprised a relatively thin stretch of territory between the Rhine-Main and Rhine-Neckar areas. In theory, Frankfurt could be supplied more cheaply from Marseille than from Rotterdam by tankers up to 100,000 tons. However, by using tankers of this size or larger, Frankfurt would be supplied more cheaply via Rotterdam.[48] With the first 100,000-ton tankers rolling off the blocks in 1959, the possibility of turning the pumps in the Rotterdam-Rhine Pipeline (RRP) to bring crude oil to the Rotterdam refineries through Marseille via the Ruhr faded quickly.[49] In 1963, Caltex Deutschland, the German subsidiary of the California Texas Oil Company (a joint venture between Chevron and Texaco), constructed a refinery in Raunheim near Frankfurt.[50] The Rotterdam-Rhine Pipeline was extended in the same year to feed the Caltex refinery.[51] By then, it was clear that Rotterdam had extended its captive hinterland to the Rhine-Main area and would not have to fear competition from Marseille and the South European Pipeline anymore.[52]

The decision-making processes of the German and Trans-European pipeline consortia clearly illustrated that multinational oil companies were in the strongest position when it came to determining where, how and when pipelines were constructed. Governmental actors had attempted to influence the decision-making process, but beyond creating favourable physical and fiscal conditions, they were fairly powerless. Nevertheless, politics and the lack of a regulatory framework did create uncertainty that affected the decision-making and planning process. Nonetheless, the strong position of private companies in pipeline decision-making created considerable uncertainty and disparate possible futures for ports and industrial clusters in the Rhine basin. The German consortium had a national orientation, potentially slicing up the Rhine basin's oil infrastructure into national fractions. The Trans-European plan presented a complete integration of the Rhine basin into a wider West European infrastructure, cutting the ties between the Rhine delta and its German hinterland that was so intimate before World War II. The realisation of the Rotterdam-Rhine Pipeline was a major step in averting either scenario, because it created a symbiotic link between the position of the Port of Rotterdam as a major industrial location and a logistical hub for the oil industry in Western Europe. As such, it retained the port's position as a gateway to the Rhine basin and created opportunities for strengthening transnational connections with urban and industrial clusters along the Rhine. It also showed that the port authority in Rotterdam gained substantially from its close relations with Royal Dutch Shell, particularly in terms of information on the timing and scale of port and infrastructural development.

Strengthening transnational connections

As a logistical hub and industrial cluster, Rotterdam's port developed into the most important gateway for the Rhine basin. Even though Wilhelmshaven and Marseille provided crude oil for substantial areas in the basin, during the 1960s the transnational connections between Rotterdam and the industrial clusters in the Rhine-Ruhr, Rhine-Main and Rhine-Neckar areas were of a wider scope. Consecutive port expansions in Rotterdam between 1955 and 1973 increased the land available for industrial settlement by 400 per cent.[53] As the prized establishment of a blast furnace and steel plant never materialised, much of the newly created port area was filled with oil and petrochemical plants, with Gulf (now Kuwait Petroleum) welcomed in 1962 and BP in 1966, adding to the existing refineries of Royal Dutch Shell, Caltex and Standard Oil. During the 1960s, Rotterdam developed into Western Europe's largest concentration of refinery capacity, exporting over 50 per cent of its production across Northwest Europe.[54] The expansion of land was matched with a continuous expansion of docks and the maintenance of waterways to keep the port and refinery sites accessible for the largest crude oil tankers. Few ports in Europe could match its capacity to accommodate the very and ultra large crude carriers (VLCC and ULCC) of the late 1960s and early 1970s. The BP refinery, which had opened in Europoort in 1966, expanded from five to 15 million tons between 1969 and 1975. Royal Dutch Shell's Pernis refinery, meanwhile, went from 18 to 25 million tons and the Standard Oil refinery from eight to 16 million tons, creating some of the largest refineries in Western Europe.

In addition, between 1955 and 1966, tank storage capacity in the port more than tripled from four to over 13 million tons, and almost doubled again to 23 million tons in 1972.[55] Much of the storage capacity was owned by independents, facilitating the growing importance of the Rotterdam port as a balancing trade hub between both geographical markets and seasonal and ad hoc demand fluctuations. Based on this capacity to store and trade, an oil product spot market developed during the 1960s, increasingly setting prices for a range of oil products across Northwest European markets. The effects of Rotterdam prices ran even deeper, because the spot market connected the barge trade up the River Rhine to West Germany, Switzerland and France, while the seaborne cargo trade drew participants from as far afield as the Mediterranean, the US, the Caribbean, South America, Eastern Europe, the Soviet Union and even the east of Suez.[56]

The port facilities and the substantial export and storage capacity of the refineries and terminals in the port combined well with the Rotterdam-Rhine Pipeline and the pattern of refining and distribution in the German hinterland.

When demand for crude oil in the Rhine-Ruhr area rose rapidly in the mid-1960s, the required additional pipeline capacity fell to Rotterdam-Rhine Pipeline and not to the Wilhelmshaven pipe. The ability of the Rotterdam port to accommodate the largest tankers made additional pipeline capacity there more sensible, leading to the construction of a second, larger pipe in 1967–1968. The smaller, original pipeline was converted into an oil products version in order to connect the export refineries in Rotterdam with the rising demand for fuels and feedstock in the hinterland. As the capacity growth and technical setup of the refineries in the Rhine-Ruhr area could not keep up with rising demand and, in particular, the changing preference for lighter oil products, West German imports of oil products grew rapidly during the 1960s.[57] In addition, the growth of petrochemical production in the main Rhine clusters required increasing volumes of feedstock. Economies of scale in feedstock processing, meanwhile, caused the strong growth of a few large-scale production plants for basic petrochemicals in the chemical clusters of the Lower Rhine basin (Rotterdam-Antwerp, Rhine-Ruhr, South Netherlands).[58] The combination of growing flows of fuels and feedstock, both domestically and internationally, and the concentrated growth of refining and processing capacity, caused the development of further pipeline connections between the Rhine delta ports – including the large chemical cluster in Antwerp – and the oil and petrochemical clusters along the Rhine.

The oil products pipeline of the Rotterdam-Rhine Pipeline, which started operating in 1968, was subsequently connected to a West German products pipeline, the Rhine-Main Pipeline (RMP), established by Deutsche Shell. The name indicates its purpose: transporting fuels and feedstock to the chemical industry and consumer markets of the areas around Frankfurt am Main and Mannheim/Ludwigshafen. Given the pattern of refinery clusters and major crude oil pipelines in West Germany and Northeast France (see Figure 5.1), the German states Hesse and Rhineland Palatinate, bordering the Middle Rhine and making up the oil-shed between the northern and southern pipeline systems, had the lowest refinery capacity per capita ratio in West Germany throughout the 1960s, leaving the area's chemical industry and fuel consumers relatively undersupplied.[59] Accordingly, when in the 1960s, demand for fuel and chemical feedstock in the Rhine-Main and Rhine-Neckar areas increased, Deutsche Shell began to ponder whether to construct a new refinery near Frankfurt or to supply the area via a pipeline from Cologne.[60] Initially, the company aimed to supply growing demand in the Rhine-Neckar and Rhine-Main regions from its refinery near Strasbourg. However, the close cooperation between Deutsche Shell with BASF and the need to satisfy the latter's growing demand for petrochemical feedstock required an increasing stream of naphtha to be supplied to Ludwigshafen. Although Strasbourg was closer to Ludwigshafen than Cologne, its naphtha stream was inadequate. Accordingly, because the naphtha yield of a refinery is closely related to its size, the additional demand in Ludwigshafen was to be supplied from the Cologne refinery, which was twice the size of the Strasbourg refinery in 1965.[61] The same reason prohibited Deutsche Shell from building a refinery in the Frankfurt area, with the company opting to expand its refinery in Cologne and combine it with an oil products pipeline to serve the Middle and Upper Rhine areas.

In 1964, Deutsche Shell sett-up the Rhine-Main Pipeline Company (*Rhein-Main-Rohrleitungstransportgesellschaft*) for the construction and exploitation of an oil product pipeline between the Rhine-Ruhr, Rhine-Main and Rhine-Neckar areas. In 1965, Deutsche BP joined Deutsche Shell, because the distribution of its refinery locations was similar, with facilities in Hamburg, the Rhine-Ruhr area, Bavaria and Strasbourg, but none in the Rhine-Main and Rhine-Neckar regions. By 1967, four more companies had joined the Rhine-Main Pipeline group.[62] With the exception of Deutsche BP, the participating firms participated in the Rotterdam-Rhine Pipeline. The expansion of the two pipelines was thus closely coordinated.

Within the Rhine-Ruhr region, the Rhine-Main Pipeline (see Figure 5.2) connected the refineries of the participating companies with the area's petrochemical plants.[63] Then, within the wider Rhine basin, the Rhine-Main Pipeline connected the Rhine-Ruhr refineries with petrochemical plants in the Rhine-Neckar (Hoechst near Frankfurt) and Rhine-Main areas (BASF in Ludwigshafen). The Rhine-Main Pipeline also connected the regional tank depots of the participating companies along the Rhine at Cologne, Koblenz, Mainz, Frankfurt and Ludwigshafen. A transport contract between the Rotterdam-Rhine Pipeline and the Rhine-Main Pipeline governed the cross-border transportation of oil products. Moreover, the connection to the Rotterdam-Rhine Pipeline enabled Deutsche Shell, BP and Caltex to pump oil products from their refineries and tank depots in the Port of Rotterdam into the Rhine-Main Pipeline, creating an integrated pipeline system for oil products between Rotterdam and Ludwigshafen.

The creation of the Rhine-Main Pipeline served two purposes. First, it solved the distribution problems of the participating oil companies and thus helped to resolve the mismatch between supply and demand on the German oil markets. In the late 1950s, the growth of German oil consumption consisted primarily of heavy fuel oil. Refineries constructed between 1958 and 1965 thus aimed for a high yield of heavy fractions to serve growing demand. During the 1960s, however, demand for lighter oil products increased relative to heavier ones. This demand could be met either domestically or via imports, for instance from Rotterdam. Domestic production would also entail a higher yield of heavy fuel oil, which could be reformed into lighter products, but this required substantial refinery upgrading. In the meantime, the growing volumes of lighter oil products were therefore covered by imports, and the Rhine-Main Pipeline's connection to Rotterdam provided an efficient and secure solution. By 1971, 70 per cent of the Rhine-Main Pipeline's transported volumes consisted of imports from Rotterdam, of which 44 per cent was destined for the Frankfurt am Main area.[64] Mostly because of the Rhine-Main Pipeline, 42 per cent of Frankfurt's supplies of oil products came from Rotterdam by 1971, with the balance supplied from a disparate collection of no less than eight other refineries north and south of Frankfurt along the German Rhine.

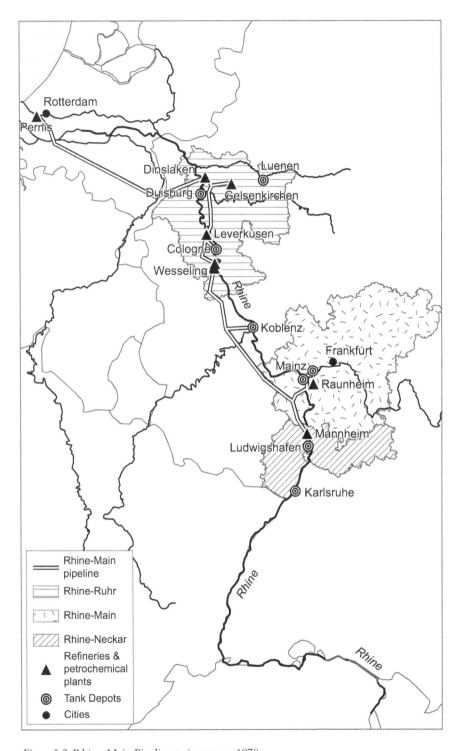

Figure 5.2 Rhine-Main Pipeline trajectory, c. 1970

Source: W. Molle and E. Wever, *Oil refineries and petrochemical industries in Western Europe: Buoyant past, uncertain future* (Aldershot 1984) 53, 164–168.

The Rhine-Main Pipeline's second purpose was to secure a continuous supply of petrochemical feedstock (naphtha) to the chemical plants of Hoechst, BASF and Bayer that dotted the Rhine between the Ruhr area in the north and Ludwigshafen in the south. The Rhine-Main Pipeline was a key piece of infrastructure to allow the rapid growth of the largest petrochemical clusters in Western Europe. So, when *Rheinische Olefinwerke* in Wesseling (ROW), which was the largest producer of basic petrochemical ethylene, expanded in 1968, it required a naphtha supply (the feedstock to produce ethylene and other basic petrochemicals) that corresponded to a crude oil distillation capacity of 20 million tons per year. The principal supplier of naphtha, Deutsche Shell's Cologne refinery, only disposed of eight million tons. The Rhine-Main Pipeline thus supplied the shortfall from Rotterdam and was therefore vital to *Rheinische Olefinwerke's* operations.[65] The situation was similar with regard to supplies to the chemical complexes of Bayer, BASF and Hoechst.

As a result, the Rhine-Main Pipeline presented significant economies of scale for the transportation of feedstock. This facilitated the further growth of petrochemical sites because it allowed for the larger naphtha crackers that provided the main source of basic petrochemicals, most importantly ethylene, which was the basis for a range of plastics. However, the trend for larger-scale refineries and naphtha crackers also made a case for the greater integration of these complexes to make them more flexible, reduce the need for expensive stock holding, lower supply and demand imbalances and reduce the disruptive effect of outages.[66] As the Rhine-Main Pipeline facilitated the smoothing out of supply and demand imbalances on the feedstock side, the exchange of basic petrochemicals such as ethylene became just as essential. On the basic petrochemical side, the West German chemical companies in the Rhine-Ruhr area took the initiative to construct an ethylene pipeline network connecting all the major producers and consumers of ethylene.[67] The pipeline added significantly to the efficient expansion of the petrochemical sector in the Rhine-Ruhr area. The *Aethylen-Rohrleitungs-Gesellschaft* (Ethylene Pipeline Company, ARG) was incorporated in 1968 by BP, the Dutch state-owned chemical company DSM and the four German chemical companies that took the initiative in 1966. In a matter of five years, ARG expanded to connect Antwerp, DSM in Limburg, the Southern Netherlands and the Rhine-Ruhr area. Around Cologne, the ARG linked up with an ethylene pipeline constructed by Hoechst, which connected in Frankfurt to a dedicated line installed by BASF and ran to Ludwigshafen. This rapidly expanding network attracted the interest of Royal Dutch Shell in 1972. It had a large petrochemical plant in Rotterdam and was developing an even larger site in Moerdijk, just south of Rotterdam. Gaining access to ARG fostered transport advantages and flexibility in the production, purchase and sale of ethylene at its two main sites, but Royal Dutch in particular saw the rationalising effect of the pipeline, as it forced participants to exchange information, coordinate investments and production slates and repair outages.

We have made a detailed study of the Northwest Europe lower olefin position and feel that a close cooperation between all ethylene producers is of utmost importance. The real key to a rationalisation in our industry lies in the opportunity to move ethylene freely through a pipeline grid and as such the initiative taken by the ARG will greatly assist the sound planning of the ethylene-based industry in Western Europe. The connection of the ARG pipeline grid in Antwerp with the DOW pipeline (later with the projected Shell pipeline) and in Wesseling with the Hoechst pipeline already gives a direct link between Rotterdam and Frankfurt. In our view, more links might be added in the future leading to extensive exchange possibilities throughout Western Europe.[68]

Although a connection to Rotterdam would not materialise until much later, nor would further expansion across Western Europe, Royal Dutch Shell clearly saw the value of the ARG as creating a unique vehicle for cooperation between the major oil and chemical companies and clusters in Northwest Europe.[69] It was this cooperation and coordination between (multinational) companies that formed the transnational connections that materialised in the pipelines of the Rotterdam-Rhine Pipeline, Rhine-Main Pipeline and ARG, providing the basis for an extraordinary collection of transnationally interconnected industrial clusters. In 1975, with the Rhine delta as its undisputed gateway for crude oil, fuels and feedstock, the clusters connected to the Rotterdam-Rhine Pipeline, Rhine-Main Pipeline and ARG systems represented 11 per cent of Western Europe's refinery capacity and 44 per cent of its ethylene production capacity.[70] Moreover, such cross-border pipelines for oil products and basic petrochemicals are unique in Western Europe, both then and now. They testify to the strong interconnected histories of urban and industrial clusters along the Rhine, in particular the Lower and Middle Rhine, and the strong transnational connections between them.

Conclusion

The chemical industry along the Rhine basin successfully switched its resource base from coal to oil over the course of the 1950s and 1960s. The cause of this transition stemmed from the sector's high level of technological advancement, its political clout and also the need for an efficient supply chain for its raw materials, primarily oil-based feedstock. The supply chain consisted of a unique, historically evolved, transnational system of pipelines for the provision and exchange of crude oil, fuels, feedstock and basic petrochemicals. This system tied together the Rhine basin's largest sea ports and their hinterlands along the Lower and Middle Rhine into a transnational conglomeration of interconnected urban and industrial agglomerations. As such, the cross-border connections that emerged from the transition to oil between some parts of the countries bordering the Rhine formed a transnational economic region. Moreover, these connections resulted from incumbent industries that formed the basis of the initial emergence of the region based on coal before 1914.

Facing the shock of World War II and the post-war struggle to recover, Western Europe embarked on a transformation of its energy balance. The replacement of domestic coal with imported oil required huge capital investments to plan and build the mid- and downstream assets for a secure supply of energy. The decision-making, the power distribution among the actors involved and the politics and economics of that planning process held the key to the question of whether the transition to oil would reinforce transnational connections in the Rhine basin or weaken them.

The decision-making process consisted of choosing *locations* for refineries and closely linked petrochemical plants on the one hand, and *trajectories* of pipelines for the supply of crude and feedstock and the distribution of fuels on the other. The major oil companies were indisputably the most powerful actors in the planning and decision-making process, which is unsurprising, given the private nature of the investments. Nevertheless, the planning and decision-making process pitted two potentially counterweighing forces against each other. Plant and storage terminal planning involved a highly localised perspective that appealed to local and national interests in terms of job creation, industrialisation and growth. Pipeline planning essentially required a transnational perspective that appealed primarily to the most efficient logistical solution for globally operating companies, partly overriding local and national interests. Indeed, the Trans-European pipeline ran into trouble because it was geared too much towards the interests of these globally operating companies. Both national governments and domestic oil companies in France and West Germany did not see their interests served by the proposed solution. The outcome was the result of perceptions of political risk and influence, a regulatory void, diverging interests among larger and smaller oil companies, different regional growth patterns and the rapidly changing economics of transporting oil.

The Wilhelmshaven and Trans-European pipelines both threatened to cut off the Port of Rotterdam from developing a similar gateway position in the Rhine basin as it had for coal, iron ore and other bulk commodities before World War II. However, as the Trans-European plan faded away, Rotterdam came back into the picture. The ensuing rapid growth of Western European oil consumption, economies of scale in the transportation and processing of oil and the fixed nature of the assets involved made the decision of Royal Dutch Shell to invest in the Rotterdam-Rhine Pipeline enormously consequential for the Port of Rotterdam and the oil and petrochemical sector in the Lower and Middle Rhine areas. Consecutive investments in capacity expansions in the hinterland required similar investments in port and transport infrastructure, increasingly concentrating oil logistics in the Lower and Middle Rhine area and transnationally integrating Rhine delta ports and their hinterland.

This historical process of change was primarily driven by changes to the macro-economic layer of our port-hinterland model. The new post-war US energy order, skilfully infused in European reconstruction and cooperation through the occupation of Germany and the European Recovery Programme, set the stage for the transition from coal to oil. This was reinforced in West Germany with the liberalisation of oil imports in the mid-1950s.

The transition gave rise to investments in a massive expansion of European refinery capacity, the localisation of which was largely determined by market access. Supply chain considerations came second. That the Lower and Middle Rhine region inherited a large market and an adaptable incumbent chemical industry was, in that respect, very important. Once long-term capital investments in processing plants started to pan out in the mid-1950s, huge investments were poured into infrastructure and transport capacity. Due to the economies of scale, the high sunk capital, asset specificity and the fixity of pipelines, the decision-making on the physical hinterland level strongly determined and restricted the range of logistical options for the actual flow of crude oil, fuels, feedstock and basic petrochemicals to and within the region. In other words, the long-term investment profile of both refineries and their supply infrastructure made for a durable, stable and highly dense integration of economic relations in the Lower and Middle Rhine region. This was primarily driven by change on the macro-economic and physical, and not the logistical level. In terms of actors, there was a strong supply push by the Rotterdam Port Authority to valorise the location and facilities of the Port of Rotterdam. These efforts were sometimes frustrated, either by nationalistic transport policies in West Germany or by the diverging logistical demands of the oil companies, particularly in the early stages of development. By the early 1950s, the port had already attained a good position as a refining hub, but its logistical function received a major boost with the Rotterdam-Rhine Pipeline, and here the major oil companies, in particular Royal Dutch Shell, were in a dominant position.

In conclusion, the years of transition to oil were both a period of continuity and fundamental change for the transnational connections in the Lower Rhine region. It was certainly a phase of change in terms of infrastructure, with a major new role for pipeline transportation. Fundamental change also occurred in the energy balance and economic structure of the region with the collapse of the coal industry and the growth of the oil and petrochemical sectors. However, it was also a period of continuity, perhaps even path-dependent continuity. The crucial link between the era of coal and the epoch of oil was the economic geography of the incumbent chemical and synthetic fuel plants in the region. The era of coal had given rise to chemical and synthetic fuel clusters along the Rhine that utilised the availability of abundant coal-based feedstock and cheap water transportation. As these clusters switched to oil after World War II, they provided a locational pull for oil refineries, essentially replicating a pre-existing economic geography dictated by the River Rhine. However, the necessary pipeline infrastructure to serve these burgeoning oil and petrochemical clusters did not follow a similar logic to the path-dependent economic geography of *locations*. As a consequence, path-dependent locations did not automatically translate into continuity in the *transnational connections* in the region. Pipelines were not determined by the trajectory of the Rhine and could connect any sufficiently tooled West European port to the refineries in the Rhine basin, which they in fact did. It was rather fortuitous that a pipeline connection from Rotterdam to the Rhine-Ruhr area materialised, but, once it had, the transnational port-hinterland relations in the Lower Rhine region experienced a renewed period of strong growth and integration.

Epilogue – after the golden age of growth

The post-war period of growth ended abruptly in 1973–1974. The first oil-price shock reverberated around the globe, resulting in a prolonged period of inflation, recession and rising unemployment in developed countries. This was only exacerbated by the second oil-price shock of 1979. Demand for oil contracted, especially after 1979. Major investments in the European refinery sector undertaken in the late 1960s and early 1970s were suddenly redundant, and many refineries and oil pipelines operated well under their full capacity throughout the 1980s. In this period, at least 10 per cent of the refinery capacity in Western Europe shut down, including three refineries in the Rhine-Ruhr area.[71] Economic revival in the 1990s and 2000s helped to alleviate the dire situation of the European refining sector somewhat, but growth rates remained low, starving the sector of the necessary investment required to upgrade. Oil companies have divested their smaller refineries in Europe or have withdrawn from the European refining sector altogether.[72] The transition to a low-carbon economy and the US shale revolution are adding to the gloom. The low-carbon transition is a long-term threat. Even though oil is not a key fuel for power production, the rise of electric vehicles might, in the long term, depress demand for motor fuels, although there seems to be some consensus that oil companies will have a significant role to play in the coming decades.[73] The shale revolution in the US, with its use of a high proportion of very light crude oil, could however seriously disrupt the export of surplus gasoline and naphtha from Europe, depressing the market environment for European refiners in the medium term.[74] Moreover, since the 1980s, the competition from refineries in oil producing countries has increased considerably. The national oil companies of major oil exporters have invested heavily in modern, large-scale refinery complexes to complement their revenues from crude oil exports with exports of refined oil products. The relatively small and dated European refineries struggle to compete with the growing volume of competitive oil products available for importation from countries like Saudi Arabia and other exporters.

Although oil appears to be playing a major ongoing role in the future energy balance, the sector faces a very difficult future in Europe, particularly the refining sector that underpins the integrated complex of oil and petrochemical clusters in the Lower Rhine region. Nonetheless, the high level of regional integration between the refining clusters in the Lower Rhine area appears to put the region in a relatively good position when it comes to remaining viable, particularly because of the competitive transport costs of the pipeline infrastructure and the high level of integration of the refineries with the region's petrochemicals sector. A recent study on the restructuring of the European refining sector found the refineries in the Lower Rhine region to be among those most likely to continue operating profitably in the future.[75] In the study's most extreme scenario, just 12 of the current 34 refineries in Northwest Europe are deemed strong enough to withstand competition from imports, seven of which are located in the Rhine Delta and the Rhine-Ruhr areas.[76] These seven Lower Rhine refineries face a brighter future than most other Northwest European refineries, because of the world-scale competitiveness of the petrochemical clusters they are integrated with. This is in turn the result of the transnational integration described in this chapter. The competitiveness of the region is also reflected in the continued importance of the Port of Rotterdam for the transhipment of oil flows to and within Northwest Europe. The port, although hit very hard by the decline after the 1970s oil shocks, has maintained a very strong position in the transhipment of crude oil and oil products, handling 50 per cent of all oil transhipped in the Hamburg-Le Havre range in 2011.[77] Moreover, whereas European consumption has been stable since 1999 and declining after 2008, the throughput of oil in Rotterdam has increased continuously over the same period: from 116 million tons in 1999 to 192 million tons in 2015, an annual growth rate of 3 per cent.[78] However, oil products made up an increasing proportion, from 19 per cent in 1999 to 46 per cent in 2015, reflecting the rising competitiveness of imported oil products on the European market. Rotterdam's hinterland transport connections (particularly the Rhine and the pipelines), which connect the port with a large hinterland market, will continue to secure Rotterdam's position in the European oil supply chain, which is a position that is supported by its role as a trading hub based on the strong independent storage sector.

In conclusion, even though the European refining industry faces a gloomy outlook, the oil and petrochemical sector in the Lower Rhine region appears to have a brighter future. A world class port, deep integration between refining and petrochemicals and a competitive transnational infrastructure linking the various clusters in the area set the stage for continued investment in the region's oil and petrochemical sectors. Indeed, in late 2015, Royal Dutch Shell and Exxon announced a plan to invest a combined € 1 billion in their refineries.[79] This will sustain for some time to come the transnational economic connections that have been forged in the three decades between 1945 and 1973. However, oil will never be a growth sector in Europe again and is very likely to decline increasingly rapidly. Although the Lower Rhine region will remain competitive based on its world class petrochemical sector, the petrochemical feedstock stream represents only up to 15 per cent of the production slate of a refinery. A declining demand for oil will therefore inevitably affect the Rotterdam refinery cluster. Meanwhile, the Rotterdam Port Authority faces the challenge of managing the decline in the coming decades, including the very real scenario of refinery closures, which would have unfolded for the Kuwait Petroleum Europoort refinery if it had not been acquired by the global oil trader Gunvor in 2016.[80] Nonetheless, three of Rotterdam's five refineries are deemed too weak to withstand competition from imports in the medium term.[81] Ultimately, the reality of the transition to a low-carbon economy will catch up with the Port of Rotterdam and force it to face the challenge of refinery closures, with the associated loss of jobs and the staggering costs of the full conversion and redevelopment of refinery sites.[82] Nonetheless, with its ready access to the large markets of the Rhine basin, and as long as hydrocarbon fuels remain a considerable part of the European energy balance, Rotterdam will continue to enjoy a strong position as a logistical and trading hub.

Notes

1 R.G. Stokes, *Opting for Oil: The Political Economy of Technological Change in the West German Chemical Industry, 1945–1961*, Vol. 1 (Cambridge: Cambridge University Press, 1994), 322.
2 David S. Painter, "Oil and the Marshall Plan," *Business History Review* 58, no. 3 (1984): 361.
3 W. Abelshauser, *Der Ruhrkohlenbergbau seit 1945: Wiederaufbau, Krise, Anpassung* (München: Beck, 1984), 16, 20.
4 Daniel Yergin, *The Prize: The Epic Quest for Oil, Money and Power* (London: Pocket Books, 1993), 424.
5 Painter, "Oil and the Marshall Plan," 362.
6 Ibid., 362–363.
7 Ibid., 364–370.
8 Ibid., 372–375.
9 R. Karlsch and R.G. Stokes, *Faktor Öl: Die Mineralölwirtschaft in Deutschland, 1859–1974* (München: Beck, 2003), 255.
10 Stokes, *Opting for Oil*, 47; Raymond G. Stokes, *Divide and Prosper: The Heirs of I.G. Farben under Allied Authority 1945–1951* (Berkeley, CA: University of California Press, 1988), 172.
11 Calculated from data provided by: Mineralölwirtschaftsverband e.V., "Rohöldestillation-sanlagen nach Bundesländern 1950–2009, Atmospärische Destillation," in *Jahresbericht Mineralölzahlen 2009*, 27, www.mwv.de/upload/Publikationen/dateien/2009_JB_KL763hj1mjg3LYm.pdf, retrieved on 11 January 2013.
12 P. Dolata-Kreutzkamp, *Die Deutsche Kohlenkrise im Nationalen und transatlantischen Kontext* (Wiesbaden: VS, Verl. für Sozialwiss, 2006), 11–12; Abelshauser, *Der Ruhrkohlenbergbau*, 90; A. Plitzko, *Bemerkungen zu den Wettbewerbsbedingungen zwischen Kohle und Erdöl* (Cologne and Opladen: Westdeutscher Verlag, 1960), 47; E. Neuffer, *Der Wettbewerb zwischen Steinkohle und Heizöl auf dem westdeutschen Energiemarkt: unter Berücksichtigung der übrigen Energieträger und unter Berücksichtigung der ausländischen Energiemärkte* (Tübingen: Eberhard-Karls-Universität zu Tübingen, 1960), 80.
13 Quoted in: Manfred Horn, *Die Energiepolitik der Bundesregierung von 1958 bis 1972. Zur Bedeutung der Penetration ausländischer Ölkonzerne in die Energiewirtschaft der BRD für die Abhängigkeit interner Strukturen und Entwicklungen* (Berlin: Duncker und Humblot, 1977), 201. Original quote: "Die von uns geförderte Konkurrenz der Energieträger untereinander wird auf die Dauer zu einer besseren und wirtschaftlichen Energieversorgung führen."
14 F. Spiegelberg, *Energiemarkt im Wandel: 10 Jahre Kohlenkrise an der Ruhr* (Baden-Baden: Nomos-Verlagsgesellschaft, 1970), 41.
15 C. Nonn, *Die Ruhrbergbaukrise: Entindustrialisierung und Politik 1958–1969* (Göttingen: Vandenhoeck und Ruprecht, 2001), 37–39; Neuffer, *Der Wettbewerb*, 60.
16 W. Molle and E. Wever, *Oil Refineries and Petrochemical Industries in Europe: Buoyant Past, Uncertain Future* (Aldershot: Gower Press, 1984), 164–169; Plitzko, *Bemerkungen zu den Wettbewerbsbedingungen zwischen Kohle und Erdöl*, 27; Neuffer, *Der Wettbewerb*, 91–92.
17 Shell Historical Archive, The Hague (SHA), Manufacturing Department (MF), inv. 48, Installations/Germany/Godorf, "Budget Revision, Return no. 513," 15 March 1957, 2.
18 SHA, inv. 82, nr. 129, Verhouding BPM en ROW, "Agreement Deutsche Shell-Badische, Article 12," October 1953.
19 M. Boon, *Multinational Business and Transnational Regions: A Transnational Business History of Energy Transition in the Rhine Region, 1945–1973* (New York: Routledge, 2018), 86–92.

20 Stokes, *Opting for Oil*, 1, 248.

21 Ibid., passim.

22 Roberto Cantoni, *Oily Deals: Exploration, Diplomacy and Security in Early Cold War France and Italy* (Manchester: University of Manchester, 2014), 193–232; Molle and Wever, *Oil Refineries*, passim; D. Mittmann, *Die Chemische Industrie Im Nordwestlichen Mittel-Europa in Ihrem Strukturwandel* (Wiesbaden: Steiner, 1974), passim.

23 Molle and Wever, "Oil Refineries and Petrochemical Industries in Europe," *GeoJournal* 9, no. 4 (1984): 424–425; M. Hubbard, *The Economics of Transporting Oil to and within Europe* (London: MacLaren & Sons Ltd, 1967), 2–3; Peter P. Waller and Harry S. Swain, "Changing Patterns of Oil Transportation and Refining in West Germany," *Economic Geography* 43, no. 2 (1967): 146–148.

24 Own calculations based on Molle and Wever, *Oil Refineries*, 164–169. The countries included are Great Britain, West Germany, France, Italy, Spain, Portugal, Switzerland, the Netherlands, Sweden, Denmark, Norway, Finland, Austria, Ireland and Belgium.

25 Italy had a similar expansion in inland locations, but its implications for the pipeline infrastructure were less severe than in France and West Germany. Being land-locked, Switzerland and Austria developed several inland refineries, but in the Swiss case, these were fairly small, while in Austria some were based on crude oil supplies from domestic oil fields.

26 P. Kirschnick, *Der Wandel in Der ökonomischen Bedeutung der grossen europäischen Seehäfen im 20. Jahrhundert* (Kiel: University of Kiel, 1969), 72–77; Rolf Oldewage, *Die Nordseehäfen im EWG-Raum: Fakten Und Probleme: Hamburg, Bremen, Wilhelmshafen, Emden, Amsterdam, Rotterdam, Antwerpen, Gent und Dünkirchen* (Basel: Kyklos-Verlag, 1963), 87.

27 Boon, *Multinational Business*, 190–192.

28 G. Manners, "The Pipeline Revolution," *Geography* 47 (1962): 157–159.

29 Ibid.

30 Ibid.

31 J.D. Makholm, *The Political Economy of Pipelines* (Chicago IL: University of Chicago Press, 2012), 29; Manners, "The Pipeline Revolution," 159–160.

32 Manners, "The Pipeline Revolution," 159.

33 Makholm, *The Political Economy of Pipelines*, 29.

34 J.R. Meyer, et al., *The Economics of Competition in the Transportation Industries* (Cambridge, MA: Harvard University Press, 1976), 130–131.

35 Ibid., 126.

36 Makholm, *The Political Economy of Pipelines*, 30.

37 Ibid., 4–6.

38 Ibid., 1–3.

39 Boon, *Multinational Business*, 103–105.

40 Ibid., 140–141.

41 F. Mayer, *Erdöl Weltatlas* (Braunschweig: Georg Westermann Verlag, 1966), 122–123.

42 Royal Dutch/Shell, *The Petroleum Handbook* (London: Shell International Petroleum Company Ltd, 1966), 252–253.

43 M. Boon, "Political Risk in Cold War France: The Case of the Trans-European Pipeline, 1956–1960," in *From Total War to Cold War: International Business and Organisational Innovation*, ed. N. Forbes, T. Kurosawa, and B. Wubs (New York: Routledge, forthcoming); Cantoni, *Oily Deals*, 209 ff.

44 Harvey B. Feigenbaum, *The Politics of Public Enterprise: Oil and the French State* (Princeton, NJ: Princeton University Press, 1985), 37–39.

45 Molle and Wever, *Oil Refineries*, 49.

46 Mineralölwirtschaftsverband e.V., *Jahresbericht 2009*, 41.

47 Own calculations based on data of Werner Pruskil, *Geographie Und Staatsmonopolistischer Kapitalismus: Zu den Auswirkungen auf die Standortverteilung der erdölverarbeitenden Industrie Westdeutschlands* (Gotha: VEB Haack, 1971), 156–175.

48 Hubbard, *The Economics of Transporting Oil*, 29.

148   *Marten Boon*

49 J. Brennecke, *Tanker: Vom Petroleumklipper zum Supertanker* (Herford: Koehler, 1980), 149.
50 E. Riffel, *Mineralöl-Fernleitungen im Oberrheingebiet und in Bayern* (Bonn-Bad Godesberg: Bundesforschungsanstalt für Landeskunde und Raumordnung, 1970), 150.
51 RRP NV, *'58–'98 Veertig jaar veilig en verantwoord transport* (Den Haag: RRP NV, 1998), 14.
52 Stadsarchief Rotterdam (SAR), AHB, 589.01, inv. 4261, L. Cohen, "Study into the consequences of the transportation by pipelines of crude oil and oil products in Europe for Rotterdam port traffic and the Rotterdam port as a location for refineries and petrochemical companies"; undated, but probably produced in 1965, 38.
53 Dirk Koppenol, *Lobby for Land: A Historical Perspective (1945–2008) on the Decision-Making Process for the Port of Rotterdam Land Reclamation Project Maasvlakte 2* (Rotterdam: Erasmus University, 2016), 53.
54 Boon, *Multinational Business*, 156; Molle and Wever, *Oil Refineries*, 60–61.
55 Figures kindly provided by Hugo van Driel. Sources: Kamer van Koophandel en Fabrieken, Rotterdam, *Jaarverslag* (Rotterdam: Kamer van Koophandel, 1946–1970); *Dirkzwager's Guide to the New Waterway* (Rotterdam and Dordrecht: 't Hooft, 1949).
56 E. Abunura, "The Structure of the Spot Oil Market and Its Implications for Sudan's Marketing Policy" (MA-Thesis, Institute of Social Studies, Rotterdam, 1984), 44 ff, http://hdl.handle.net/2105/13198, retrieved on 30 April 2019; J. Roeber, "The Rotterdam Oil Market," *Petroleum Economist* 26 (1979): 1–8.
57 Boon, *Multinational Business*, 63–9, 161–167.
58 Molle and Wever, *Oil Refineries*, 88–89.
59 With 0.4 and 0.7 million tons of refinery capacity per 1,000 inhabitants, Hessen and the Rhineland Palatinate had a significantly lower local oil product supply than the West German average of 1.3 million tons in 1965. In 1970, the gap was even larger. Own calculations using population data from J. Sensch, "Bevölkerungsstand, Bevölkerungsbewegung, Haushalte und Familien in der Bundesrepublik Deutschland, 1947 Bis 1999," Histat-Datenkompilation online (Cologne: GESIS, 2007). Refinery data from Molle and Wever, *Oil Refineries*, 164–169.
60 Riffel, *Mineralöl-Fernleitungen*, 114; E. Bockelmann, H.J. Burchard, and H. Streicher, "Ursachen und Wirkungen der veränderten Standortstruktur der Mineralölraffinerien in der Bundesrepublik Deutschland," *Brennstoff – Wärme – Kraft* 20 (1968): 356–361; H.J. Burchard, "Neuere Entwicklungen im Rohrleitungstransport," *Erdöl und Kohle – Erdgas – Petrochemie* 18 (1965): 1008.
61 Molle and Wever, *Oil Refineries*, 165–169; Riffel, *Mineralöl-Fernleitungen*, 114.
62 *Mineralöl-Fernleitungen*, 115. The company's shares were divided between Deutsche Shell AG (55 per cent), Deutsche BP AG (29), Chevron Erdöl Deutschland GmbH (5), Texaco Oel GmbH (5), Gelsenkirchener Bergwerks AG (4) and Mobil Oil AG (2).
63 Ibid., 116.
64 Boon, *Multinational Business*, 192–197.
65 "Die ROW als Beispiel fruchtbarer Zusammenarbeit zwischen Mineralöl- und chemischer Industrie," *Erdöl und Kohle, Erdgas, Petrochemie* 22 (1969): 11, 721–723.
66 M.F. Cantley, *The Scale of Ethylene Plants: Background and Issues* (Laxenburg: International Institute for Applied Systems Analysis, 1979), 17, 33–34; A. Melamid, "The European Ethylene Pipeline System," *The Professional Geographer* 22 (1970): 326–328.
67 Bayer Archive Leverkusen (BAL), 369–203, ARG, Memo Farbenfabrik Bayer AG, "Aktennotiz betr.: Äthylenverbund, Besprechung in Hüls," 25 October 1966. Besides Bayer, representatives from three major chemical plants in the Rhine-Ruhr area took part: Chemische Werke Hüls, Scholven Chemie and Erdölchemie Dormagen (50/50 Bayer and BP).
68 BAL 369–203, ARG, Shell International Chemie Maatschappij N.V. to Farbenfabriken Bayer AG, "Membership Aethylen Rohrleitungs Gesellschaft," 28 December 1971.
69 Kenneth Bertrams, Nicolas Coupain, and Ernst Homburg, *Solvay: History of a Multinational Family Firm* (Cambridge: Cambridge University Press, 2012), 367.
70 Own calculations based on data reported in Molle and Wever, *Oil Refineries*, 164–169, 172.

71 Pierre Drouet, "The Restructuring of the Petroleum Refining Sector and Its Social Consequences," *International Labour Review* 123 (1984): 423–440; Molle and Wever, *Oil Refineries*, 185.
72 Concawe, "Developments in Eu Refining: Looking Ahead to 2020 and Beyond," *Concawe Review* 23 (2014): 4–7.
73 Aad Correljé, et al., *Transition? What Transition? Changing Energy Systems in an Increasingly Carbon Constrained World* (The Hague: Clingendael International Energy Programme, 2014), 12.
74 Amrita Sen, *US Tight Oils: Prospects and Implications* (Oxford: Oxford Institute for Energy Studies, 2013), 34.
75 Robbert van den Bergh, Michiel Nivard, and Maurits Kreijkes, *Long-Term Prospects for Northwest European Refining: Asymmetric Change: A Looming Government Dilemma?* (The Hague: Clingendael International Energy Programme, 2016).
76 Ibid., 30.
77 Rotterdam Port Authority, "Port Statistics 2011," 3.
78 Data sources: Database on cargo flows in the Port of Rotterdam, 1880–2000, persistent identifier urn:nbn:nl:ui:13-n6w-g4s, accessed 13 October 2009; Port Authority Rotterdam, *Tijdreeks Goederenoverslag Rotterdamse haven 1989–2015*; BP *Statistical Review of World Energy* 2015.
79 "Haven Rotterdam moet het dit jaar hebben van fossiele brandstoffen," *Het Financieele Dagblad*, 8 December 2015.
80 "Gunvor Acquires Rotterdam Refinery," *Oil & Gas Journal* (2 February 2016), www.ogj.com/articles/2016/02/gunvor-acquires-rotterdam-refinery.html, retrieved on 25 November 2016.
81 Van den Bergh, Nivard, and Kreijkes, "Long-Term Prospects for Northwest European Refining," 31.
82 Ibid., 43 ff.

Bibliography

Abelshauser, W. (1984), *Der Ruhrkohlenbergbau seit 1945: Wiederaufbau, Krise, Anpassung* (München: Beck).
Abunura, E. (1984), "The structure of the spot oil market and its implications for Sudan's marketing policy" (MA-Thesis, Institute of Social Studies).
Bertrams, Kenneth, Nicolas Coupain, and Ernst Homburg (2012), *Solvay: History of a Multinational Family Firm* (Cambridge: Cambridge University Press).
Bockelmann, Erwin, Hans-Joachim Burchard, and Heinz Streicher (1968), "Ursachen und Wirkungen der Veränderten Standortstruktur der Mineralölraffinerien in der Bundesrepublik Deutschland." *Brennstoff – Wärme – Kraft* 20, no. 8: 356–361.
Boon, Marten (2018a), *Multinational Business and Transnational Regions: A Transnational Business History of Energy Transition in the Rhine Region, 1945–1973* (New York: Routledge).
Boon, Marten (2018b), "Political risk in cold war France: The case of the trans-European pipeline, 1956–1960." In *From Total War to Cold War: International Business and Organisational Innovation*, edited by N. Forbes, T. Kurosawa and B. Wubs, 196–213 (New York: Routledge).
Brennecke, Jochen (1980), *Tanker: Vom Petroleumklipper Zum Supertanker* (Herford: Koehler).
Burchard, Hans-Joachim (1965), Neuere Entwicklungen im Rohrleitungstransport." *Erdöl und Kohle – Erdgas – Petrochemie* 18, no. 11: 1008.
Cantley, Mark F. (1979), *The Scale of Ethylene Plants: Background and Issues* (Laxenburg: International Institute for Applied Systems Analysis).
Cantoni, Roberto (2014), *Oily Deals: Exploration, Diplomacy and Security in Early Cold War France and Italy* (Manchester: University of Manchester).

Correljé, Aad, et al. (2014), *Transition? What Transition? Changing Energy Systems in an Increasingly Carbon Constrained World* (The Hague: Clingendael International Energy Programme). "Developments in Eu Refining: Looking Ahead to 2020 and Beyond." *Concawe Review* 23, no. 1 (2014): 4–7.

Dolata-Kreutzkamp, Petra (2006), *Die Deutsche Kohlenkrise im nationalen und transatlantischen Kontext* (Wiesbaden: VS, Verein für Sozialwissenschaft).

Drouet, Pierre (1984), "The restructuring of the petroleum refining sector and its social consequences." *International Labour Review* 123, no. 4: 423–440.

Feigenbaum, Harvey B. (1985), *The Politics of Public Enterprise: Oil and the French State* (Princeton, NJ: Princeton University Press).

Horn, Manfred (1977), *Die Energiepolitik der Bundesregierung von 1958 bis 1972: Zur Bedeutung der Penetration ausländischer Ölkonzerne in die Energiewirtschaft der BRD für die Abhängigkeit interner Strukturen und Entwicklungen* (Berlin: Duncker und Humblot).

Hubbard, Michael Edmund (1967), *The Economics of Transporting Oil to and within Europe* (London: MacLaren & Sons Ltd).

Karlsch, Rainer, and Raymond G. Stokes (2003), *Faktor Öl: Die Mineralölwirtschaft in Deutschland, 1859–1974* (München: Beck).

Kirschnick, Peter (1969), *Der Wandel in der ökonomischen Bedeutung der grossen europäischen Seehäfen im 20. Jahrhundert* (Kiel: University of Kiel).

Koppenol, Dirk (2016), *Lobby for Land: A Historical Perspective (1945–2008) on the Decision-Making Process for the Port of Rotterdam Land Reclamation Project Maasvlakte 2* (Rotterdam: Erasmus University).

Makholm, Jeffrey D. (2012), *The Political Economy of Pipelines* (Chicago, IL: University of Chicago Press).

Manners, Gerald (1962), "The pipeline revolution." *Geography* 47: 154–163.

Mayer, Ferdinand (1966), *Erdöl Weltatlas* (Braunschweig: Georg Westermann Verlag).

Melamid, Alexander (1970), "The European ethylene pipeline system." *The Professional Geographer* 22, no. 6: 326–328.

Meyer, John R., Merton J. Peck, John Stenason, and Charles Zwick (1976), *The Economics of Competition in the Transportation Industries* (Cambridge, MA: Harvard University Press).

Mittmann, Detlef (1974), *Die chemische Industrie im Nordwestlichen Mittel-Europa in ihrem Strukturwandel* (Wiesbaden: Steiner).

Molle, Willem, and Egbert Wever (1984a), "Oil refineries and petrochemical industries in Europe." *GeoJournal* 9, no. 4: 421–430.

Molle, Willem, and Egbert Wevers (1984b), *Oil Refineries and Petrochemical Industries in Europe: Buoyant Past, Uncertain Future* (Aldershot: Gower Press).

Neuffer, Ernst (1960), *Der Wettbewerb zwischen Steinkohle und Heizöl auf dem westdeutschen Energiemarkt: Unter Berücksichtigung der übrigen Energieträger und unter Berücksichtigung der ausländischen Energiemärkte* (Tübingen: Eberhard-Karls-Universität zu Tübingen).

Nonn, Christoph (2001), *Die Ruhrbergbaukrise: Entindustrialisierung und Politik 1958–1969* (Göttingen: Vandenhoeck und Ruprecht).

Oldewage, Rolf (1963), *Die Nordseehäfen im EWG-Raum: Fakten und Probleme: Hamburg, Bremen, Wilhelmshafen, Emden, Amsterdam, Rotterdam, Antwerpen, Gent und Dünkirchen* (Basel: Kyklos-Verlag).

Painter, David S. (1984), "Oil and the Marshall plan." *Business History Review* 58, no. 3: 359–383.

Plitzko, Alfred (1960), *Bemerkungen zu den Wettbewerbsbedingungen zwischen Kohle und Erdöl* (Cologne and Opladen: Westdeutscher Verlag).

Pruskil, Werner (1971), *Geographie und staatsmonopolistischer Kapitalismus: Zu den Auswirkungen auf die Standortverteilung der erdölverarbeitenden Industrie Westdeutschlands* (Gotha: VEB Haack).

Riffel, Egon (1970), *Mineralöl-Fernleitungen Im Oberrheingebiet Und in Bayern* (Bonn-Bad Godes-berg: Bundesforschungsanstalt für Landeskunde und Raumordnung).

Roeber, Joe (1979), "The Rotterdam oil market." *Petroleum Economist* (April): 1–15.

Royal Dutch/Shell (1985), *The Petroleum Handbook* (London: Shell International Petroleum Company Ltd).

RRP NV (1998), *'58–'98 Veertig jaar veilig en verantwoord transport* (The Hague: RRP NV).

Sen, Amrita. (2013), "Us tight oils: Prospects and implications" (Oxford: Oxford Institute for Energy Studies).

Sensch, Jürgen (2007), *Bevölkerungsstand, Bevölkerungsbewegung, Haushalte und Familien in der Bundesrepublik Deutschland, 1947 bis 1999* (Cologne: GESIS).

Spiegelberg, Friedrich (1970), *Energiemarkt Im Wandel: Zehn Jahre Kohlenkrise an der Ruhr* (Baden-Baden: Nomos-Verlagsgesellschaft).

Stokes, Raymond G. (1988), *Divide and Prosper: The Heirs of I.G. Farben under Allied Author-ity 1945–1951* (Berkeley CA: University of California Press).

Stokes, Raymond G. (1994), *Opting for Oil: The Political Economy of Technological Change in the West German Chemical Industry, 1945–1961* (Cambridge: Cambridge University Press).

Van den Bergh, Robbert, Michiel Nivard, and Maurits Kreijkes (2016), *Long-Term Prospects for Northwest European Refining. Asymmetric Change: A Looming Government Dilemma?* (The Hague: Clingendael International Energy Programme).

Waller, Peter P., and Harry S. Swain (1967), "Changing patterns of oil transportation and refining in West Germany." *Economic Geography* 43, no. 2: 143–156.

Yergin, Daniel. (1993), *The Prize: The Epic Quest for Oil, Money and Power* (London: Pocket Books).

Archives

Shell Historical Archive, The Hague (SHA).
Bayer Archive Leverkusen (BAL).
Stadsarchief Rotterdam (SAR).

6 Port competition and the containerisation of hinterland transport, 1966–2010

Klara Paardenkooper

Introduction

Containerisation is a spectacular phenomenon, and has been pinpointed by some as the most important invention of the 20th century and one of the causes of globalisation.[1] It has certainly had a major impact on the Lower Rhine region. On the maritime side of the port, container transport meant that Rotterdam joined the globalising economy by linking it to growing worldwide networks, thereby connecting production and consumption within the Lower Rhine region to global economic processes. On the hinterland side of the port, containerisation caused an initial loosening of the ties between the Port of Rotterdam and its Lower Rhine hinterland area until the 1990s, followed by increasing integration. This chapter explains the roles of the most important actors and forces with respect to these processes and discusses the following three research questions:

1 How did maritime container transport develop between Rotterdam and its hinterland areas compared to the German ports?
2 Which activities generated the transport flows in the hinterland?
3 What kind of effect did container transport have on the competitive position of the Port of Rotterdam?

In this chapter, economic integration is quantified as networks, which are defined as connections created by flows of goods, people and information.[2] It is assumed that economic integration causes network growth – in this case, the growth of transport networks in the Lower Rhine region. To determine the effect of containerisation on transport networks in this area, network growth within the region is compared to the relative growth of transport networks in other geographical locations. The chapter therefore not only analyses the network dynamics within the Lower Rhine region, but also its ratio to network connections with respect to other relevant hinterland areas. The chapter considers two regional scenarios for the effect of containerisation on the transport network within the Lower Rhine region. On the one hand, globalisation causes the growth of the worldwide transport network relative to the network density in the region. On the other, regionalisation is defined here as the intensification of network connections within a region relative to the outside world.

The first section discusses the phenomenon of containerisation and its introduction and economic effects in the Lower Rhine region. The second analyses the container flows between the Port of Rotterdam and its hinterland and the competition from other West European ports. Section three discusses container flows in the context of the deindustrialisation of the German Ruhr area and its consequences for transport network integration and port competition in the Lower Rhine region. Section four concludes the chapter.

Containerisation in the Lower Rhine region

The first American maritime container arrived in Rotterdam in 1966. Although the use of maritime containers has since become standard in global trade, it is not the only container standard. In Europe, there has been a tradition of continental container transport going back to the 19th century. The result of this was a standard that is slightly different to that of the United States. This difference is due to the fact that the dimensions of US maritime containers are based on that country's highway regulations, while European dimensions are based on European international railway agreements. The most important transport route for European continental containers is within the so-called blue banana, comprising the busy transportation routes across Western Europe between the United Kingdom and Northern Italy. Continental containers rarely leave Europe, because their size is incompatible with the standard used in maritime transport. These containers are therefore almost exclusively used for the distribution of European industrial products. Continental container flows are indicative of production- and consumption-based economic relations within Europe, unlike maritime containers in which, often generic, Asiatic products are transported. Maritime container flows are footloose; the products they contain are required by all European consumers and can take alternative routes through different ports given even small differences in transport costs. As maritime container flows represent globalisation more than their continental container counterparts, the focus of this chapter is on maritime container flows between Rotterdam and its hinterland in the period 1966–2010. Unfortunately, the statistics used for this analysis sometimes include, and sometimes exclude, continental containers, and separating the two flows is not always possible. To identify the continental container flows in this chapter, if they are not explicitly mentioned in the statistics, assumptions are made based on a thorough knowledge of European cargo flows.

The hinterland transport of maritime containers takes place by means of three modalities: truck, barge and rail. The choice of modality is determined by numerous factors. These include a mix of hard economic metrics, for example transport costs, distances and the structure and position of the various actors involved in container logistics, such as company structure or relative power within the network. Laws and regulations regarding the transportation of goods also play an important role. Of the three modalities of container transport, the truck is often considered to be the cheapest and most flexible option. This modality was especially preferred in the early days of container transport, when there were no line or shuttle services available. However, truck transport is most profitable over relatively short distances, within a range of 150 km, which equates to just reaching the Ruhr area from Rotterdam. Truck transport is, nonetheless, frequently used for longer distances, especially when other criteria matter, such as speed or a lack of alternative modes of transport. Trucks transport was initially mostly performed by relatively small companies and was quite straightforward, as road haulage went from door to door. Therefore, unlike with barge and rail transport, there was no need to arrange separate cover for the last mile. On the one hand, road transport has low fixed costs and the greatest expense is hiring the driver. On the other hand, road haulage incurs high infrastructural costs that go towards paying for the development and maintenance of the road infrastructure through road and fuel taxes. The greatest challenge, however, is to identify return cargo in order to optimise the efficiency of this mode of transport.

Barge transport is also considered to be relatively cheap, especially because of the low social costs and the fact that, because of the Act of Mannheim (1868), the sector has barely paid for the use of the infrastructure. In the early days of containerisation, barge transport was only considered to be cost-efficient over longer distances, which is why the first container terminals on the Rhine were opened in Mannheim and Basel on the Upper Rhine. Later, shorter distances also became cost-efficient and, in the 1990s, in the Netherlands even the domestic transport of maritime containers by barge became common. Barge transport was considered to be environmentally friendly, which is why, from the 1980s onwards, when environmental issues became important to the public, there was increasing pressure from local administrations, such as the Rotterdam Port Authority, to use barge transport. This form of transport did, however, have only have limited penetration, as it was restricted to existing waterways. The main challenge for barge transport was to arrange the last mile and achieve a loading capacity of 70–80 per cent to reach break-even. Barge transport was performed by a few large and numerous small companies, with the latter mostly chartered by the former. Barge companies on the Rhine cooperated greatly and divided the market between them. For a long time, Combined Container Services (today Contargo) was the market leader. Barge transport was the Port of Rotterdam's trump card. The Rhine, the most navigable waterway in Europe, was a cheap hinterland connection without congestion. Indeed, the only obstacle for this modality was incidental low or high water levels.

Rail transport was an entirely different sector. It was the most expensive of the modalities, because of its costly infrastructure, which the sector had to pay for in full. This was because, unlike road haulage, the rail infrastructure had no alternative use, other than passenger transport, which was rarely cost-efficient. Rail cargo transport was only considered to be value for money for distances over 300 km. Such transport distances hardly existed in the Netherlands, which is why the transport of containers by rail targeted cross-border destinations from the outset.

In order to make rail transport cost-efficient, in the 1990s the shuttle concept was developed. A shuttle service involves cargo trains in constant combinations travelling regularly between two destinations. Unlike the other modalities, rail transport was fully performed by national rail companies until the 1990s. These also built and maintained the infrastructure. The German seaports did not have a good barge connection with their hinterland. The Weser and the Elbe had more unstable water levels than the Rhine and often froze over in the winter. As a result, the German ports were best connected with their hinterland by rail. Port competition in the Hamburg-ARA (Antwerp-Rotterdam-Amsterdam) range with respect to hinterland access for maritime container flows centred on competition between Dutch barge and German rail transport. Rail is a relatively expensive modality and requires some form of government subsidy to compete with barges. Throughout the research period, German rail transport was dominated by Deutsche Bahn, the German state-owned rail operator. Port competition over access to Rotterdam's traditional Lower Rhine hinterland was therefore, in reality, competition between the Rhine and Deutsche Bahn. However, for other hinterland areas – Southern Germany and Eastern and Central Europe – port competition was mainly played out on the railways. Rail transportation is therefore the key modality in this chapter, even though it formed the smallest of the modal split of hinterland transport for the Port of Rotterdam.

While Rhine navigation has been subject to a liberal regime of supranational regulation ever since the Treaty of Mannheim (1868), the construction of railways was predominantly a national affair. This posed a problem for cross-border transport in which international cooperation was necessary. This led to numerous problems, especially between the Netherlands and Germany, as both governments used their rail transport to serve their own national policy goals, which were in conflict: for the Netherlands, it was the stimulation of cross-border hinterland rail connections to improve the access of the Rotterdam port to hinterland areas beyond those served by the Rhine; for Germany, meanwhile, it was the stimulation of the German ports of Hamburg and Bremen, which relied on their railway connections for any hinterland access. At the same time, there was also a third party involved: the state of North Rhine Westphalia. It had a different approach, as it was dependent on cheap transport from the North Sea ports.

The most eye-catching case of conflicted cooperation within this complex divergence of national and local economic interest was the construction of the Betuwe Route. This was a dedicated rail freight line from Rotterdam to the German hinterland, providing the Dutch with access to the German rail network. The Betuwe Route was built by the Dutch government between 2000 and 2007 at a cost of 4.7 billion Euros to facilitate hinterland transport to Germany. The Port of Rotterdam had lobbied for this new connection, as it was concerned about the quality and capacity of those connections already in existence. Furthermore, it was thought that the choice of specific ports by sea-shipping companies depended on the quality of the available rail connections.

In order to construct this cross-border connection, arrangements had to be made with Germany about the trajectory on the other side of the border. In 1990–1991, both the Dutch and German parties made prognoses about expected transport volumes. Based on these reports, the German side concluded that it was essential to construct the Betuwe Route to keep pace with the growth of freight transport. Finally, in 1992, the transport ministers of the two countries signed the Agreement of Warnemunde, which provided for the two nations to coordinate their efforts to build the route.[3] The precise location of the connection was established in 1996 and ran from Maasvlakte to the German border at Zevenaar. In the Agreement of Warnemunde, Germany agreed to update the connection through Emmerich to Oberhausen by adding a new third track. This track was to be used by high speed trains for passenger transport, leaving the remaining two tracks for freight. This would keep the German part of the Betuwe Route dedicated to freight transport, just like in the Netherlands. The German part of the route, however, was never built. Although this could be seen as a breach of the Agreement of Warnemunde, that agreement was actually only a declaration of intent.

Initially, the German government had showed good will, even though it represented national interests. This included those of the German ports, which were clearly against building a good hinterland connection for the Port of Rotterdam with German money that would make container transport less dependent on the geographically fixed Rhine. In the Netherlands, meanwhile, there was a strong suspicion that the German lobby was blocking decisions. At the end of 2010, there were still no definitive plans to complete the third track. Furthermore, the terminal in Valburg on the Dutch side of the Dutch-German border has, despite previous plans to develop it into a major logistics centre, remained a simple emplacement location where container shuttles waiting for a slot on the overcrowded German rail network can be parked. The bottleneck formed by the lack of the third track was especially disadvantageous for the Port of Rotterdam's shuttle connections coming from and going to destinations that were relatively far away, in the parts of the hinterland it competed with the German ports. The volumes of transported containers from Rotterdam remained relatively low, because of the cumbersome cross-border connection, which made it difficult and expensive to run regular shuttles. Moreover, because of the congested connection, the time advantage that Rotterdam had as the first port of call for the powerful shipping companies like Maersk could not be exploited to the full. This gave an advantage to the German ports and their hinterland access, in particular to hinterlands beyond the Lower Rhine region.

Such cross-border transport issues persisted despite the liberalisation of the European transport sector that was pursued by the European Union in the 1990s. Before liberalisation, the transport policies of Germany and the Netherlands had been consistently different, but both underwent significant change due to the opening up of the European transport sector in the 1990s.

Harmonisation of transport regulations had been attempted ever since the advent of European integration after World War II, but only seriously began in the 1990s and continues to this day. Most relevant for this chapter is the opening of the transport markets of the Netherlands and Germany. Liberalisation in this sense took place between 1991 and 1994; it began in the rail sector in 1991 and continued with road haulage in January 1993, while the fixed transport tariffs of all three of the container transport modalities were abolished in Germany in 1994. In the years before and after this period, some other measures had been and were put in place, but the most important were implemented between 1991 and 1994.

Although the liberalisation of the European transport sector could not hinder the enduring Dutch-German rail connections, it was nevertheless a major discontinuity in the history of containerisation in the Rhine region. Containerisation caused an initial and rapid expansion of the hinterland transport connections of the Rotterdam port from the 1960s onwards, and, as a consequence, a relative loosening of economic connections between the Port of Rotterdam and the Lower Rhine hinterland. However, from the early 1990s onwards, this was followed by growing network integration within the Lower Rhine region. This was reflected in a contraction of the hinterland of Rotterdam, the intensification of flows between the port and relatively closer areas such as Antwerp, the domestic hinterland and the Lower Rhine region and the reduction of flows between the port and relatively further away areas such as the Upper Rhine, Northern Italy, Southern Germany and former Eastern European countries. This contraction of the hinterland was the result of the interaction of containerisation, globalisation, liberalisation and port competition. The arrival of maritime containers in Rotterdam in 1966 meant the introduction of a cheap and flexible transport system to which the port was unaccustomed. The entire European transport sector was forced to adjust to the new flows and forwarded transhipped boxes to the hinterland. This was a major push factor, which stimulated the extension of the transport network of the Port of Rotterdam, but also of the other ports in Northern Europe. Containerisation, together with the development of information and communication technologies, encouraged globalisation, the extension of networks and the intensification of transport flows within those networks on a global scale. The introduction of maritime containers in Rotterdam meant that the port was included in a newly emerging transatlantic network. This encouraged companies within the port to extend their networks within Europe.

Prior to liberalisation, the extension of such networks was hindered by restrictive post-war transport policies, especially in Germany, which put obstacles in the way of cross-border transport. This created transport patterns based on political, not economic, principles. Liberalisation gradually removed most of these hurdles. This initially enhanced the extension of hinterland transport and ownership networks, but, in the long run, liberalisation caused the intensification of intramodal and intermodal rivalry, which led to growing port competition. Particularly in the case of footloose maritime containers, the competition increasingly became a rivalry between alternative transport routes that could bring containers to the hinterland without much difference in price. This port competition was a major factor in shaping port-hinterland regions. Port competition was strongly influenced by major sea-shipping companies, especially Maersk, which orchestrated hinterland transport from the seaport. Port competition made the captive hinterlands of ports shrink and the contested hinterlands grow. Indeed, it was not only Rotterdam, but also all other Northern European ports that started to expand their hinterland container transport networks. In Central Europe, the networks met and competition was most intense. As a result, most hinterland areas became contested and fewer were served by a single port; in effect, ports retreated to their backyards. The contraction of the captive hinterland of Rotterdam accelerated in the first decade of the 2000s. This meant, for the city, that its transport flows were growing relatively faster within the Lower Rhine region. Additionally, a logistics triangle emerged between Rotterdam, Antwerp and the Lower Rhine region. Antwerp, with its tradition as an industrial port, developed its volumes based on production and served as an export port for the German industry, while Rotterdam, which was strong with respect to Asiatic routes and imports, increasingly specialised in logistics flows connected to European distribution centres in the first decade of the new century.

Hinterland areas of the Port of Rotterdam

In this section, the position and role of different hinterland areas of the Port of Rotterdam are analysed. The hinterland is the region from which a port derives most of its throughput. Most of the hinterland areas of the Port of Rotterdam can be grouped around two axes. One is formed by a curved line connecting the ports of Le Havre, Antwerp and Rotterdam, as well as the German ports. These are port areas, but they generate transhipment for the Port of Rotterdam by way of logistics processes. Due to the focus of this chapter, the analysis of these areas is omitted here. The other axis goes along another curved line, comprising the United Kingdom, the Netherlands, the German Lower, Middle and Upper Rhine areas and Northern Italy. There is a third category consisting of relatively distant areas that are not situated along this curved line, namely Southern Germany (most importantly Bavaria) and the countries of Central and Eastern Europe (Figure 6.1). Due to the focus of the chapter, the emphasis is on the three Rhine areas, Southern Germany and the Central and Eastern European countries. Other hinterland areas will only be discussed briefly. This section summarises the dynamics of the geographical patterns of container transport by the three modalities of hinterland container transport – rail, barge and truck – before and after the liberalisation of the European transport sector per hinterland area.

Lower Rhine: from industry to logistics

The Lower Rhine was the traditional focal point of the cargo throughput of the Port of Rotterdam. Nevertheless, for the transport of maritime containers, it remained less important than other hinterland areas for several decades, at

Figure 6.1 An overview of the hinterland areas of the Port of Rotterdam

Source: Map produced by Cartographic Studio/Annelieke Vries-Baaijens (2018).

least before the liberalisation of the European transport sector. The relatively short distance between Rotterdam and the Lower Rhine region meant that this area was not of interest to rail transport in the early years of containerisation, as it had a competitive advantage at distances of over 300 km. This is enhanced by the fact that the majority of the cargo transported by the first container ships to Rotterdam had the Middle Rhine region as their final destination, because they were mostly cargo destined for the military depots situated in that area. The transport of maritime containers by barge was also aimed at areas beyond the Lower Rhine from the outset. Accordingly, in the early period of containerisation, maritime containers with destinations in the Lower Rhine region travelled by truck. Truck transportation was complicated by the compulsory cross-border licences required between Germany and the Netherlands for transport between the two countries until the liberalisation of the road haulage sector in 1993. However, the importance of the Lower Rhine for the Port of Rotterdam started to increase from 1990–2010. In this period, the gravity point of container barge transport moved slowly down the Rhine. This included rail transport. As liberalisation allowed new entrants to the rail market, *ERS Railways*, a joint venture by the major sea-shipping companies and the first competitor to *Nederlandse Spoorwegen* (Dutch Railways), took advantage of this opportunity to break the rail shuttle market wide open and establish cheap shuttles to areas relatively close to Rotterdam from 1994 onwards. This meant that, after liberalisation, the Lower Rhine region could be served cost-efficiently by all three modalities, which increased competition.

The development of the German inland Port of Duisburg into a major inland transport hub played a major role in this process. The Port of Duisburg – originally named Ruhrort – started in 1926 as a joint venture of the municipality of Duisburg and the state of Prussia for the transhipment of supplies for local heavy industry. In 1950, the port had to adjust to the changes caused by the energy transition from coal to oil.[4] Containers arrived at the Port of Duisburg in 1984, when the first container terminal was built by the Duisburger Container Gesellschaft (DeCeTe), along with a roll-on-roll-off facility for short sea transport.[5] In 1988, the federal government decided to turn Duisburg into a European logistics hub, for which 150 million *DM* of government subsidies were reserved. Duisburg also acquired the status of a free port, where transit goods could be stored, processed and forwarded without duties.[6] Previously, only the ports of Hamburg and Bremen had had this status.[7] As a result of these investments in the early 1990s, the total transhipments (in tons) of the Port of Duisburg continued to grow, despite the reduction of coal transhipment.[8]

The next step was to integrate the growing port into European transport networks and set up a cooperation agreement with West European ports. In 1991, when the EuroLogistik-Terminal of Kühne & Nagel was opened, Duisburg was included in the network of this major German forwarder with five centres in Europe. A rail connection was constructed for the terminal, from where it transported expensive consumption goods, including televisions and radios.[9] In the early 1990s, the Port of Duisburg increasingly realised its dependence on the Port of Rotterdam and enhanced its cooperation with this port. The saying went: "If Rotterdam coughs, Duisburg contracts pneumonia."[10] In the middle of the 1990s, the cooperation focused on multimodal transport. Duisburg had the goal of collecting containers coming in from Rotterdam and forwarding them by train to their final destination.[11] The director of the Port of Duisburg-Ruhrort in the 1990s, K. van Lith, expected that the Port of Rotterdam would become overcrowded, its infrastructure jammed and that Duisburg would offer an escape. He also argued that it was easier to load shuttles in Duisburg, where volumes were concentrated. A good rail connection from Duisburg to the German ports was also seen as an absolute necessity and a new rail yard was built and the number of tracks increased. Rotterdam was also willing to cooperate. In 1999, European Container Terminals (ECT), the largest stevedore in Rotterdam, established a container terminal in Duisburg. The motivation was that this would give ECT a good connection to the German rail system, although it did not make use of this opportunity until 2000, when it merged with the first container terminal in Duisburg, DeCeTe.[12] A formal cooperation with the port of Antwerp was also established in 2005, with Duisburg opening its own terminal in this port, the Antwerp Gateway Terminal, for the transhipment of volumes with a destination of Duisburg.[13] The port expanded rapidly from the 1990s onwards.

The name Duisport was introduced in 2000, and in the same year the growth of the port accelerated.[14] Indeed, its turnover grew from 34 million Euros in 2000 to 58 million in 2005, which represented annual growth of approximately 12 per cent. The total transhipment in 2001 was 36.4 million tons, which grew at an average annual rate of 5 per cent to 45 million tons in 2005. The transhipment of containers almost doubled between 2002 and 2004 from 38,000 to 61,000 TEU, and in 2005, for the first time more tons of containers than bulk were transhipped. The transhipment of containers reached 1 million TEU in 2008.[15] Duisburg's target of creating employment was also quite successful. In 2006, the port provided direct and indirect employment to 17,000 people in Duisburg and 36,000 in the region.[16] The growth of the port was the result of major investments. Indeed, in the period between 2001 and 2004, 54 million Euros were invested in the port by the federal government, and in 2006 another 70 million was spent on expanding the port area (Logport II). Then, between 2006 and 2008, 155 million Euros was spent on the extension of the rail infrastructure and expanding the container transhipment capacity.[17]

Between the mid-1980s and 2010, the Port of Duisburg turned into a terminal cluster. Eight terminals were built in that period.[18] At the same time, a company cluster emerged. The port area Logport I acted as a magnet for logistics companies. Indeed, 50 companies settled at Duisburger Hafen between 1996 and 2006.[19] This was a classic clustering effect, with companies with similar activities co-locating to profit from the positive externalities of their cluster.[20] In 2010, Duisburg, which tried to become the most important inland barge terminal cluster in Germany, proved itself to be a pivotal port, developing an elaborate barge network connected to 160 trimodal terminals. With its terminal and company cluster, it was the only port area that had shown spectacular growth, despite the fact that in the rest of Germany the transport of containers stagnated in the late 2000s.[21] The most concentrated connections were with Rotterdam and Antwerp, which could both be reached from Duisburg by barge (Figure 6.2). The connection to the German ports was

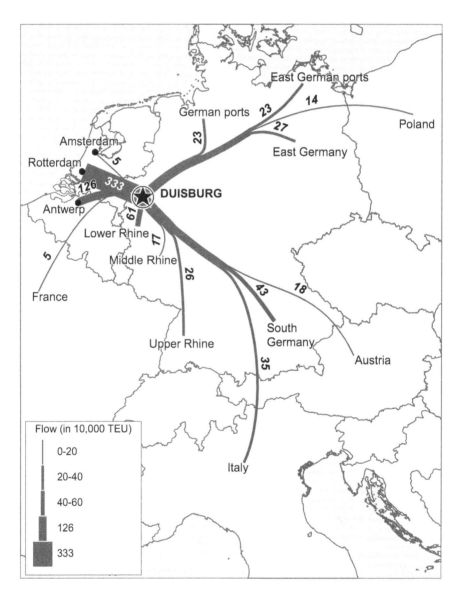

Figure 6.2 Container transport by rail and barge to and from the Port of Duisburg, 2010

Source: Deutsches Statistisches Bundesamt, *Kombinierter Verkehr*, Fachserie 8 Reihe 1.3 (Wiesbaden 2004–2011). Map produced by Cartographic Studio/Annelieke Vries-Baaijens (2018).

less important, as were those to the hinterland areas in Germany and Central and Eastern Europe, even though Duisburg targeted all the major contested hinterlands of Rotterdam and the German North Sea ports. Flows of volumes between Antwerp and Duisburg were also growing, but they started at a lower level and grew slower than those of Rotterdam. The remaining areas, including the German ports, mostly stayed under 50,000 TEU, and none of them showed spectacular growth between 2004 and 2010.

A comparison of the container transport flows by barge and rail to and from the Port of Duisburg with the containers flows of the entire Lower Rhine region (Figure 6.3) demonstrates that Duisburg was more oriented towards Rotterdam than the Lower Rhine area in general.[22] The latter had approximately equal transport flows with Rotterdam and Hamburg, and a much less intensive flow going to Antwerp. The distribution flows followed the Rhine Valley, but there was also an important stream going to Italy and a rail connection to Southern Germany. The development of container transport in the period 2004–2010 by rail and barge in the Lower Rhine area shows that the role of the most important flows to Rotterdam and the German ports increased during the period, with the exception of a minor dip for Rotterdam in 2008. Italy and Antwerp, meanwhile, were left behind and declined from 2007 onwards. Southern Germany and the Upper Rhine never reached the 100,000 TEU level.

The Lower Rhine area increasingly became a contested hinterland for the Port of Rotterdam and was targeted by both Antwerp and the German ports. Antwerp's weapons were its cooperation with Duisburg in the form of German investments in the Belgian port and the Belgian logistics companies establishing themselves in Duisburg. Rotterdam competed with its cheap barge connection on the Rhine and the German ports with their good rail connections and Deutsche Bahn. Unfortunately, the official German statistics of the *Deutsches Statistisches Bundesamt* are only available for the last seven years of the research period. These show that, in this period, Antwerp was losing its position and the competition between the German ports and Rotterdam was more or less balanced between them.

Companies that had distribution centres in the Lower Rhine region benefitted from this competition. They had a choice between four ports for their transhipment, while a logistics cluster provided all possible high-quality logistics services in Duisburg. Prior to the liberalisation of the European transport sector, when cross-border transport was submitted to a number of restrictions, companies could best organise the distribution of their products per country. After liberalisation, the majority of the problems of crossing national borders were resolved, resulting in increasing intermodal competition and lower transport costs. Furthermore, as a result of liberalisation, the distribution of the products of multinationals no longer needed to take place by country, but could be arranged from one central warehouse. As a consequence, warehouses and the European distribution centres of multinationals settled in the Lower Rhine region.[23] The distribution centres of IKEA, Hewlett Packard, Konica-Minolta,

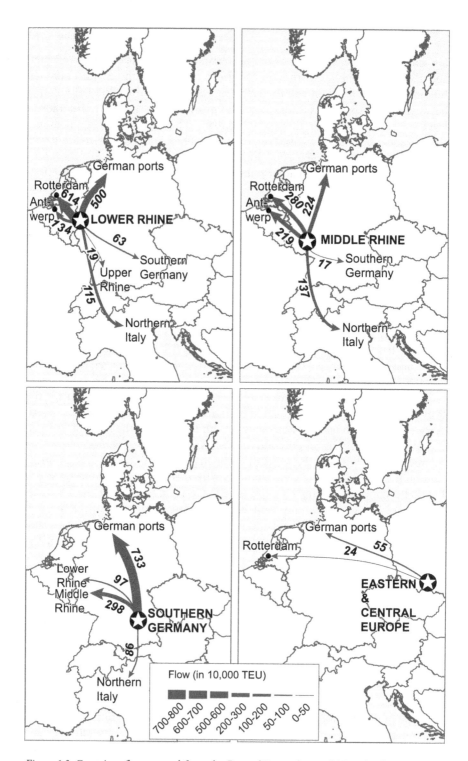

Figure 6.3 Container flows to and from the Port of Rotterdam and hinterland areas, 2010

Source: Deutsches Statistisches Bundesamt, *Kombinierter Verkehr*, Fachserie 8 Reihe 1.3. (Wiesbaden 2004–2011). Map produced by Cartographic Studio/Annelieke Vries-Baaijens (2018).

Metro (Makro) and the largest centre of the toy manufacturer Hasbro were situated there, for example.[24] As a result, transport between Rotterdam and the Lower Rhine region increasingly depended on the logistics activities of these companies. At the same time, production gradually disappeared from the Lower Rhine area, because the traditional Ruhr industry was lost. As a consequence, municipalities tried to create employment in logistics. Accordingly, in combination with the growth of production in Southern Germany, the industrial gravity point of the country was moving south, away from the Lower Rhine region.

In conclusion, it can be seen that, before liberalisation, the Lower Rhine area was less important than the Middle Rhine area for container transport from and to the Port of Rotterdam. This changed after liberalisation, when the restrictions on cross-border transport disappeared and *ERS Railways*, the first serious competitor to the Dutch state-owned railways, started a shuttle to the Lower Rhine area. As a result, the gravity point of container transport moved slowly down the Rhine. The emergence of Duisburg as a logistics hub played an important role in this process. It exploited its geographical position between Antwerp and Rotterdam and the German ports by hosting European distribution centres for multinationals. The policy in Duisburg, aimed at replacing production employment with logistics, was a major catalyst in this process. However, this also contributed to the fact that the area shifted from being a macro-economic, i.e. productive, hinterland to a logistical one. This meant that, even though the transported volumes were growing, footloose container transport could take alternative routes without major tariff differences, making the position of the Port of Rotterdam in relation to European container flows insecure.[25]

The Middle and Upper Rhine: US military bases and industrial production

From Bonn to Karlsruhe, the Rhine is 300 kilometres long. At Mainz, near the mouth of the River Main, the Middle Rhine flows into the lower section of the Upper Rhine, which stretches between Mainz and Karlsruhe. In this context, this latter section is the most important part. Along the Middle Rhine, between Cologne and Koblenz, there were only two barge terminals (at Bonn and Koblenz), while in 2010, there were eight along the Upper Rhine. The reason for this is that there was less demand for transport on the Middle Rhine, because the Rhine Valley between Koblenz and Mainz is too narrow for industrial activities. There is a large transport demand generated by US army depots and the machine, automobile and chemical industries between Mainz and Karlsruhe.

The lower Upper Rhine area played an important role as the macro-economic hinterland for the Port of Rotterdam, as the supplies for the US troops stationed in the region were transhipped in Rotterdam from 1956 onwards. In fact, this was one of the reasons why Rotterdam, instead of Bremen became the first container port in Europe, which was initially favoured by the US army for currency reasons. If the flow of military cargo had not been redirected from the German port to Rotterdam, Bremen could have become the pioneering container port on the continent. Military cargo supplied basic volumes to create economies of scale, which is key to profitable container transport. Germany was divided into different occupation zones after World War II. In the American zone, there were numerous military bases along the Rhine, because the river used to be a major demarcation area. The largest army depots were situated in the neighbourhood of Mannheim,[26] which could be served either from Rotterdam by barge or from the German ports by rail. In 1945, the goods destined for the American zone were transhipped in Bremen. Transport costs via Rotterdam were substantially lower, but had to be paid in foreign currency, which was scarce at that time. The choice of Bremen was seen in Rotterdam as discrimination against the Dutch port.[27] The Dutch transport attaché in Bonn, C.A.F. Kalhorn, intervened in 1954, but it was only two years later, when the Americans had to pay all transport costs from their own resources instead of German reparation funds, that they became receptive to Kalhorn's arguments about promoting cheaper transport through Rotterdam. The transportation of military goods on the Rhine started in 1956, and 20,000 tons of supplies were soon going upstream and 30,000 tons of military goods were travelling downstream.[28] In 1956, one third of the military cargo destined for US troops was transhipped in Rotterdam. Nevertheless, refrigerated cargo, cars and passengers still came through Bremen, because of the investments made there for this purpose.[29]

Rotterdam had become a major port for the transhipment of US military goods by the time maritime containers arrived in Europe. The first maritime container arrived in Rotterdam in 1966 while McLean was engaged in setting up container services between the US and Vietnam. These first maritime containers were filled with jeans, tyres, cotton and electric appliances, and there were more to follow.[30] The US army learned a lesson in Vietnam about logistics, and its goods were increasingly containerised. Indeed, half of the military cargo going to Europe was containerised by 1970 and its share grew further afterwards.[31] The transfer of the activities of a German road haulier, Erich Kieserling, from Bremen to Rotterdam in 1974 was another factor that led to the shift of military cargo. Kieserling became involved in barge transport on the Rhine at that time, including handling containers for Hapag Lloyd, which had already been his customer in Bremen. At the same time, he started transporting military goods for Sea Land, which gradually relocated its services from the German ports to Rotterdam. Kieserling played an important role in this process, as he attracted his former customers from Bremen to Rotterdam. There were more than 200,000 US soldiers stationed in Germany during the Cold War, but their number was reduced after the end of Soviet dominance in Central and Eastern Europe. The presence of the US troops was still essential for Rhine barge container flows between Rotterdam and the Middle and lower Upper Rhine. In 2010, there were still more than 50,000 US military personnel in Germany, who, because of the tendering system of the US army, received their supplies almost entirely from their homeland. Supplies did not mean just military items; as the manager of the Germersheim barge container terminal of Contargo, Jasmin Daum, put it: "American soldiers eat American brownies and use American toilet paper."[32]

Apart from the military volumes, the products of the major chemical companies BASF, Bayer and Hoechst were important in the Middle and lower Upper Rhine area. Transporting the exports and supplies of these companies, which were increasingly moved in tank containers – tanks suspended in a frame with standardised measures – contributed to the local transport demand. The same was true for the automobile and machine industries in the region. In Koblenz, the transport demand consisted of products of and supplies for light industry and agricultural goods, but machine industry was also present in the neighbourhood, such as a rolling machine plant (Bomag) and Aleris Aluminium Koblenz GmbH.[33] Daimler Benz had a car factory in Germersheim and a truck plant in Worth. Meanwhile, Mercedes, Daimler, Roche and Boring had plants in Ludwigshafen, and John Deere, the producer of agricultural machines, had one in Mannheim.[34] The tyre company Goodyear also had a warehouse in the neighbourhood.[35]

The combined demands of the US military and local industries meant that the lower Upper Rhine area, especially the surroundings of Mannheim, were of great importance for maritime container transport from and to Rotterdam. The first barge terminal was built in Mannheim in 1968, while the ones that followed were mostly also constructed in the Upper Rhine area, as barge transport was initially only thought to be cost-efficient over longer distances. This view later changed, but the lower Upper Rhine area remained a major centre for container transport. This was due to the fact that all modalities were attracted by the opportunities in the region. No fewer than eight container terminals between Mainz and Worth were in operation in the early 1990s. Liberalisation made it easier to transport goods between the Middle Rhine area and Rotterdam, but also between this region and other ports. In the long run, this led to more competition between the modalities and the ports, and the amount of rail and truck transport between Rotterdam and the Middle and lower Upper Rhine has decreased in the past decade as a consequence. Barge transport, however, was growing, but Antwerp's share was rising faster than that of Rotterdam, apparently giving the former the upper hand in this area of the Rhine. The port of Antwerp was able to derive its success from its history as an industrial port hosting a major chemical cluster and its traditionally strong relationship with German car manufacturers. As is clear from Figure 6.3, the Middle Rhine area is served in almost equal measure by ports in the Rhine delta (Rotterdam and Antwerp), the German North Sea ports and ports in Northern Italy.

Along the upper parts of the Upper Rhine, between Karlsruhe and Basel, Switzerland was already a hinterland area for the Port of Rotterdam before the introduction of maritime containers. In 1965, the Dutch Railways established a rail connection to both Basel and Chiasso. Switzerland also played an important role in barge transport in the early years of containerisation, when it was still only thought to be profitable over longer distances. Consequently, after the construction of the first container terminal in Mannheim in 1968, the second was built in 1969 in Basel at the same time as the barge terminal in Strasburg. Later, when barge transport became profitable over shorter distances, Switzerland's share fell. Even though rail transport could have been profitable to this area, the share of rail shuttles between Rotterdam and this region varied between 4 and 7 per cent, which means that it was not a major hinterland area. Moreover, Rotterdam lost its market share in this region to Antwerp. The same was true for road haulage; Switzerland was not an important destination for most companies. The liberalisation of the European road haulage sector did not make much difference to the accessibility of this hinterland area, because Switzerland imposed heavy restrictions on truck transport within the country at the same time.

The Upper Rhine area's low share of maritime container transport flows was a missed opportunity for Rotterdam, because it had a lot to offer. An important industry cluster, for example the pharmaceutical company Sandoz and the multinational food concern Nestle, was situated in the Basel neighbourhood. These had an interest in cheap transport for both their exports and supplies, and a cluster of terminals formed around Basel to serve that demand. They imported their raw materials, such as cocoa and chemicals, and exported finished products along the Rhine.[36] In the case of these and other flows based on productive activity in the Upper Rhine area, the distinction between maritime and continental containers matters. Switzerland was important for Rotterdam in relation to the export of the products of Swiss industry, the importation of raw materials and the transport of continental containers to and from the United Kingdom or overseas, because these were transhipped in Rotterdam. Nonetheless, continental container flows between Switzerland and the Netherlands were more important for the Dutch economy in general than for the Port of Rotterdam. The results of the research suggest that continental flows dominated container transport between the two countries. The footloose maritime flows could go either through Italy, Antwerp or the German ports. Switzerland thus turned out to be a minor hinterland of Rotterdam, especially in comparison with Italy, which is situated even further away.

Although not located in the Rhine Valley, Northern Italy belonged to the contested hinterland of the Port of Rotterdam. There had been volumes transported between the United Kingdom through Rotterdam to Italy even before the introduction of the maritime container, and many such containers followed the same trajectory after 1966. The majority of transport was performed by rail, as this modality had a competitive advantage at distances above 300 km. There had been a spectacular growth of connections between Rotterdam and Italy in the 1980s. Indeed, in the period 1994–2010, the share of rail shuttles going to or coming from Italy amounted to around 20–30 per cent of the total number of shuttles, with the country becoming the third most important cross-border destination for containers from Rotterdam. Volumes were still growing at the end of this period, but the share of maritime containers fell; it was continental containers that made volumes rise. Italy could not be reached by barge from Rotterdam, but much of the volumes that were transported by rail probably sailed the first part of the track on the Rhine. Incidentally, before liberalisation, trucks went to Italy carrying maritime containers, despite the long distance and the obstacles posed by the Alps. After liberalisation, when many of the hurdles to cross-border transport were lifted, the number of trucks travelling to Italy even grew. As a result of growing port competition, however, their number fell again in the 2000s.

Central and Eastern European countries

The third and final category of hinterland areas discussed herein consists of destinations relatively far away from Rotterdam that do not belong to the Rhine region, namely Central and Eastern European countries and Southern Germany (Bavaria). The Central and Eastern European countries of the former German Democratic Republic, Poland, the Czech Republic, Western Russia and Hungary traditionally belonged to the hinterland of the German ports. This is unsurprising, as Prague, which was the most important contested hinterland destination, is approximately 600 kilometres from the German ports and 900 kilometres from Rotterdam. In spite of this, after World War II, when transport resumed on damaged roads, Czechoslovakia was the first important cross-border destination. Indeed, between 1955 and 1960, this country was the Eastern European destination to which the Dutch railways, *Nederlandse Spoorwegen*, transported goods. An average of 140,000 tons of goods was transported annually between the two countries in this period. This amounted to 1.6 per cent of total Dutch cross-border rail transport. This was due to the fact that the industry in the occupied Czech territories was encouraged and spared by the Germans in World War II, because the Nazi regime needed this industrial production for its warfare. As a result, it was relatively easier to restart this production in Czechoslovakia after the war, for example in Sudetenland, where heavy industry was located.[37] Due to the lack of data, it is impossible to discover how many containers travelled to Central and Eastern European countries between 1966 and 1997. It is therefore difficult to say how liberalisation actually influenced transport to these destinations. Indeed, as its effects were intertwined with the outcomes of a complex political and economic transformation in these countries, it would be a difficult conclusion to reach in any event.

The Rhine Main Danube Canal opened in 1992 as a new trajectory to Czechoslovakia, Hungary, Romania and Bulgaria, but it remained of minor importance because of nautical restrictions and the low speed of transport on the canal. It is likely that the removal of numerous restrictions on road haulage caused the growth of volumes to destinations in these countries, but the economic transformation also made these nations partners again. Furthermore, the activities of ERS Railways in the late 1990s saved some shuttles going to Poland, the Czech Republic and Slovakia.

After the implosion of the Soviet system, the Port of Rotterdam and Dutch transport companies had become increasingly interested in the emerging markets in Central and Eastern Europe. Rotterdam had a trump card to play because, despite the fact that the German ports were situated closer to Central and Eastern European countries, it was the first port of call on the Western European coastline on both the Asiatic and Atlantic routes. This meant that goods arrived one or two days earlier in Rotterdam than the German ports. With a good rail connection, a time advantage of 24 hours could be achieved which could undo the effect of the vicinity of the German ports to this hinterland area. Still, it was not easy to start a transport connection to Central and Eastern European countries, as cargo to this area was scarce. Starting a rail shuttle service was a precarious business, as it needed to be shared with other modalities and there was hardly any return cargo. The latter issue was due to the fact that, while Western Europe was keen on using Central and Eastern Europe as an outlet for its own products, it had less need for industrial goods produced there. The return cargo therefore mostly consisted of canned fruit, vegetables and other agricultural products.

Ever since the introduction of maritime containers, the Dutch railways had been busy setting up a wide container shuttle transport network. They also tried to gain ground in Central and Eastern European countries, and started a shuttle connection to Prague in 1994. This was one of many attempts to establish a connection to these countries, followed by an attempt to launch a shuttle to Poznan. Prague and Poznan were not always the final destinations of goods from Rotterdam; from Poznan, they were often transhipped to Malaszevicze on the Russian border, and from Prague to Bratislava in Slovakia or Sopron and Budapest in Hungary.[38] ERS Railways saved these connections in the late 1990s, which were on the verge of bankruptcy, with ERS making them feasible by adding volumes supplied by Maersk and combining these with continental containers. Maersk acquired the majority of the shares of ERS Railways, which was promoting the Rotterdam rail connection to the Central and Eastern European hinterland from its head office in Copenhagen. Maersk was initially interested, but it became increasingly difficult to explain why it should choose Rotterdam over the German ports, whose rail connections were improving. Maersk was not a stakeholder in Rotterdam; it just wanted to transport its containers as cheaply and efficiently as possible. When the majority of the containers with destinations in Central and Eastern European countries went to German ports, why would Maersk send a fraction through Rotterdam? Nonetheless, in the second half of the 1990s, ERS Railways managed to increase the number of departures from three to four times a week to seven to eight times a week and the connection was exploited more or less successfully. It rode six times a week in 2004. At the same time, there was a connection between Prague and the German ports travelling seven times a week.[39]

Figure 6.3 shows the port competition for the Central and Eastern European hinterlands between Rotterdam and the German ports. This clearly demonstrates that this area was more the hinterland of the German ports than of

Rotterdam. Indeed, despite the efforts of Rotterdam to hold its ground in these hinterland areas, with their increasing economic importance, it lost its opportunity. Figures 6.4 and 6.5 show how rail container transport to these countries developed in the period between 2004 and 2010. For the German ports, this market in 2004 was more important than for Rotterdam and the transported volumes grew steadily. The transport to these countries from Rotterdam has never reached the total volume of 300,000 TEU and, after a brief period of growth in 2005, the transported volumes fell back to 18,000 TEU. Unfortunately, there is no data available for later years; however, as the number of shuttles fell, there is no reason to assume that the volumes would have grown in this period.

From the late 1990s onwards, the Central and Eastern European hinterland areas had more to offer. As a result of rising standards of living, it is to be expected that the demand for diverse transatlantic and Asiatic goods would grow. Furthermore, as a result of multinational companies opening new plants in Central and Eastern Europe, it is likely that acquiring return cargo would become easier. Due to the construction of new infrastructure in these new markets, it is increasingly possible that more European distribution centres belonging to other multinationals will follow the example of Lego – which moved its distribution headquarters from Germany to the Czech Republic – and move east to get closer to new consumers. The key for this market lies in good rail connections. This was traditionally the strong point of the German ports, where almost the entire hinterland transport was performed by rail. Rotterdam, which had more advantages in terms of barging, depended on the Betuwe Route, which is still hampered by the absence of a functioning connection to the German rail network.

Southern Germany: the backyard of the German ports

The German ports of Bremen and Hamburg performed their hinterland transport almost entirely by rail. This formed an important part of German transport policy during the entire research period. Southern Germany was connected to the German ports even in the 1850s, and when maritime containers arrived in Bremen in 1966, most of them had this area as their final destination. After the liberalisation of the rail sector, ERS Railways founded a subsidiary, BoxXpress, which ran shuttles between the German ports and Southern Germany. This activity was successful, as even in 2004 it was transporting 900 TEU per day, which made it the largest container transporter in Germany.

It is also easier to serve Southern Germany by rail from Rotterdam; it is only in exceptional cases that truck transport goes beyond 300 km, and at a distance of between 800 and 900 km, Southern Germany is too far away to be served cost-efficiently by truck from Rotterdam. It only became possible to reach Southern Germany directly by barge when the Rhine Main Danube Canal was opened in 1994, but there were still no major volumes sailing on the canal in 2010 because of its nautical restrictions. Rail transport thus remained

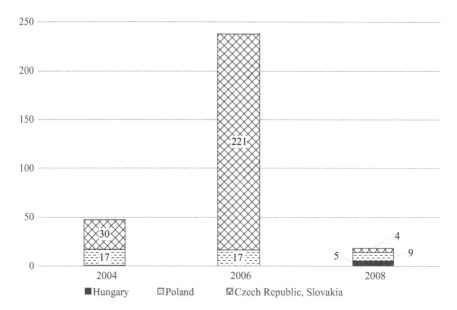

Figure 6.4 Number of containers transported between Rotterdam and the Central and Eastern European countries in 1000 TEU, 2004–2006

Source: Centraal Bureau voor de Statistiek, Containerstatistiek (Heerlen 2011). Map produced by Cartographic Studio/Annelieke Vries-Baaijens (2018).

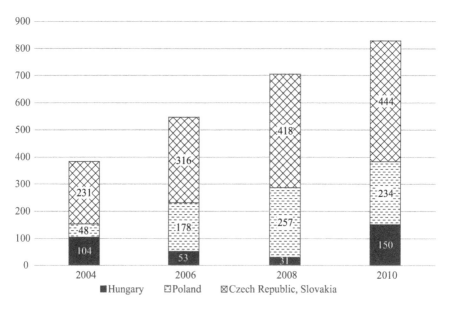

Figure 6.5 Number of containers transported between Hamburg and Bremen and the Central and Eastern European countries in 1000 TEU in 2004, 2006, 2008 and 2010

Source: Deutsches Statistisches Bundesamt, Kombinierter Verkehr, Fachserie 8 Reihe 1.3. (Wiesbaden 2004–2011). Map produced by Cartographic Studio/Annelieke Vries-Baaijens (2018).

Note: Data for Figures 6.4 and 6.5 come from different sources and were not available for the same years.

the only feasible alternative. In 1991, the Dutch railways tried to conquer this area with the Delta Bayern Express, which connected the Rotterdam port with, among others, Nurnberg, Augsburg and Munich, and from there with 50 other destinations in Southern Germany. Still, the transport of containers between Rotterdam and Southern Germany was not a major success. While the share of container shuttles between Rotterdam and Germany in general increased in the period 1994–2010 – especially after ERS Railways opened up the market – the share of shuttles to Southern Germany fell dramatically. This fits into the picture of a retreating hinterland caused by competition between the Northern European ports.

The loss of Southern Germany as a hinterland area seemed to be a missed opportunity for Rotterdam, as the region, especially Bayern, became an increasingly interesting hinterland area. Southern Germany was an underdeveloped area in terms of industry until the 1950s, as a result of its lack of raw materials. The major economic activity in Bavaria was agriculture and, as it offered enough revenues, there was no need for industrialisation, while Baden-Wurttemberg was one of the poorest areas in Europe. Baden-Wurttemberg had started to industrialise in 1900, with Stuttgart as a centre, and cheap labour attracted Daimler and Bosch. Bavaria started to industrialise in 1950, when numerous companies such as Siemens fled to Southern Germany from the zones occupied by the Soviet Union, Eastern Germany and Sudetenland, which was occupied by Soviet troops.[40] Transport to this peripheral area of Germany became easier in the 1950s as a result of growing road haulage transport. Companies such as Siemens, BMW and MBB – an aeroplane and Space Shuttle factory – grew rapidly and an industrial cluster formed around them. Large firms attracted smaller ones as their suppliers. The agglomeration effects of this emerging cluster enhanced innovation and created new jobs. The companies were export-oriented and Southern Germany accelerated in terms of foreign direct investment.[41] Indeed, from 1973 onwards, the industrial growth of Southern Germany surpassed the average of the general level of German industrialisation. As the opposite happened in North Rhine Westphalia in this period, this development was given the name *Süd-Nord Gefälle*, or South-North gradient. In the period 1975–1987, unemployment fell substantially in Southern Germany and the share of the area in relation to German GDP grew.[42] In the following two decades, the self-reinforcing clustering effects persisted and the gravity point of German industry moved further southwards. In the 1990s and the first decade of the new century, unemployment rates in Southern Germany remained well below the country's average. Furthermore, Bayern and Baden-Wurttemberg paid an increasing share to the German federal government, much of which was reinvested in the poorer north, especially North Rhine Westphalia. Moreover, it was Southern Germany in which the largest investments were made in research and development.[43] German industry played a major role in generating containerised flows of goods and its role became even more apparent in the economic crisis of 2008, when it was hit less hard than other countries' industries.

As a result of a combination of deindustrialisation in the Lower Rhine region and industrialisation in Southern Germany, Bayern and Baden-Wurttemberg became the industrial centres of the Federal Republic. There was electric engineering, as well as automobile and machine industries. Companies such as BMW, which had its headquarters in Munich, Audi in Ingolstadt, Heilbronn Siemens in Stuttgart and Nixdorf Computer AG had their plants in Southern Germany.[44] Oil refineries and chemical industries were also situated in the area. Moreover, Southern Germany had a food industry and Ober Bayern was a fast-growing, high-tech sector. The entire area was very export-oriented, and much of the transport was executed through the German sea ports. As a consequence, the region could be seen as a gold mine for container transport. The German ports could not have agreed more. When comparing the number of transported containers between the two most important German ports and Southern Germany between 2004 and 2010 (Figure 6.3), it is clear that the latter belonged to the captive hinterland of the German ports. There was only a minor flow from and to Rotterdam, but a part of the flows from the Lower and Middle Rhine areas probably also originated from Rotterdam or Antwerp.

Deindustrialisation and logistics flows

Rotterdam had the advantage of having a wealthy and productive Lower Rhine hinterland for over a century, but as the Ruhr deindustrialised and the Middle and Upper Rhine and Southern Germany became the centres of capital and consumer goods' production, the port faced greater competition to attract production-based flows of goods. Transport liberalisation in the early 1990s increased port competition and Rotterdam lost out in these hinterland areas, especially after the first decades of the 21st century. While the hinterland network for maritime containers from the Port of Rotterdam had extended before liberalisation, the network contracted thereafter and Rotterdam increasingly depended on its traditional Lower Rhine hinterland again. As such, the traditional place of the industry as the main provider of transit flows in the port was increasingly taken over by logistics. From the 1990s onwards, Duisburg turned into a logistics hub and the surrounding area attracted warehouses and European distribution centres from major multinational companies. Liberalisation played an important role in the emergence of these distribution centres, as it opened national markets and allowed for the centralisation of distribution flows. As a result, transport flows became more dependent on logistics and could take multiple routes through the Dutch ports, as well as through Antwerp or the German ports. This one-sided dependence on logistics instead of production meant that the Port of Rotterdam was vulnerable, because logistical flows of maritime containers are footloose and shift routes from one day to the next. Areas where Rotterdam did retain a foothold were mostly also created by logistical processes, such as in the case of Northern Italy, where the flow of maritime containers from Rotterdam was caused by the *main port effect*, i.e. Rotterdam was the first port of call forwarding container flows to Italy instead of maritime container vessels sailing onwards and calling at ports in Northern Italy. Rotterdam also retained a position in container flows based on European production deriving from the fact that they were mostly shipped in continental containers, some of which were transhipped in Rotterdam, usually destined for the UK. Most continental flows, however, did not pass through the Port of Rotterdam and were thus of less importance than the maritime container flows.

Another area where Rotterdam experienced increasing port competition following liberalisation was Central and Eastern Europe, where rising standards of living and increased economic activity provided for growing volumes of containerised transport.[45] This could have meant that more European distribution centres moved eastwards to be closer to the emerging market. This would have favoured the German ports, as the countries referred to belong to their captive hinterland. For Rotterdam, because of the distance, the only way to contest the German ports in Central and Eastern Europe and Southern Germany would be by rail shuttle. However, a good connection to the German rail system is essential for this and in 2010 had not yet materialised; without a good rail connection, the geographical advantage of Rotterdam, being situated on the Rhine estuary, would become a disadvantage, because the Rhine cannot be moved.

The inflexibility of waterways was demonstrated by the history of container transport on the Rhine Main Danube Canal. The nautical restrictions of the canal meant that it was only navigable by barges with a carrying capacity of less than 100 TEU. When the canal was opened in 1994, many Rhine barges could transport three times as many containers and increasing numbers of fast rail shuttles crossed Europe. Slow barge transport can only attract major container volumes, because its large scale keeps costs low. Due to the failure of the connection of the Betuwe Route in Emmerich, distant hinterlands unconnected to the Rhine remain out of reach for Rotterdam. That this connection was never realised was an enormous advantage for Germany and the German ports and railways. As the rail infrastructure in Germany is only partially split from railway exploitation, it is clear that Dutch interests were dependent on the cooperation of its competitors. It is only when Germany and *Deutsche Bahn* build a railway track from Emmerich to the main German rail network that the Dutch port will be able to compete with German ports and railways. It is clear that German interests were opposed to any strengthening of Rotterdam and their cooperation can hardly be expected. European liberalisation thus proved to be a weak shield against the national interests of the most powerful state in Europe.

The competitive position of the Port of Rotterdam vis-à-vis the German ports can be explained by Germany's rail policy. The effect of this policy can be demonstrated by a thought experiment on the map of Western Europe (Figure 6.6). Line A visualises all the points of equal distance from the Dutch and German ports. On this line, transport costs from all three ports should be equal when excluding geography, differences between transport modalities and transport policies. If the transport costs of the ports of both countries on this line were the same, the majority of transport from Rotterdam would

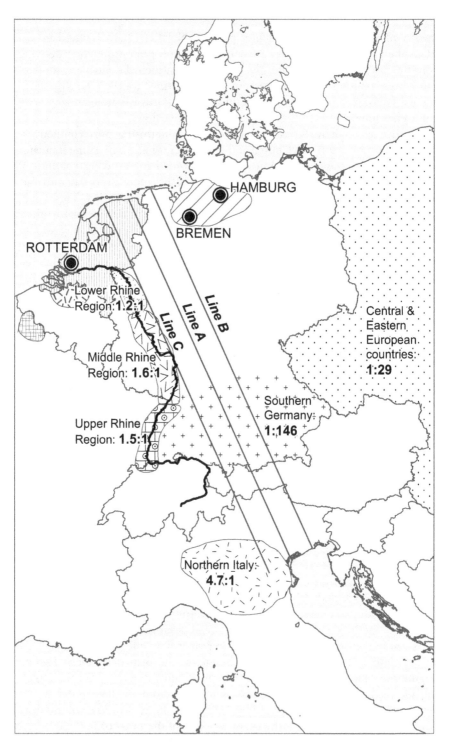

Figure 6.6 Map of Western Europe with the line of equal distance, and equal transport costs before liberalisation and the ratio of transported containers per hinterland area between Rotterdam and the German ports in 2010

have its origins and destination on the western side of line A and that of the German ports on the eastern side. Transport costs were, however, not equal. As Rotterdam provided hinterland transport predominantly by barge, it could be cheaper than the German ports, which performed its hinterland transport over longer distances almost exclusively by rail. This means that the line of equal transport costs would have to be situated more to the east, considering the average reach of the Rhine terminals for the last mile by truck, which was 50–60 kilometres (line B). Prior to liberalisation, the *Seehafenausnahmetarife*, the preferential rail tariffs for rail hinterland transport between the German ports and their hinterland, and the restrictions on cross-border transport neutralised the price differences. This would move the line of equal transport costs to the west, for instance to the Rhine (line C). After liberalisation, when all the conditions obstructing free intra-and intermodal competition disappeared, the line of equal transport costs could be expected to have moved in the direction of line B. According to the calculations based on German container transport data, however, this did not happen. The ratios of the German and Dutch ports on the two sides of the line indicate that the line of equal transport costs was situated closer to line C than to line A, notwithstanding the fact that Rotterdam had a very competitive hinterland connection in the Rhine.

Considering the calculations of the share of the individual hinterland areas, the Lower Rhine region, being less than 300 kilometres away for both Rotterdam and the German ports, is inefficient for rail transport from all three ports. Nevertheless, there has been rail transport from the German ports to this area. Prior to liberalisation, this can be explained by preferential German rail tariffs, which are not related to the transport costs but to the importance of areas for the German ports. After liberalisation, there were still major container flows between the Lower Rhine region and the German ports. This concerned the pivotal position of the logistics hub in Duisburg. Although the Lower Rhine region was situated closer to Rotterdam than the German ports, and could be reached from there by cheap barge transport, it attracted much transport from the German ports. Before liberalisation, the transport market was obstructed by restrictive transport regulations and the German ports could easily cross this line. After liberalisation, the hinterland areas of Rotterdam were situated on the western side of line A and that of the German ports on the eastern side. There was one exception to this, the Lower Rhine region, where Rotterdam and the German ports had an almost equal share. The Dutch hinterland was hardly contested by the German ports, and the Middle and Upper Rhine region belonged more to Rotterdam than to the German ports' hinterland.

Note: The ratio represents the share of the Port of Rotterdam versus the share of the German ports. For example, in the North of Italy the Port of Rotterdam had 4.7 times as much share in the transported containers in TEU as the German ports. In Southern Germany the German ports had 146 times more share in the transported containers in TEU. The map is an approximation to illustrate the point. The data is not precise enough to determine the exact line. The actual line would be curved.

Source: Deutsches Statistisches Bundesamt, *Kombinierter Verkehr*, Fachserie 8 Reihe 1.3. (Wiesbaden 2004–2011); Rail Cargo Information Shuttle Timetable www.railcargo.nl/uploads/tekstblok/timetable_september_2010.pdf, seen on 7 December 2011. Map produced by Cartographic Studio/Annelieke Vries-Baaijens (2018).

The German ports also had only a minor interest in Northern Italy. On the other side of the line, the Central and Eastern European countries belonged more to the hinterland of the German ports than to Rotterdam, and Southern Germany was almost exclusively served by the German ports. It is conspicuous that, while the ratio of the share of the Dutch and German ports in the case of the Central and Eastern European ports in 2010 was 1:29, it was 1:146 in Southern Germany. This means that Rotterdam had less success in contesting the areas belonging to the German ports than the other way round. Rotterdam was actually completely unimportant in those regions. The ratio between the position of Rotterdam and the German ports in the Lower Rhine region was 1.2:1, 1.6:1 in the Middle Rhine and 1.5:1 in the Upper Rhine. It was only in Northern Italy that was it higher, at 4.7:1.

Rotterdam was less successful in contesting the German ports' hinterland than the German ports were in contesting Rotterdam. The major difference in the ratios on the two sides of line A suggests that the German ports could still use rail transport in port competition efficiently, despite the fact that Rotterdam was blessed with the opportunities of cheap barge transport. This implies that liberalisation did not lead to equal competition. Dutch rail transport was disabled by the lack of a good rail connection to the German rail network, which would have made it possible to exploit Rotterdam's position as the first port of call on the Atlantic and Asiatic routes. This means that there must have been a force that counteracted equal competition between the ports in the hinterland in 2010. This force is probably the pressure of the German ports on the German government, which hinders the construction of the third track in Emmerich. This connection would give the Port of Rotterdam a chance to compete in hinterlands unconnected to the Rhine and at distances of 300 km and over, which would bring Southern Germany and Central and Eastern Europe within the range of efficient container transport from and to the Port of Rotterdam.

Conclusion

This chapter raised three questions:

1   How did maritime container transport develop between Rotterdam and its hinterland areas in comparison with the German ports?
2   Which activities generated the transport flows in the hinterland?
3   What effect did it have on the competitive position of the Port of Rotterdam?

Although the chapter predominantly focused on the 2000s (in light of data limitations for earlier periods), the analysis makes clear that Rotterdam was an early adopter of maritime container transhipment. Its position in the early phase, starting with the establishment of the first container terminal in the port in 1966, was aided by the Rhine connecting Rotterdam with the major American military bases along the Middle and Upper Rhine. The containerisation of military goods was taking off at the time and provided Rotterdam with considerable volumes. Container transport was primarily thought of as long-distance transportation and barge terminals shot up along these relatively far off stretches of the Rhine. Rail container transport was similarly developed for longer distances and the Dutch railways established regular shuttle services to Central and Southern Europe. In the period from 1966 to the early 1990s, the hinterland of the Port of Rotterdam grew and its competitive position strengthened. However, from the limited data available, it seems that it was the rail connections in particular that struggled to grow volume and most of the hinterland growth relied on the Rhine. In the Rhine basin, the relatively far off destinations along the Middle and Upper Rhine were more important than the Lower Rhine area, which was traditionally Rotterdam's principal hinterland.

However, from the early 1990s, Rotterdam's hinterland contracted again. When the European Union enacted the liberalisation of the European transport sectors between 1991 and 1994, port competition increased, with varying results for the Rotterdam facility. The rail connections between the port and the hinterland faltered and most of the hinterlands at distances of over 300 km, i.e. those predominantly served by rail, fell to the German North Sea ports. The gradual decommissioning of US military bases and the rise of Duisburg as a logistical hub for rising volumes of containerised Asian-produced consumer goods caused the Rotterdam hinterland to contract and container flows to and from Rotterdam to concentrate on the Lower Rhine area. Most of these flows were derived from logistics and were therefore footloose, i.e. they were flows that were oriented to consumer markets for which transport routes were mainly determined by cost. Minor cost differences could lead to the flows shifting routes – a tendency that was strengthened by liberalisation. Deindustrialisation in the Ruhr area reduced opportunities for the Port of Rotterdam to attract flows that derived from productive activities in the hinterland, i.e. flows that are presumed to be more stable because production sites are less mobile than warehouses and distribution centres. The relative and absolute growth of industrial centres along the Upper Rhine area and in Southern Germany provided limited opportunities for Rotterdam. The port of Antwerp traditionally had better connections than Rotterdam with the industrial areas along the Upper Rhine, and the rail connections of the German North Sea ports left Rotterdam with very few opportunities in Southern Germany. Intra-European flows of continental containers only partially offset Rotterdam's reliance on logistical container flows.

The analysis of the container transport flows for the period 2004–2010 makes it clear that container transport networks in the Lower Rhine region have intensified relative to other hinterland areas after liberalisation. Port competition has in general pushed back the extent of Rotterdam's captive hinterland, with the effect that economic integration in the Lower Rhine region appears to be growing due to the significance of the Rhine and the rise of Duisburg as Europe's largest inland container port. Rotterdam's status as the first port of call on the major Atlantic and Asiatic container lines and Duisburg's role as an intermodal transhipment hub are mutually reinforcing. However, the predominance of barge transportation in Rotterdam's hinterland connections is not entirely due to free inter- and intramodal competition. The ongoing German inaction with regard to the agreed dedicated rail connection on the Dutch-German border continues to obstruct Dutch cross-border transport links to other hinterland areas served by rail. The comparison of market shares of Rotterdam and the German North Sea ports makes it clear that the German ports are better able to compete in the Rhine-based hinterlands of Rotterdam than Rotterdam is able to in the rail-based hinterlands of the German ports. It appears that, despite liberalisation, the failure of the Dutch-German rail connection to materialise has served German port and rail interests and functions as a de facto protectionist measure. The cross-border rail connection could provide Rotterdam with the opportunity to fully exploit its *main port* position, i.e. the advantage of being the first port of call, including for further away hinterlands served by rail.

Other challenges have emerged in the decades after 1990. Major container terminals in Mediterranean ports threaten Rotterdam's position and have weakened its share in Northern Italy, the one rail-based hinterland where it had retained a relatively strong position. Moreover, economic growth in Central and Eastern Europe could start drawing warehousing and the European distribution centres of multinationals eastwards, following growing opportunities in those markets. This would weaken the position of Duisburg as a logistics hub and so lay bare the vulnerability of Rotterdam's reliance on logistical container flows over the Rhine. The German North Sea ports stand to gain from such a shift to the east.

Notes

1 B. Kuipers, "Ja, de container is uitvinding van de eeuw," *NRC Handelsblad*, 11 October 2014.
2 D. Held, Anthony McGrew, David Goldblatt, and Jonathan Perraton, *Global Transformations* (Oxford: Polity, 2001).
3 Gerrit Nieuwenhuis, *De Betuweroute goederen sporen van zee naar Zevenaar* (Alkmaar: De Alk, 2012), 56.
4 M. Boon, "Energy Transition and Port-Hinterland Relations: The Rotterdam Oil Port and Its Transport Relations to the West German Hinterland, 1950–1975," *Jahrbuch für Wirtschaftsgeschichte Economic History Yearbook* 52, no. 2 (2012): 215.
5 Willie Morhs, "Geschichte in Zahlen," 16 September 2016, https://www.wp.de/staedte/duisburg/300-jahre-duisburger-hafen-ein-historischer-rueckblick-id12088954.html?seite=4&displayDropdownTop=none&displayDropdownBottom=block, retrieved on 30 April 2019.
6 "The Rhine-Ruhr Port of Duisburg," *Logistic Management and Distribution Report* 36, no. 7 (1999): 11.
7 "Duisburg wil centrale rol in Europees transport spelen," *Nieuwsblad Transport* (6 June 1992). www.nieuwsbladtransport.nl/Archive/Article/tabid/409/ArchiveArticleID/10029/ArticleName/DuisburgwilcentralerolinEuropeestransportspelen/Default.aspx, retrieved on 28 October 2013.
8 "Duisburg wil samenwerking met Rotterdam uitbouwen," *Nieuwsblad Transport* (3 January 1995). www.nieuwsbladtransport.nl/Archive/Article/tabid/409/ArchiveArticleID/7469/ArticleName/Duisburgslaatfractiemeergoederenover/Default.aspx, retrieved on 28 October 2013.

9 "Duisburg wil centrale rol in Europees transport spelen." www.nieuwsbladtransport.nl/Archive/Article/tabid/409/ArchiveArticleID/10029/ArticleName/DuisburgwilcentralerolinEuropeestransportspelen/Default.aspx, retrieved on 28 November 2013.

10 Quoted in: "Duisburg wil centrale rol in Europees transport spelen." Own translation: Als Rotterdam hoest, krijgt Duisburg longontsteking.

11 M. Gonlag, "Shuttle Rotterdam-Duisburg moet (beter) aansluiten op Duits spoor Havens willen samenwerking tussen spoor en binnenvaart," *Nieuwsblad Transport* (16 September 1995). www.nieuwsbladtransport.nl/Archive/Article/tabid/409/ArchiveArticleID/33314/ArticleName/SHUTTLEROTTERDAMDUISBURGMOETBETERAANSLUITEN OPDUITSSPOORHavenswillensamenwerkingtussenspoorenbinnenvaart/Default.aspx, retrieved on 28 November 2013.

12 "Fusie ECT en DeCeTe Duisburg Mag," *Nieuwsblad Transport* (15 February 2002). www.nieuwsbladtransport.nl/Archive/Article/tabid/409/ArchiveArticleID/74658/ArticleName/FusieECTenDeCeTeDuisburgmag/Default.aspx, retrieved on 21 October 2013.

13 Anonymous, "P&O invests in new Antwerp container facility," *Flanders Investment & Trade*, 24 April 2004, https://www.flandersinvestmentandtrade.com/invest/en/news/po-invests-in-new-antwerp-container-facility, retrieved on 19 April 2019.

14 "Havenbedrijf Duisburg tevreden over jaarcijfers," *Nieuwsblad Transport* (15 April 2003). www.nieuwsbladtransport.nl/Archive/Article/tabid/409/ArchiveArticleID/82704/ArticleName/HavenbedrijfDuisburgtevredenoverjaarcijfers/Default.aspx, retrieved on 19 October 2013.

15 "Opnieuw sterk toeneming containeroverslag Duisburg," *Nieuwsblad Transport* (23 March 2005). www.nieuwsbladtransport.nl/Archive/Article/tabid/409/ArchiveArticleID/94645/ArticleName/OpnieuwsterketoenemingcontaineroverslagDuisburg/Default.aspx, retrieved on 19 October 2013; "Nieuwe en andere klanten voor Duisburg," *Nieuwsblad Transport* (9 March 2005). www.nieuwsbladtransport.nl/Edition/tabid/321/ArticleID/10051/PageID/3909/PageTitle/12/EditionID/197/Default.aspx?ArticleTitle=Nieuwe+en+andere+klanten+voor+Duisburg&EditionTitle=Edition+9-3-2005, retrieved on 20 October 2013; "Duisburg is bulkhaven af," *Nieuwsblad Transport* (12 April 2006). www.nieuwsbladtransport.nl/archief/2006/04/12/duisburg-is-bulkhaven-af/, retrieved on 19 July 2018.

16 Anonymous, "Duisburger Hafen ist Jobmotor für die gesamte Region," *Deutsche Verkehrs-Zeitung*, 29 June 2011. https://www.dvz.de/rubriken/logistik/detail/news/duisburger-hafen-ist-jobmotor-fuer-die-gesamte-region.html, retrieved on 30 April 2019.

17 "Opnieuw sterk toeneming containeroverslag Duisburg"; "Nieuwe en andere klanten voor Duisburg"; "Duisburg is bulkhaven af."

18 Intermodal Terminals in Europe, http://www.intermodal-terminals.eu/database/, retrieved on 30 April 2019.

19 "Havenbedrijf Duisburg tevreden over jaarcijfers."

20 M.E. Porter, "The Economic Performance of Regions," *Regional Studies* 37, nos 6–7 (2003): 562.

21 Buck Consultants International, *Notitie groei containerbinnenvaart en kansen nieuwe initiatieven (concept)* (Den Haag: Buck Consultants International, 2012), 11.

22 The Lower Rhine region is defined here as the province of North Rhine Westphalia.

23 Theo Notteboom, "The Relationship between Seaports and Their Intermodal Hinterland in Light of Global Supply Chains," in *Port Competition and Hinterland Connections ITF-Round Table No. 147* (Paris: OECD, 2008), 25–76, here: 34–35.

24 Interview with Michael Mies, Managing Director, Contargo, Rhein Waal Terminal Emmerich, and Heiko Vollmer, Sales Manager, Contargo, Rhein Waal Terminal Emmerich, 2 May 2012; interview with Kees Kleijn, Director Kleijn Transport, 3 July 2013; David Taylor, "Case 4 Hasbro Europe," in *Global Cases in Logistics and Supply Chain Management* (London: International Thomson Business Press, 1997), 47–60.

25 Notteboom, "The Relationship between Seaports," 20, 29.

26 Interview with Konrad Fischer, Contargo, Managing Director Terminal Ludwigshafen, 6 June 2012.

27 M. Lak, *Tot elkaar veroordeeld: de Nederlands-Duitse economische en politieke betrekkingen tussen 1945–1957* (Hilversum: Verloren, 2015), 188–190; M. Lak, "Because We Need Them . . . German-Dutch Relations after the Occupation: Economic Inevitability and Political Acceptance, 1945–1957" (PhD diss., Rotterdam, 2011), 165.

28 Nationaal Archief, The Hague, 2.05.118 BuZa Code Archief, inventarisnr. 8617 Vervoer van goederen, bestemd voor Amerikaanse troepen, via Rotterdam naar Duitse Rijnhavens, 1955–1960, from C.A.F. Kalhorn to MVW DGV 1–7.

29 Nationaal Archief, The Hague, 2.05.118 BuZa Code Archief, inventarisnr. 8617 Vervoer van goederen, bestemd voor Amerikaanse troepen, via Rotterdam naar Duitse Rijnhavens, 1955–1960, from J.A.M.H. Luns to Washington, 4 December 1956.

30 M. van Baal, "Containerrevolutie," *Maritiem Nederland* (21 February 2007). www.maritiemnederland.com/nieuws/containerrevolutie/item854, retrieved on 19 July 2018.

31 Marc Levinson, *The Box: How the Shipping Container Made the World Smaller and the World Economy Bigger* (Princeton, NJ: Princeton University Press, 2006), 183.

32 Interview with Jasmin Daum, Manager Contargo Terminal Germersheim, 7 June 2012.

33 Interview with Arndt Puderbach, Terminal Manager Contargo Rhein-Main Terminal Koblenz, former Terminal Manager Contargo Terminal Aschaffenburg, 5 June 2012.

34 Interview with Jasmin Daum, Manager Contargo Terminal Germersheim, 7 June 2012.

35 Interview with Konrad Fischer, Contargo, Managing Director Terminal Ludwigshafen, 6 June 2012.

36 Interview with Leo Roelofs, Sales and Intermodal Products, Contargo, DIT Duisburg Intermodal Terminal GmbH, 13 April 2012, 26 June 2012.

37 Hein A.M. Klemann and Sergei Kudryashov, *Occupied Economies: An Economic History of Nazi-Occupied Europe* (London: Berg, 2012), 47, 173, 234, 435.

38 Interview with Cees van Altena, Interim Manager Rail Cargo Information, former manager ERS, Maersk 23 March 2013.

39 Ibid.

40 Ibid.

41 Ibid.

42 Ibid.

43 M. Greive, C.C. Malzahn, L. Rethy, D. Siems, D.F. Sturm, and T. Vitzhum, "Die unheimliche Kraft des Südens," *Die Welt* (26 January 2014), 1–5. www.welt.de/politik/deutschland/article124225959/Die-unheimliche-Kraft-des-deutschen-Suedens.html, retrieved on 19 July 2018.

44 Ibid.

45 H.W. Hoen, "Crisis in Eastern Europe: The Downside of a Market Economy," *European Review* 19, no. 1 (2011): 31–41, here: 32; M.M.C. Allen and M.L. Aldrecht, "The Impact of Institutions on Economic Growth in Central and Eastern Europe," in *The Changing Geography of International Business*, ed. G. Cook and J. Johns (London: Palgrave Macmillan, 2013), 35–53, here: 37–38, 42; A.A. Levchenko and J. Zhang, "Comparative Advantage and the Welfare Impact of European Integration," *Economic Policy* 72, no. 27 (October 2012): 567–607; W. Wilinski, "Internationalization of Central and Eastern European Countries and Their Firms in the Global Crisis," in *Emerging Economies and Firms in the Global Crisis*, ed. M.A. Marinov and S.A. Marinova (London: Palgrave Macmillan, 2013), 83–101, here: 92, 98.

Bibliography

Allen, Matthew M.C., and Maria L. Aldrecht (2013), "The impact of institutions on economic growth in Central and Eastern Europe." In *The Changing Geography of International Business*, edited by G. Cook and J. Johns, 35–53 (London: Palgrave Macmillan).

Boon, Marten (2012), "Energy transition and port-hinterland relations: The Rotterdam oil port and its transport relations to the West German hinterland, 1950–1975." *Jahrbuch für Wirtschaftsgeschichte/Economic History Yearbook* 52, no. 2: 215–235.

Buck Consultants International (2012), *Notitie groei containerbinnenvaart en kansen nieuwe initiatieven* (Den Haag: Buck Consultants International).

Held, David, Anthony McGrew, David Goldblatt, and Jonathan Perraton (2011), *Global Transformations* (Oxford: Polity).

Hoen, Herman W. (2011), "Crisis in Eastern Europe: The downside of a market economy." *European Review* 19, no. 1: 31–41.

Klemann, Hein A.M. with Sergei Kudryashov (2012), *Occupied Economies: An Economic History of Nazi-Occupied Europe* (London: Berg).

Lak, Martijn (2011), *Because we need them . . . German-Dutch relations after the occupation: Economic inevitability and political acceptance, 1945–1957* (PhD diss., Rotterdam).

Lak, Martijn (2015), *Tot elkaar veroordeeld: de Nederlands-Duitse economische en politieke betrekkingen tussen 1945–1957* (Hilversum: Verloren).

Levchenko Andrei A., and Jing Zhang (2012), "Comparative advantage and the welfare impact of European integration." *Economic Policy* 72, no. 27: 567–607.

Levinson, Mark (2006), *The Box: How the Shipping Container Made the World Smaller and the World Economy Bigger* (Princeton, NJ: Princeton University Press).

Nieuwenhuis, Gerrit (2012), *De Betuweroute goederen sporen van zee naar Zevenaar* (Alkmaar: De Alk).

Notteboom, Theo (2008), "The relationship between seaports and their intermodal hinterland in light of global supply chains." In *Port Competition and Hinterland Connections ITF-Round Table no. 147*: 25–76 (Paris: OECD).

Porter, Michael E. (2003), "The economic performance of regions." *Regional Studies* 37.nos 6–7: 549–578.

Taylor, David H. (1997), "Case 4 Hasbro Europe." In *Global Cases in Logistics and Supply Chain Management*, edited by D.H. Taylor: 47–60. (London: International Thomson Business Press).

Wilinski, Witold (2013), "Internationalization of Central and Eastern European countries and their firms in the global crisis." In *Emerging Economies and Firms in the Global Crisis*, edited by Marin A. Marinov and Svetla A. Marinova: 83–101 (London: Palgrave Macmillan).

Index